THE TROUBADOURS

*Translated from the French
by the author*

Edited by

LAWRENCE F. KOONS

ROBERT S. BRIFFAULT

The Troubadours

1965

Indiana University Press
BLOOMINGTON

Contents

Illustrations

(following page 2)

MAPS

Editor's Preface

THE only prefatory comment in the original French version of this work is the following "Editor's Note":

> In his work, "The Mothers: A Study of the Origins of Sentiments and Institutions" (3 volumes, Allen and Unwin, London, and Macmillan, New York, 1927), Robert Briffault devoted a chapter, the twenty-ninth, to the poetry of the troubadours. Returning to this theme, he develops its historical and philological aspects, all the while regarding it from the viewpoint of the history of human customs and of the *sentiment romanesque*.

Inasmuch as the work is self-contained, perhaps this is the only comment needed, but a truly adequate appreciation of this treatise requires some degree of familiarity with the author himself, his philosophy, indeed his very psyche. Unfortunately, it is impossible to offer even a partially adequate presentation of these in the space available, and it would be very difficult to do so in the compass of a full volume, for like many men of genius, Briffault remained an enigma even to those who were closest to him.

In a philosophical and humane sense, Briffault believed that the individual counted for little in the progress of the human race, and possibly because of this he was rather secretive about the details of his personal life. In his lifetime the only available biographical sketches pertaining to him, in addition to the entries in "Who's Who," were those which appeared on the dust jackets of his books and some material in an article by Huntington Cairns. Recently these have been augmented by a Biographical Note in G. Rattray Taylor's abridgement of Briffault's *The Mothers* (Macmillan, New York, and Allen and Unwin, London, 1959). Early biographical sketches contain the statement that he was born in London in 1876, but he told his confidants that in fact he was born in Nice in 1873. In any event, he seems to have been a British citizen. His father, Charles Frederic Briffault, a former French diplomat during the presidency of Louis Napoleon, broke with the latter on his seizure of power, and apparently acquired British citizenship. Briffault's mother was a devout Presbyterian of Scotch origin.

Briffault was brought up in Florence, although he was sent to England to complete his education. After his father died, his mother emigrated to New Zealand in 1892, and took Robert with her. There, in 1897, he married one Anna Clark. He took up the study of medicine about the same time, subsequently receiving the degree of Bachelor of Medicine from Dunedin University in 1901 and the degree, Bachelor of Chirurgery from Christ Church University in 1905. Upon graduation he set up private practice in Auckland. He never seemed to have been content in the colonial atmosphere of New Zealand, far from the great European centers of culture. He made one trip to Europe, via the United States in 1905, but was unable to break away from New Zealand until the War provided the opportunity. He enlisted as as army medical officer, and served with distinction (he was twice decorated) in Gallipoli and later in Flanders. His health was impaired as the result of his having been gassed. Incidentally he spent some time in a staging area in Egypt and there acquired his manifest interest in Arab civilization. While there, he added Arabic to his store of languages. Having been bought up in a trilingual situation, he spoke English, Italian and French. Sometime in the course of his career, he also learned German, Dutch, Latin, Greek, Provençal and some Spanish.

Anna Briffault died of pneumonia shortly after the end of the war, so that Robert returned to New Zealand late in 1919 only long enough to arrange for the return to England of his two daughters. His only son, Lister, is still living in New Zealand. For approximately five years following his return to England Briffault supported himself by working as a *locum tenens* in a London hospital while doing research for, and writing *The Mothers*. During this period he was beset by a series of tragedies, including the deaths of his mother and his daughter.

In 1930 he married Herma Hoyt, an American. He resided briefly in New York, but after 1932 Paris was his chief place of residence. He and his wife were trapped in Paris during the Nazi occupation. After the war his wife returned to the United States, but Briffault was unable to obtain a visa in order to join her, and his apparent compulsive need for access to the libraries and cultural attractions of the European capitals precluded his acceptance of his surviving daughter's offer to join her in Chile. During the last four years of his life he led an incredible existence as a homeless wanderer through France, Italy and England. In 1948 while in Paris he became seriously ill with tuberculosis, the malady which had proved fatal to his daughter. With the assistance of some friends he was sent to a hospital in Hastings where he died in December, 1948.

The bare facts listed above hardly convey any impression of the man. Some additional indication of, at least, his versatility may be obtained from a consideration of his major published works:

The Making of Humanity, Allen and Unwin, London, 1919. This treatise on cultural evolution was written largely in the trenches during World War I. Chapters discussing the contribu-

tion of Arab civilization to that of Europe foreshadow some of
the material in *Les Troubadours*.

*Psyche's Lamp: A Revaluation of Psychological Principles as
Foundation of All Thought*. Allen and Unwin, London, 1921.
This work, which considers the question of the importance of the
individual vis-à-vis that of the race, was written largely on board
ship.

*The Mothers: A Study of the Origins of Sentiments and Insti-
tutions*. This three-volume, one-and-a-half-million-word treatise
was a masterpiece of scholarship and ingenuity which earned
Briffault a reputation as an anthropolgist of note. It is an uncon-
ventional study of just that which is stated in the subtitle. It has
been much praised and much criticized, often by people who
apparently have not bothered to read it. Much of the criticism
centers around Briffault's thesis that human sentiments and insti-
tutions developed from a form of society in which the male
played a minor role in family life.

The Mothers, Macmillan, New York, 1931. This is not an
abridgement of the previously listed work, but an attempt to present the major theses thereof without ancillary material and
without the supporting evidence. On occasion the two works have
been confounded by critics.

Rational Evolution, Macmillan, New York, 1930. A completely rewritten version of *The Making of Humanity*.

Breakdown: The Collapse of Traditional Civilization, Bren-
tanos, New York, 1932. As with many of Briffault's books, the
subtitle presents a fair idea of what it is about. He said of this
book that it contained a fresh idea on each of its 273 pages
which, he claimed, meant that it contained at least 272 more ideas
than each of the 30,000 other books published in America in
1932.

Sin and Sex, McCauley, New York, 1937. A rather moderate
plea for a more enlightened view of sex than that of the puritan.
See the concluding passage in *The Troubadours*.

Reasons For Anger, Simon and Schuster, New York, 1938. The title is a humorously sarcastic reply to a not-so-humorously sarcastic remark in a review of *Sin and Sex.* The book is a collection of essays by Briffault which had previously appeared in the periodical literature.

The Decline and Fall of the British Empire, Simon and Schuster, New York, 1938. This small book was all that resulted when Briffault found it necessary to abandon a projected "Gibbonesque" treatise on the British Empire. Briffault's choice for the title was "The English Myth."

Europa, Scribners, New York, 1935. This was Briffault's first novel. Vaguely autobiographical in character, it became a bestseller.

Europa in Limbo, Scribners, New York, 1937. Sequel to *Europa.*

Fandango, Scribners, New York, 1940. A novel set in the Spain of the thirties. It was not very well received.

The New Life of Mr. Martin, Scribners, 1947. A fantastic novel which hardly admits of description. Its style betrays Briffault's interest in James Joyce, whom he had lampooned in *Europa.* A Dante-Beatrice theme which runs through the complex plot betrays his interest in Dante which is also evident in *The Troubadours.*

Les Troubadours et le sentiment romanesque, Briffault's last published work, was written in Paris during the Nazi occupation under conditions of considerable hardship. It was published in elegant form, richly illustrated, both in boards and in paperback versions, in Paris in 1945. Occasionally copies of it, wrapped as new, are still to be seen in the bookstalls along the banks of the Seine. It apparently received wide distribution. I have seen copies of it in most of the large municipal and university libraries that I have been in during the past fifteen years, and the copies usually show signs of use. In fact, *Les Troubadours* is one of the three major works by Briffault to be found in the Lenin Library in Moscow; the other two are the three-volume *The Mothers* and *Europa*. Yet citations to the work are rare and it is probably safe to say that knowledge of its existence has been largely confined to persons interested either in the particular topics treated or in Briffault himself.

Be that as it may, it appears to this amateur at least, that the book has had considerably more influence than references to it would indicate. American scholars generally seem to have fewer qualms about acknowledging the debt Western civilization owes to the Moors than do their European counterparts, but even on this side of the Atlantic, the topic seems to be more often encountered in popular treatises than was the case two or three decades ago. Similarly the broadcasting of paeans to the troubadour conception of idealized love seems to be much less widespread than it was as recently as my own high school days. This could, of course, only be the result of a general change in attitude, but a comparison of recent and early encyclopedia articles on the troubadours indicates that today there is actually a better understanding of the real nature of the troubadours and their works. In view of the lack of evidence, it would be more than rash to charge *Les Troubadours et le sentiment romanesque* with some responsibility for the general improvement in the quality of references to the troubadours, but it would be wrong to summarily dismiss this possibility.

All such abstract considerations aside, however, there are abundant good reasons for making the book available in English translation. The account of the appearance, growth and decline of the troubadours, and of the effect their tradition exerted on subsequent literature, is a peculiarly interesting one. Briffault, combining his native skill at writing with real scholarship and an irrepressible, wry humor, has told it in a way that only he could have done. Quite in addition to the matter of esthetics and interest, however, there is a fundamentally sound reason for the consideration of such matters as the accuracy of the traditionally held views on historical topics, including such apparently trivial ones as the troubadours' "conception of love." The reason is expressible in terms of a cardinal point in Briffault's philosophy which is nicely stated in the conclusion of an article by him which appeared in a New Zealand newspaper before World War I, the oldest item by Briffault that I have seen in print. The passage reads: "There can be no faith but in the assurance that who loves the one [the good] loves the other [the true]; that the truest and the highest and the best are indissoluble." Briffault equated "good" with "truth," and "virtue" with "intellectual honesty." I believe that he was correct in so doing. Ultimately evil stems from the acceptance of untruth as verity.

It may not matter whether Guiraut de Bornelh espoused the concept that disembodied love is the only true love. But if it is easy, for reasons frivolous or tendentious, to falsely spread the idea that he did, then it is also easy to scatter misinformation on more important matters. It would hardly be reasonable to assume that Briffault has said the "last words" on the many points of controversy which appear in this book, or that he has completely resolved the uncertainties regarding issues beclouded by time, language problems, prejudice, and a host of other factors. Here as elsewhere, however, he has given a fine example of the diligence with which it is necessary to search for facts that are not in accord with prevailing thought. One need not agree with his every conclusion in order to be inspired by the thoroughness of his investigations and his ability to weave little items of evidence together to form plausible support for ingenious inferences.

Briffault undertook the translation of *Les Troubadours* into English when he apparently became dissatisfied with the efforts of a professional translator. In the course of doing so, he made several revisions in the text. The changes in the first five chapters are rather slight. They include the occasional replacement of the included specimens of poetry by others he apparently deemed

more appropriate, a few additional references to English authors, slight expansions of the discussions of the derivations of
the terms "jongleur" and "troubadour," and occasional variations in the order of presentation. The last chapter, however, differs materially from the corresponding passage in the original
version. Many paragraphs have been rewritten, the order of
presentation of much of the material has been altered, and new
material has been added. The passage on Dante, which certainly
is interesting and, I believe, unique, has been considerably expanded. The passage on Shakespeare and the English poets did
not appear in the original version in any form. I have a copy of
a letter from Briffault in which he states that his translation has
ten times the worth of the original French version. Hyperbole was
no doubt intended, and a serious claim of improvement by even
a factor of two might bring rebuttal. There is no doubt, however,
that the expansion added significantly to the value of the book.

My own contributions to this volume have been very slight,
namely the translation of the notes, which unfortunately seem
not to have been translated by Briffault, and a very small amount
of editing of some ambiguous passages in the text. I was guided
by the feeling that the work was Briffault's, and his it should remain. To this end I was very reluctant to make any alterations,
however much of an improvement they might have seemed to
represent, unless it was apparent that an oversight was involved.
In some of the new material, there were instances of alternate
versions from which it was necessary to make a selection, but the
differences generally involved matters of style and not of content.
In the one important instance where content was involved, both
versions are given, one in an appendix.

In one of Briffault's translations from Provençal into Old English, some of the obscure terms have been replaced by their
more familiar equivalents. What prompted Briffault to express
the translations in Old English is a matter for conjecture, but I
suspect he felt that such renditions better retained the spirit of

the original. In any event, many of these passages which have a distinctive charm when presented in archaic terms (albeit with Briffaultian flair) would appear coarse, at best, if rendered into straightforward modern English.

The references did pose a bit of a problem. The straitened circumstances under which Briffault wrote the original version, and the apparent haste with which it was printed, resulted in the appearance of a number of typographical errors. The English translation was done while Briffault was an impoverished wanderer in postwar Europe, and there was little opportunity for careful editing on his part. Moreover, the notes to the material added in translation are usually penned in the margin of the manuscript in Briffault's not very legible handwriting, and they are often in some sort of shorthand notation which he intended to amplify later. I mention all this not to condone any blunders on my part, but to warn of the possibility that there may be some.

Briffault was a controversial figure. Some of the reviews of each of his books were quite hostile. Sometimes these hurt him; often they amused him. (An advertisement for *Rational Evolution* on the flyleaf of *Psyche's Lamp* includes without comment two sarcastic statements from unfavorable reviews.) Still it was exceedingly dangerous to do verbal battle with Briffault, and I cannot recall of an instance in which an adversary of his came out the victor. Although he is no longer here to defend his position, he needs no champion among the living. His work stands on its own merits, and his arguments are clear and ready for discussion. Such errors and oversights as may have occurred in the technical aspects of the preparation of this volume should be charged directly to myself. It would have been far better if the preparation and translation had been done by someone with detailed knowledge of the topics treated, and preferably by someone with a good knowledge of Arabic. Happily, however, Briffault had carried the work to the point that such a specialist was not indispensable.

In his preface to *The Mothers,* Briffault states that since he worked single-handed he had been denied the gratification of offering acknowledgements of indebtedness. Fortunately, I have not experienced this denial. I am indebted to Mrs. Joan Briffault Hackelberg for having retyped her father's manuscript and having made both her copy and the original available to me, as well as for countless other forms of assistance; to Morris Justice for having offered his usual incisive, crititical comments; to Mrs. Herma Briffault for having first made me aware of the desirability of the publication of an English translation; to Mrs. Frances Joyner for having retyped my translation of the notes; to Mrs. Alice R. Jwaideh for editorial assistance, and to Bill Hixson for having been an assiduous coworker in the ferreting out of biographical data.

THE TROUBADOURS

1 Spanish minstrels

2 Cercamon

3 Perdigon

4 Peire Vidal

5 Arnaud Daniel

6 Cercamon

7 The Count of Poitiers

8 Jaufré Rudel

9 Marcabru

10 Bertram de Born

11 Gaucelm Faidit
   & Marie de Ventadorn

12 Guilhem de Cabestanh

13 Bernard de Ventadorn

14 Upper figures show Blanche of Castile and Louis IX

15 Montanhagol

16 Capture of Béziers. Chanson
de Croisade Albigeoise. Design in
ink to be covered with paint

auos que no no sabetz. Tan
len ter sauenon en sems. Lo
senz el prez el abeutatz. Eiz
francz cors canc bona fos
natz.

S im sueill eu tener clam. Co
uassalz delors bons seingn
ors. Enomen son del tortlais
satz. Quel nesus cors abque
bataill. fris contra leis euas
mi quetz. Que dis quellam
son uele reinis. De manz
en con bruetz cui passatz. En
quem fora desesperatz.

Gro de cabrol ode dam. Si
precz entendes mela morz.
Cuiera fos a vo mesiatz. Mas
uos ma dompna non assaill.

L ams ni mer cez
car non ueres. Los mals qui
en trac nils plantz nil gems.
Que fag la nuet em sol col
gatz. Al orn non puesc estar
en patz.

S i per dieu en sotz estam. No
us pluz quem enspas la vo
lors. Que mausira si non

pen satz. Ereu merses orgoull
nous tfail. Epassa tam sino
sentez. Con es lors frolitz
esteins. Can de seruizi non
uengtatz. Sellm quenez mor
trebaillatz.

S im tenes prez elliam. Eno
ual forsa niualors. Nom deu
ualer humilitaz. Si ca pos
estren. Costres mans esim
destrignetz. Qui mais me
uol gra ser rezeins de mas
muntz ode reuelatz. Quen
tal trebailla foluitatz.

P er uos dompna quem de
strignetz. Cuier ben en esser
rezeins. De mas untz ode
reue laz. Anz caissi fos uiste
ziatz. Dompna merces car
pen satz. Com eu non fos tos
temps forsatz.

Giraut de burnel.

I l cors nom lus tan oregz.
Emal son grat non la fra
ing. Enun chantaret soul
nomez uns quem safraing
na. Si non es forsatz. En n

17 Provençal chansonnier, 13th century

Guiraud de Bornelh and two jongleurs.
Page of manuscript, 13th century

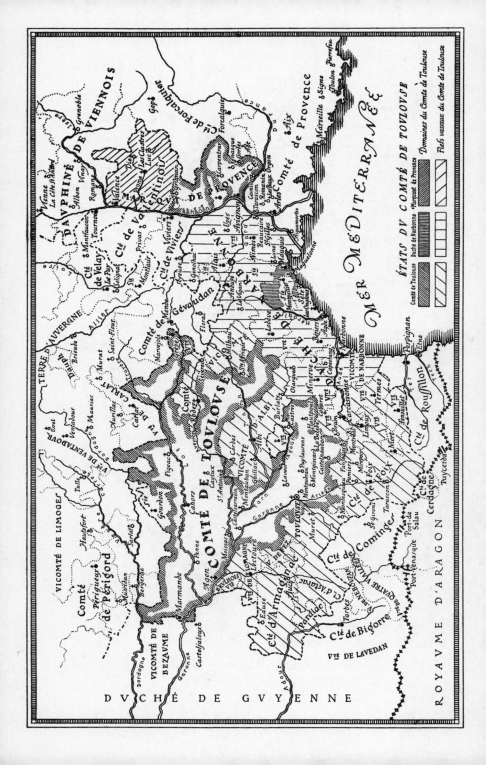

Introduction

WHILE in the North, the tales and sagas of Celtic paganism were flowering into the romances of chivalry which captured the imagination of the Middle Ages, a literary form equally alien to the classical tradition was unfolding in southern France. The poetry of the troubadours answered the mood of a feudal society newly awakened to a sense of its native uncouthness by contact with the luxury of the Orient, and beginning to advance claims to the airs and graces of ornate leisures. Throughout Europe blew the aura of a new lyrical inspiration. Provençal song brought fertility to the flinty soil of the vernacular tongues, and stood as a pattern to their nascent productiveness. It was echoed in the lays of the Northern *trouvères*.[1] It kindled the luster of Italian verse, which was in turn to shed a reflected luster far and wide over the literatures of the new Europe. It begot in outlying Germanic lands and in England the first lilts of rich poetical successions.

The crusaders sang the songs of Provence as they marched east along the Danube. The people of the medieval world, accustomed to distant pilgrimages, were singularly given to travel. Poetry partook of that vagrant disposition. It was not, in the twelfth century, a specialized and somewhat precious taste confined to relatively small circles of cultivated persons. The songs of the medieval *jongleur* (in Caxton's English, *"jogler"* or *"jogeler"*), the professional itinerant minstrel, discharged most of the functions of current literature in our age—novels, periodicals, dramatic spectacles. The *nouvelles* which he descanted were at times truly the latest news of the day. He was the world's reporter and practically the sole provider of entertainment. As he passed, singly or in groups, from court to court, from castle to castle, where his coming was always a welcome event, the singer of verse took no account of frontiers and found ready access to every lordship. He was a vagabond by vocation.

The earliest troubadour-jongleur whose memory has reached us is known only by the nickname of "Cercamon" (Scour-the-world). This designation, which recalls that of the Old English *skop*, "Widsith" (the far-travelled), applies no less aptly to most of his brethren of the craft, peddlers of poetry. Spain and Italy were their second homelands. Peire Vidal lodged for a time with Aymeric, King of Hungary, and lived for a considerable period in Cyprus, where he married a Greek.[2] One of the surviving songs of Bernard de Ventadorn was composed in England.[3] Marcabru too paid a visit to London.[4] Almost every company of travellers included jongleurs. No prince would think of setting out on a journey without a train of minstrels in his retinue. When Raymond Bérenger V, Count of Toulouse, went to Turin to be invested by Frederick Barbarossa, "he presented his poets to the Emperor," says master Jean de Gaufridi. "He had brought with him the most famous among them, both in order that he should be the more honored for his province's uncommon distinction and so as to please the Emperor, who was himself given to the composition of occasional verses."[5] So delighted was the monarch that he assigned to Count Raymond a number of estates whose titles the Count's rival, the Lord of Baux, had sought to obtain for himself. The troubadours thus extended, in a literal as well as figurative sense, the boundaries of their native land. Moreover, proud of being able to display his talents, the

Emperor improvised for the occasion a ditty in the Provençal tongue which has come down to us.

The troubadours and the Germanic bards met again some years later, when Barbarossa came to be crowned King of Arles and sojourned for a time in Provence. It was during this period that the first German Minnesingers made their appearance in the castles of the Danube. They were in every respect the disciples of the troubadours. The songs of Heinrich von Weddeke, Friederich von Hausen, Reimar der Alte and Heinrich von Morungen are copies, in form and content, of those of Languedoc.[6]

Like the Swabian emperors, the Plantagenet kings claimed, as part of their Angevin dominions, the lands of poesy, and showered favor upon its adepts. Aliénor of Aquitaine, granddaughter of the first troubadour, Count Guilhem of Poitiers, and mother of the minstrel king, Richard the Lion-Hearted, was among the first and most ardent patrons of Provençal poetry. She was reputed to be "wondrous couth of merit, courtesy, and well-dight saying of praises"—*bien dire de louanges*. The lady Aliénor (never otherwise designated until David Hume vandalized her name into "Eleanor")—who, addressing the Pope after her divorce from King Louis and her marriage to Henry of Anjou, writes herself: "I Aliénor, by the wrath of God, Queen of the English"—was of a temper and authority to impose her tastes. As Queen of France, she was responsible, together with her daughter, Countess Marie, for the spread of the new poetry in the castles of Champagne, Picardy and Artois. As Queen of England, she invited the poets to cross the Channel and introduced them to the English Court. The oldest English lyrical poetry, whence derives in unbroken succession the great poetic heritage of England, obtained its original models, both directly and through French versions, from the Provençal songs. Modern research has shown that the first stamp of that influence was scarcely less profound than upon Italian verse, and as indelible, and its full measure is far even now from having been fully computed.[7] Already the Augustan Age had some inkling of this. Pope placed the "Provençal school" first in the lineage of English poetry.[8] And Dryden writes: "Chaucer first adorned and amplified our barren tongue from the Provençal, which was then the most polished of all modern languages."[9] The idiom of the troubadours was on the point of becoming the universal language of poetry. In Italy and Spain, up to the fourteenth century, the poets knew no other.[10]

It is not easy for the modern reader to share the enthusiasm raised in its day by that poetry, and ratified under the seal of such high judges as Dante and Petrarch. For one thing he is brought up against the linguistic obstacle; nothing could be more futile than to try the merits of any poetry desiccated to the dust of translation. That obstacle is not insurmountable, however. Given a Latin grounding, it is very much less formidable than that encountered by one sufficiently reverent of his mother tongue to want to learn it *per origines*. Once let the profit be deemed worth the painstaking, the construing of Provençal is small trouble in comparison with that of Old English.[11]

The major stumbling block lies not in the language, but in the staple theme of the poetry. The sighs and mannered tropes, the mincing measures of love, be they rhymed by the troubadours or by Petrarch, by Elizabethan sonneteers or seventeenth-century madrigalists, no longer have the ability to stir our emotions farther than to raise an indulgent smile. The troubadours are indeed mainly indictable for some six centuries of that poetic confectionary. But the very extent of the mischief with which they are indictable is witness to the magnitude of their influence, and offers, in the view of critical history, a problem which peculiarly invites inquiry.

The merits of troubadour poetry are not, in any case, adequately appraised by taking single cognizance of the fusty sentimental fashions of its matter. The matter, incidentally, was not wholly of the poet's election; it was imposed on the professional amorist by the circumstances of his calling. Noble lords with a genuine relish for versing, such as Bertram de Born or Peire Cardenal, who were at large to choose their own subjects, did so as they pleased, and amatory themes hold a subordinate place, if any, in their production. When occasion served, and he was free to take a truce, the vocational poet too was ready enough with other matter. He could express sentiments, as does Peire Vidal in the following strophes, which have not aged:

> *Ab l'alen tir vas me l'aire*
> *qu'eu sen venir de Proensa;*
> *Tot quant es de lai m'agensa,*
> *si que, quan n'aug ben retraire*
> *eu m'o escout en rizen*
> *e.n deman per un mot cen:*
> *tan m'es bel quan n'aug ben dire.*
>
> *Qu'om no sap tan dous repaire*
> *con de Rozer tro qu'a Vensa,*
> *si com clau mars e Durensa,*
> *ni on tan fis jois s'esclaire.*
> *Per qu'entre la franca gen*
> *ai laissat mon cor jauzen*
> *ab leis que fa.ls iratz rire.*[12]

I hale and breathe the air / that blows from Provence way; / for aught from there / me glads and maketh gay; / when to its praise I list / I smile, ears pricked, and whist, / and for each word / would I'd a hundred heard, / so fain am I to hear its praise.

For there's no land so sweet / as between Rhône and Vence / between the sea and the Durance, / where all is bright, / folk blithe and meet to hold my heart, / and her whose gentle art / on rueful mien a smile can raise.

Nor did Bertram de Born dip his quill in sugary sentiment
when he dashed off this battle-piece in the manner of Ucello:

Massas e brans, elms de color,
escutz trauchar e desguarnir
veirem a l'entrar de l'estor
e maintz vassals ensems ferir,
  Don anaran arratge
chaval de.ls mortz e de.ls nafratz;
e quan er en l'estorn entratz
  Chascus hom de paratge
no pens mas d'asclar chaps e bratz,
que mais val mortz que vius sobratz.

Ie. us dic que tan no m'a sabor
manjar ni beure ni dormir
com a, quan auch cridar: "A lor!"
d'ambas las partz, et auch ennir
  chavals vochs per l'ombratge,
et auch cridar: "Aidatz! aidatz!"
e vei chazer per los fossatz
  paucs e grans per l'erbatge,
e vei los mortz que pe.ls costatz
an los tronzos ab los cendatz.[13]

Maces and brands shatter and cleave
high painted helms and blazoned shields;
closing in combat-clash, men-at-arms, reave,
fell down or fall, strowing the fields,
and wildly race across the plain
riderless steeds of maimed and slain.
Once in the thick of it, hard blows to take or give,
  no man of ought else recks
  than hewing limbs and necks.
Liefer be dead than vanquished live.

  Troth! there's more taste to life
  in height and heat of strife
  than meat and wine;

"Have at them!" both sides yell;
and from forth fozely dell
come cries of "Help" and horses whine.
In tumult and din, grapple-locked, battle waves;
in tall grass and ditches,
stilled the last twitches,
Great and small lie, flanks pierced with pennoned staves.

Within the very framework of their conventions, the troubadours speak at whiles in lyrical accents which belong to all time. No formula, for instance, is of more conventional order than the practice of introducing a song by an allusion to the season of the year, to the flowers that bloom, or to the notes of the nightingale. Yet Arnaud Daniel, availing himself of this convention, gives us a series of songs, headed by reference to the four seasons, which may fairly challenge very modern comparisons. Here is "Autumn":

L'aur'amara fa.ls bruoills brancutz
clarzir, que.l doutz espeissa ab fuoills,
e.ls letz becs dels auzels ramencs
ten balps e mutz, pars e non pars;
per queu m'esfortz de far e dir plazers
a mains per liei que m'a virat bas d'aut,
don tem morir, si.ls afans no m'asoma.[14]

The bitter air
strips panoply
from trees
where softer winds set leaves.
The glad
beaks
now in brake are coy,
scarce peep the wee
mates
and un-mates.
What gaud's the work?

What good the glees?
What curse
I strive to shake!
Me hath she cast from high;
in fell disease
I lie, and deathly fearing.
                    (Ezra Pound's rendition)

The poetry of the troubadours is, to be sure, archaic, inasmuch as of all post-classical European literature, it is the oldest. Yet it is certainly more modern, in the same sense as is the work of François Villon, than any poetry since produced in France down to the nineteenth century. As Gaston Paris justly remarks. "It was the troubadours who created the modern style."[15] The French language, after developing from its origin as a living Romance tongue, underwent, in fact, a change when pundits undertook to graft upon that ancient stem a dead language and one which was probably never spoken, the forensic declamatory Latin of the Ciceronian vintage. Jurists and pedants repudiated the Romance vernacular, whose growth had been largely poetic, and by dint of grammatical trituration took to framing a tongue born of court records and notaries' deeds. They would have it logical at all costs, even though perforce allowing in every instance the precedence of usage, that is, the living quality of language, over logic.

Thence French clarity and an admirable vehicle of prose, but thence also the embarrassment of Frenchmen when set to wondering who is their great poet. For a long time they took rhetoric for poetry, the stilts of pomposity for the surge of inspiration, and were nurtured on the noble circumlocutions of Racine's alexandrines. And when they bethought themselves of retracing their steps and of returning to truly poetical expression, by rescuing themselves from that contagion, they found themselves with the impossibility of achieving lyrical speech without doing violence to the French language and thus betraying what Dante, the pupil of the troubadours, declared to be the poet's first duty: to keep jealous ward over the purity of his native tongue.

The troubadours who sang those tongues to life stand at the pole opposite from peruked Augustan "classicism." Yet their songs, startling as the conjunction may be thought, meet the highest model of authentic Grecian antiquity on the level of one cardinal virtue that is paramount in both. Speaking of another archaic poet, or aggregate of poets—ballad-singers, they have been called—Matthew Arnold singles out one quality to place it in the forefront before all others. He calls it "rapidity." It is a far cry from the troubadours to Homer, but as it happens, that same quality, swift movement, no dawdling over unessentials, no slackening of the lyre's strings, is the outstanding excellence of the Provençal minstrel-songs also. The troubadours brought no elevated vision, no profound interpretation, no rich colored imagery to European poetry, but they gifted it with what has been called, by Nietzsche, the whole of style—tempo, the vitality of flowing and flexible rhythm. In lending words to music, they lent music to words. "This vivacity," says Sir Arthur Quiller-Couch, "this new beat of the heart of poetry, is common to Chaucer and the humblest ballad-maker; it pulses through any book of lyrics printed yesterday. And it came straight to us out of Provence."[16]

And, without wishing to strain the analogy, archaic Provençal poetry touches archaic Greek poetry—perhaps because they are both archaic—at another vital point: directness and simplicity. The troubadours ventilated, far back in the twelfth century, a question which is even today not finally resolved, that of poetical obscurity. Arnaud Daniel, the most eminent exponent of the *trobar clus,* refused the devalued coin of ready-made eloquence. But his quest of the unlooked-for bears no sort of affinity to preciosity or the flowery ornaments into which Italian virtuosity was to fall, even while imitating the troubadours. Quite on the contrary; he sought a concision that should cut to the quick, the unloading of all ballast, the elision of the superfluous, preferring, if circumlocution were thereby avoided, the common, even the coarse word. However affected and artificial the sentiments expressed by the troubadours, as needs they had to be, being avowedly "praise" (otherwise said, flattery), their language was not. That was filed down to the minimum of verbiage. For its effect it relied on the right word in the right place, not like Petrarch and the Elizabethans, on ornament. Those are the characteristics of the style of Arnaud Daniel, and they are to be those of Dante.

That compression draws more largely on the attention of the reader, accustomed, in our over-excited age, to literary cake which levels down to his quick luncheon habits, and he feels injured when unable to snap up at one bite the meat of a period or a page. But the "obscurity" serves in fact one of the essential ends of poetry. Guiraut de Bornelh, though having dipped in the *trobar clus* manner, joins issue on the question. "When one uses words," he says, "it is after all in order to be understood." That facile logic, for all its color of truism, is in point of fact specious. Merely to be apprehended as ideas is not the sufficient end of poetry. Prose itself, emotional in its origin, and indeed the daughter of poetry, reverts to its primal nature when it seeks to convey moods and tempers, and in doing so aspires to being an art. Poetry is under the obligation of being one, an art intermediate between verbal and musical communication, aiming at enriching each with the emotional qualities of the other. The poet does not finger the elements of language as the key of a calculating machine, but as the strings of a lute. That his words should convey ideas is not enough; they must also stir by their vibrations the fibers of emotional sensibility to pleasurable or exciting purpose. The intellectual content is, in poetry, an instrumental part in the concerted symphony. The purpose of all art being to lift the mind's excitement above the oppression of actuality, that function is not served by M. Jourdain's prose when he calls for his slippers.

The fusion of its consubstantial elements, of form and content, in a total and indivisible effect is the rightful end of poetry; its perfect attainment is the stamp of great poetry. The troubadour lyrics are not great poetry. They are but songs; songs of which for the greater part, the words have come down to us amputated from their musical stem, but which were not composed to meet the eye in written form; songs largely descanted and delivered by strolling singers, common crowders who had been wont to collect their audiences at fairs and the junketings of yokels, before a boon of fortune sent them basking in memorial halls and princely courts. The ambition to create great poetry never entered their heads. Their highest design did not aim above providing pleasant entertainment. But within the relatively modest compass of that purpose, the song-makers were certainly in earnest, and strove, like conscientious craftsmen, to excellence. Their concern for form assigned to it an undue preponderance, and craft came to dominate inspiration. But to that solicitude, excessive to a fault, is largely owing the sway which their poetry bore over the early growth of European literatures. It is manner rather than matter that summons such influence. That fault was almost a requisite condition for the fashioning of the instrument with which Provençal poetry equipped succeeding centuries, and which furnished the burthen of poetry with resources that gave it larger and freer play. The musical instrument must needs be fashioned by the craftsman before it can be handed to the musician. And the art of the Provençal song-makers, trifling as we may account it, and removed as it is from the highest order of poetry, proved—from the outset of the wide-reaching posthumous influence it exerted—its aptness to the needs of the very greatest poetry. It answered the ends of Dante.

The considerations which engaged the attention of the troubadours in the twelfth century carry us a long way from archaic ingenuousness. Provençal technical mastery was, in point of fact, not only in advance, as by a miracle, of its time, but of the literary production of most European countries for centuries to follow. Abstracting our knowledge of dates and our concern for content, say we set the gawky, heavy-footed gait of laggard England in the fourteenth century, of Lydgate, Gower, Hoccleve, yea, of Chaucer, beside the light easeful trip and nimble sleight of the troubadour songs, there can be little question which of the two we should count the more archaic. Which is more beforehand and which is callower, this of Gower:

> And that was in the monthe of Maii,
> When, every brid hath chose his make,
> An thenkth his merthes forto make
> Of love that he hath achieued;
> Bot so was I nothing relieued,
> ffor I was further fro my loue
> Than Erthe is fro the heuene aboue.
>   *(Confessio Amantis,* I, 100 sq.)

or this of Bernard de Ventadorn?

> *Quan l'erba fresch' e'lh folho par,*
> *e la flors botn' al verjan,*
> *e'l rossinhols autet e clar*
> *leva sa votz e mou son chan,*
> *joi ai de lui, e joi de la flor,*
> *joi ai de me e de midons major.*
>
> I joy in the song, I joy in the flower,
> I joy in myself, but in my lady more.[17]

In respect of its intrinsic quality, troubadour poetry is today above all a poetry for poets, for artists, whether practitioners of verse or of prose or of neither, who are interested in art and able to appreciate technique. While few might choose those lyrics for their bedside book, poets like Rimbaud, Laforgue, Ezra Pound, have drawn from them profit and pleasure. It was Goethe who plucked them from the neglect of five centuries and introduced the serious study of them into Europe.

The very themes that alienate us, I had almost said repel us, by their factitious sentiments, constituted in the twelfth century a recommendation at least as weighty as the elegance of lyric love. Unlike the chivalric narratives of deeds of derring-do, that poetry was levelled at a feminine public. The oft-quoted saying of Dante, that lyrical poetry was composed in the vernacular because women did not understand Latin,[18] is erroneous; neither the men nor the poets themselves, in Provence, understood Latin any better than did the women. But the gist of lyrical poetry, which was accounted equivalent with love-poetry, was imposed by the tastes of the audiences to which it was addressed. The treatment of that theme contrasts with the classical tradition even more violently than the form that clothes it. The poetical expression on which our modern tongues were nurtured, has, together with its cast and mouth, transmitted to a whole literary progeny, down to the eighteenth and nineteenth centuries, an attitude towards amatory sentiment which has been termed, misleadingly as it happens, a "new conception of love."

Love-poetry did not hold an important place in pagan Europe. As is the rule in the lower cultures, erotic lays were regarded among the barbarian tribes in the light of charms. A love-song was counted as a magical incantation whereby the lover sought to work theurgically upon the object of his desire. Among Nordic peoples the composition of verses addressed to a woman amounted to an offense which exposed the author, like any other practitioner of sorcery, to punitive measures. Instances are on record of poets being formally charged, proscribed, or subjected to heavy penalties for having written verse to a young woman whose family had rejected their suit. The Scandinavian poet,

Ottar the Black, found guilty of having dedicated a song to the daughter of King Olaf, was condemned to death. He owed his reprieve only to the lucky inspiration of singing the praises of the king on his way to execution.[19] In one of the numerous variants of the story of Tristan, the hero is killed by King Mark for having sung a love poem to Iseult.[20]

Those barbaric lays were devoid of merit, and bore little resemblance to what we understand by love-poetry. The conventions of Provençal love-songs are the first expression of a profound difference in the treatment of erotic themes which divides our literatures from those of classical antiquity or of barbarian cultures. When, for instance, Racine imparts to a paraphrase of Euripides a sentimental delicacy which has no analogy in the original, he is unconsciously drawing from a tradition which had its cradle in Provence. And Shakespeare's ideal female figures, his Perditas, Imogens, Mirandas, have no sisters in the imaginative works of Greece or Rome, nor are they sib to the Diarmaid, Etain, or Essylt of Celtic saga. They are the nonesuch Lady-liege of the troubadour-knight, the paragons of every feminine charm and perfection with which the flattery of lyrical homage painted and bedecked her. The Provençal song-makers did not then frame anew the form only of poetical expression; they enacted a change which has struck deeper into the European mind, a change in the whole of its emotional and imaginative cast. They did not pour new wine into old bottles; they poured new wine into new bottles. Both form and content were, in their poetry, a new departure, in all respects, foreign from the tradition of Greco-Roman literature.

Much rather than with assessing, far less recommending, the qualities of that half-forgotten poetry, it is with placing in its historical perspective the remarkable action that it exerted that our present purpose is concerned. The intrinsic merits of troubadour poetry lie open, as does all literary production, to divergence of judgment contingent on diverse tastes and standards. But that is not the case with regard to the fact of that poetry's historical importance. The importance is enormous. It is perhaps greater than that of any other single agency that has been influential upon the course of development of our literatures.

Down to the eighteenth century, all discussion in matters literary pivoted on the tiresome opposition between the "ancients" and the "moderns." The assumption which lay at the base of that insistent antithesis was that European literature is essentially continuous with that of Greece and Rome. Whatever deviations its course has been put to were not seen as effects of qualitative cultural differences, but of deficiencies and disabilities, of barbarism, ignorance, and untutored license. In the later Middle Ages, thoughtful men suffered under a crushing sense of inferiority. And small wonder! They looked about them upon a world that had mouldered in the night of five centuries. They held, at the same time, the imperishable remembrance of another world that had gone before and had grown to a mythical mirage in their haunting nostalgia. Beside that splendor, its wealth of achievement, of thought, of art, of masterpieces, what were the puny and stunted fruits the present had to show, but penury? "Antiquity" did not stand in their minds for a peculiar form or phase of culture; it stood for human culture in an absolute sense, for the mental cultivation that raises man above brutishness. That there could ever be a new world, a new Europe, a new culture, a new literature was to them a notion devoid of meaning. The Renaissance, when it came, was seen as a restoration, a rebuilding. It was the resumed flow of the stream of human culture, which had its upper waters in Rome and Greece, which had for a time slumbered in hidden backpools, been sucked in the slop of swamps, but was about to take up its even course towards the changeless goals set by the great masters.

The facts are somewhat different. The contrasts between the trends of modern Europe and those of Greco-Roman tradition are not primarily effects of barbaric shortcomings and the disabilities of ignorance; they are the outcome of wholesale cultural importations and immigrations from without. Our literatures have not been shaped by adaptation and modification of the classical heritage, but by drawing from entirely distinct sources, having no sort of connection or cognateness with that heritage. There was no going back on the effects of those accessions. For better or worse, they had entered the blood and fiber of European culture, and no opinion, no debate, no pronouncement could eradicate or purge them. Despite every effort to follow in the steps of the "ancients," whom their would-be disciples were incapable of comprehending, whom they grossly and grotesquely travestied until the rousing of the critical historical sense of archeology, comparative anthropology, and comparative religion in the nineteenth century, despite the pathetic misconceptions of psuedo-classicism, the development of our literatures has been paramountly determined by the nurture which they sucked during the impressionable period of their infancy.

As regards lyrical expression and the attitude towards amatory emotions, both categories of far wider reach and scope than narrow definitions imply, the spring at which those literatures drank was not situated in Greece or in Rome, but in Provence.

In speaking of "Provence," I am following the example set in the Middle Ages by the inhabitants of those regions where the *langue d'oc* was spoken, geographically much more extended than the district now known as Provence. Those territories included the Roman "provinces" of Narbonne, the "first" and the "second" Aquitania, and reached north as far as the Loire. "The name 'Provençal,'" says Raymond d'Agyles, "was given to the peoples of Burgundy, Auvergne, Gascony, Gothia and Provence."[21] Those were the native lands of the Provençal troubadours.

The emergence in the twelfth century of a new lyrical art in Provence was among the privileges conferred upon those lands by their favorable situation. While Christendom as a whole still lay palled in the darkness of barbarism, Provence—and more particularly the country of Toulouse, a feudal parcel of the domains of Aragon, the most Arabized of the Spanish kingdoms—stood open as no other to the influence of Hispano-Mauresque civilization. It was the mart where the rich products of Moorish industry came for distribution to northern countries. It was the intermediary through which Islamic culture at its palmary height filtered through the darkest Europe. Prominent among the manifestations of that culture, in respect to the ardor with which it was cultivated, was a lyrical art, accompanied by music. With that source of inspiration, particularly rife among the Moorish population of Aragon, the Provençal dependencies of that kingdom were in far closer contact than Northern France with Wales or Ireland. It was inevitable that the widespread popularity of Moorish music and song should instill their form and fashion into *langue d'oc* minstrelsy.

Many specialists in Romance philology have followed Friederich Diez, professor at the University of Bonn, and the founder of modern Provençal studies, in denying the influence of Hispano-Mauresque poetry on that of the troubadours, or have, more often than not, passed over the question in ostentatious silence. Jeanroy, the most eminent French authority, makes one reference to it, and as far as I know only one, relegated to a popular article, and couched in these terms: "As for Arabian influence, which used to be much discussed so long as summary judgments did duty for the close study of facts, it is more and more likely that this is nothing but a fable."[22] I do not know whence Professor Jeanroy derived the impression of that waxing probability; not, certainly, from the study of facts bearing in favor of an extraneous influence on Provençal poetry, which he had no interest to study, closely or at all. But the effect of the close study of facts, which he himself carried out with admirable industry, has not been to bring confirmation to views touching an autochthonous origin of that poetry. On the contrary, as he has shown, the effect has been to reveal the insecurity of the suppositions on which those speculations were poised, and to impair what measure of confidence, limited and half-hearted at the best, they may for a moment have commanded.[23]

The first and by far the most general assumption—it cannot be called a theory or even a hypothesis, for it was held as axiomatic on such bright conviction as to need no confirmation from references to the most accessible facts—was that Provençal poetry arose out of Latin poetry. Romance languages are derived from Latin, not as once was believed, by corruption of the speech of peoples who had once spoken Latin, but as the modified form of Latin which they and their forebears had for centuries used. But linguistic derivation is one thing, and literary derivation quite another. The English language is derived from Low German, but Anglo-Saxon productions, such as *Beowulf* or the *Proverbs* of King Alfred have left no mark or inheritance in English literature. The view that Provençal poetry had its origin from Latin, which was clung to for a longer time and with more sufficiency than any other, is today so completely abandoned that to refer to it is but to thrash a dead horse. Apart from the singular tidings that Latin poetry contained at any time an incitation to the contrivance of rhyme-patterns and strophic novelties, the main pertinent facts are: firstly, that few if any troubadours knew Latin; and secondly, that what tags of Latin verse are assignable to the period and the localities in cause, do not suggest the remotest resemblance to troubadour poetry.[24]

Nothing in the records of Christian Europe affords a glimpse, even the dimmest, of troubadour poetry in the making. That there existed previously to the twelfth century, as at all periods, popular chants of some kind is a legitimate assumption. None have come down to us. But what slivers may be gleaned of relatively studied verse, composed by clerks, are rude in cast and manner and bear no sort of comparison with the most ancient Provençal songs. There is no reason for supposing that popular songs surpassed "learned" poetry in quality.

The well-known theory of Gaston Paris, which refers the
origin of troubadour poetry to the chants sung at the great pagan
Celtic festivals of May Day, has found favor in England from
such high authorities as Sir Edmund Chambers. Invocations and
references to the Spring are a staple in the poetry of troubadours
and trouvères. Among the latter those songs bore a special name;
they were called *reverdies;* among the Arabs they were known as
neherye. That the spread of the new Provençal style ousted what
uncouth psalmodies may have previously been intoned at May
celebrations is only natural. But those facts, if facts they be, contain no tittle of indication that can help to trace the Provençal
Muse up to her spring. They elucidate in no way the origin and
development of the distinctive characteristics of that new poetry.
They explain nothing. To say that it had its origin in the songs of
people who went a-maying no more touches the question of its
flowering than if one were to say, because troubadour poetry
treats largely of amatory themes, that it had its origin from love.

The close study of facts, as we shall have occasion to note
further, shakes every conjecture that attempts to explain troubadour poetry as an autochthonous growth. These attempts have
failed simply because that poetry was not an autochthonous
growth. Just as it would be odd to search Petronius and Apuleius
for the source of the narratives of Chrestien de Troyes, were the
derivation of these from the "matter from Britain" not avowed,
so is it equally idle to derive the song of the Comte de Poitiers
from the poems of Ausonius or Sidonius Apollinaris, or from
the flight off and away from every trend of local tradition of some
historically mute inglorious Miltons. In the one case as in the
other, if the origin of Romance works differing profoundly from
Latin tradition is to be accounted for, that difference must exist
in the source, and we must needs look to an influence alien from
that tradition. The question is not one to be exclusively determined by the authority, however high, of specialists in the Romance languages, since its solution calls for some acquaintance
with poetical activities outside the range of the Romance idioms,

concerning which information was almost entirely lacking at the time when Diez wrote.

This is no longer the case. While not a parcel of proof is to be found in support of the hypotheses which were advanced relative to the activities akin to the art of the troubadours in Christian Europe, we now dispose of a considerable amount of information concerning the rich literature of Moorish Spain from the tenth century on, and our knowledge in this direction has of late years advanced to such a degree that to ignore it is no longer excusable. Signs are not wanting of a more enlightened attitude slackening the hold of the views which have long prevailed in academic circles. Those views, it may be observed, presented but a particular instance of a much more ancient and comprehensive aberration of historical judgment, born of reluctance to owning the debts of barbarous Christendom to a miscreant civilization. No hypothesis was so wild and unsubstantial that zealots would not flee to it in pursuit of a refuge from that distasteful acknowledgement.[25] But while those prejudices have now lost much of their force, many cultivated Frenchmen, including distinguished writers and professors of general history whose training never offered them any encouragement to acquire a personal judgment, are readily disposed to rest on the authority of eminent scholars' views which are agreeable to national sentiment.[26] They find no difficulty in believing that Provençal lyric art flowered by a spontaneous generation within a few leagues from Paris,[27] and never perceive the need, in accounting for its origin, of having recourse to the Moors.

The singers of those lyrics, however, did not scruple at resorting to the Moors for the musical instruments on which they accompanied their lays. The patrons of the troubadours obtained from the Moors the luxury and elegance which helped refine their tastes; those privileged leisures which cradled their courtly diversions, they owed to the wealth which their country derived from commerce with the Moors. Europe borrowed in the twelfth century from the Moors the new industries, the sciences, the arts of navigation which were to transform it. The studious and the learned resorted to the Moors to acquire the new mathematical sciences, medicine, chemistry, and to gain access to Aristotle and Averroes. Daniel de Morley, Michael Scotus, Gerard of Cremona, Gerbert d'Aurillac, Raymon Lully resorted to the Moors for the seeds of a new world of thought and science. Regiomontanus depended on the ephemerides of Al-Batáni for the data destined to enable Henry the Navigator, Vasco da Gama, and Christopher Columbus to extend tenfold the area of the known world. Adelhard of Bath went to Cordova to procure the copy of the works of Euclid which supplied, until the year 1533, all the schools of Europe; Plato of Pisa and Fibronacci went to Moorish Spain for algebra, algorism, the abacus and the almanac. The Church itself drew its system of scholastic dialectics from Moorish authors; Albertus Magnus and Thomas Aquinas, both Arabic scholars, had resort to Avicenna, Al-Farabi and Averroes for casting the philosophy of the Catholic faith into a systematic mold. While the troubadours were intoning their song on the doorsteps of Moorish Spain, Roger Bacon was proclaiming at Oxford that no science and no thought was possible without an acquaintance with the books of the Arabs.

Medieval Europe, sunk in the night of five centuries of barbarism, the darkness of which we have difficulty in piercing, was suddenly recalled to life. She owed, in that critical hour, everything to the world of Islam. She owed almost nothing to Rome, which had hitherto transmitted to her, in literature, little more than a few selections from Ovid, Cassiodorus and Boethius. To suppose that the new poetry which made itself heard on the edge of Andalusian gardens constituted a singular exception is, properly considered, an eccentricity which it would take far more cogent reasons to color than the unsupported guesses offered in explanation of the origin of that poetry.[28]

Moorish Origin

T HE theologians of Damascus discussed the abstruse question of "universals," raised by a passage in the *Isagogos* of Porphyry, and developed a new system of dialectic derived from Aristotle a full century before the doctors of the University of Paris took up the debate in the same terms, using the same authorities and the same methods. About a century before the first troubadour song soared in Languedoc, the men of letters in Moorish Spain were engrossed in trying the merits of a new style of poetry, the spread of popularity of which amounted, for them, to a literary revolution.

"True to the tradition of their family, the Spanish Umayyads," writes Professor Nicholson, "loved poetry, music and polite literature a great deal better than the Koran."[1] In the earliest days of the Western Caliphate, the ancient Arabian poetry, devoted in general to the glorification of the tribe, the praise of battles and horses, continued to be cultivated by a number of poets, of whom Ibn Hani of Seville (d. 973) is named as the most noted. But that consecrated hieratic manner, in honor since the "days of ignorance" among the Arabs, gave place before long to another and very different poetical form. H.A.R. Gibb, paraphrasing Jan van Goeje, states, ". . . a galaxy of poets . . . released themselves from the old conventions and made their verse a vehicle of self expression ... it was practically confined to erotic verse."² The most interesting features of Spanish-Arabian poetry," says Nicholson again, "are the tenderly romantic feeling which not infrequently appears in their love-songs, a feeling that sometimes anticipates the attitude of medieval chivalry, and in the second place, an almost modern sensibility to the beauties of nature. On account of those characteristics, the poems in question appeal to many European readers who do not easily enter into the spirit of [ancient Arabic poetry]."³ King Al-Mu'tamid of Seville and Ibn Zaidūn of Cordova were counted among the most eminent poets who lent luster to that new poetry. It celebrates love as the highest form of happiness and the noblest source of inspiration; it sings of the beloved's beauty, the sorrow of the rejected lover and the cruelty of the lady. It introduces new fashions in composition, as in its hymns to Spring. Anticipating Provençal lyrics by close on two centuries, Hispano-Moorish poetry was the only one, in Europe, to cultivate those themes and to exhibit those characteristics. Nowhere else did a lyrical literature exist, popular or learned, offering a like resemblance to Provençal poetry. The *prima facie* implication of these facts is, without more ado, obvious.

No belief could be more uninformed than the notion, not infrequently entertained, that the Arabs knew nothing of love beyond its sensual aspect. Veneration for women and their idealization counted among the most ancient traditions of the race, and dated from further back than Islam. In earliest times, poetical competitions were held in the tents of cultivated women, themselves poets, who were the judges in those contests.⁴ When, therefore, in the tenth and eleventh centuries, a form of poetry characterized by a chivalrous spirit unknown to Greco-Roman tradition made its appearance in Spain, the ground had been prepared for that efflorescence by the traditions and disposition of Arabic poetry from the first. Licentious poetry is, to be sure, found in Arabic literature as in most others, and poets were not lacking who scoffed at the ethereal refinement of their colleagues. But far from being alien to the Islamic world, the puritan spirit, particularly during the period with which we are more immediately concerned, was one of its most prominent and widespread characteristics. Sects such as the Beni-Odra, or "Sons of Chastity," and the Ikhwan as-Safā', or "Brothers of Purity," whose tents were disseminated in Spain by Maslem of Madrid towards the close of the tenth century, carried that tendency to the point of extravagance.

Most important, however, among the manifestations of Arabian mysticism was the Sufi doctrine, which arose in the second century of Islam and spread throughout all countries and all social classes of the Muslim world. It may, some think, have owed something to contact with the Cenobites of Sinai. Among the oldest documents of Sufism are cited the *Sentences* of an Islamic Saint Theresa, Rabi'a of Basra, who assimilated divine to profane love. Sufism adopted an erotic and even bacchic terminology in its highly colored symbolic language. In the intoxication produced by the wine of the true doctrine, God was revealed to the adept under the likeness of love and of the Mystic Vine. The whole imagery of Sufi idealism rests indeed on the conception of love. Love is, according to Yusuf u Zulaikha, the primary cause of creation. Divine love cannot be understood by him who has not experienced the transports of profane love.

The Sufis of eleventh-century Spain not only devoted themselves to the composition of love-poems, an exercise which they accounted almost prescriptive, but they furthermore discussed at length in the scholastic manner the metaphysics of the sentiments which inspired their lyrics. This peculiar erotic philosophy is, in fact, as closely connected with Hispano-Moorish love poetry as are the dialectics of "courtly love" with that of the troubadours. The piety of Sufi puritans had at any rate the merit of not being dismal; it was a manner of *gai saper,* of "gay science." Poetry, song and dance were its current manifestations. Disseminated in innumerable forms and varieties throughout the Islamic world, the Sufi doctrine gathered force from the study of Plato and the neo-platonists. Several among the philosophers, including the illustrious Ibn Sina, whom the Rumi call Avicenna, transposed Sufi symbolism and drew their inspiration from passages in the *Phaedrus* and the *Symposium,* making profane love the subject of their writings and comparing it to love divine. There exists a whole series of such dissertations,[5] curious products of the oriental mind, in which realism and mysticism are mingled. One of those works, the *Kitāb az-Zahra* of Abū Bakr Ibn Dawūd (868-909), head of the Zaharite school, of Bagdad, is permeated throughout with the theories of Plato. The Arabian author quotes in detail the Platonic conception of pre-established affinities, according to which souls that have been created by the bisection of the same sphere find themselves attracted to their complementary halves. He insists on "the submission of the lover to the beloved," this being, he says "the mark of refined love," and above all on purity, declaring that "he who is well born should be pure and chaste."[6]

It was in Spain that these trends of thought reached the peak of their vogue and influence. 'Ali Ibn Hazm of Cordova (994-1065), an author remarkably modern in his critical style—*vir immensae doctrinae*, as Dozy calls him[7]—and whose philosophical writings provide one of the most valuable bodies of evidence we possess on the history of Arabian thought, composed, among other treatises, one *On Love,* bearing the poetical title of *Tauk al-Hamama*, "The Dove's Neck-Ring."[8] This work, which runs to thirty chapters, treats, among other subjects, "Of Love from Description," "Of Love Messages," "Of Hints from the Eyes," "Of Loyalty," "Of Fidelity," "Of the Submissiveness due the Lover to his Lady," "Of the Signs of Love," etc. Ibn Hazm observes that "love often begins jestingly but its end may be very serious."[9] He reverts, in almost the same terms as Ibn Dawūd, to the theories of Plato. He has a chapter on "Slanderers," another on the "Helping Friend"; he declares that lack of trust in love-relations is the mark of "a person of low birth and one devoid of refined feelings."[10] In one poem the lover declares himself satisfied with a look.[11] The author is above all devoted to the extolling "the excellence of Chastity." "The union of the spirit," he asserts, "is more beautiful than the union of the body, a thousand times."[12] And he relates, in his chapter on love at first sight, how the poet Ibn Hārūn ar-Ramādī, well known in the literary annals of Moorish Spain, after having met his lady on a single occasion, near the Gate of the Druggists at Cordova, dedicated his love poems to her for the rest of his life.[13] Some of Ibn Hazm's anecdotes, which recall the romanticized biographies of the troubadours, relate to love for a "distant lady," known only by hearsay.[14] On descanting upon the various ways in which love comes to birth, he dwells on the impression of sight, "for love enters most often through the eyes, which are the gateways of the mind, and thence spreads throughout the whole soul,"[15] a doctrine much in vogue among the troubadours. The Arab author of the eleventh century goes, in fact, much farther on the path of idealization than any troubadour. He is much closer in his ideas to the Italian poets of the fourteenth century.

Like the majority of Arab works, Ibn Hazm's book is abundantly larded with verses. Sufi mysticism and its predilection for expressing itself in verse exercised in fact a profound and widespread influence on Hispano-Moorish poetry. As a sample we may cite from a poem of the tenth century by Ibn Darrach (d. 976). After having drawn a picture of the seductive charms of his lady, "who sets wide the gates of passion," the poet concludes:

> She is like an orchard of which I taste
> only the beauty and the perfume;
>
> for I am not as the beasts of the field,
> to whom a garden is but a pasturage.[16]

That idealization of passion, though entirely absent from the Western amatory poetry of the following centuries, remained current in the Islamic world down to the thirteenth century and later. One of the most popular among the later poets, Umar Ibn al-Farīd (1185-1235), sings of his beloved in the following terms:

> Far from me be the chill love that leaves the
> eyelids dry, the passion that does not kindle
> the fires of frenzy! . . . .

> Inflict upon me what trials and travails
> soever you will, save only that of banishment
> from your presence; I shall ever remain
> your faithful and submissive lover; I shall
> ever employ my industry to forestall your wishes.

> Take this last breath of life which it has
> been your pleasure to leave to me. No love
> is perfect that would pause before yielding
> what of bare life remains. To die of love
> for the beloved is to claim an honored place
> in the regard of all true lovers. . . .

> Should my beloved move away,
> then forsake, O my blood, the heart which you
> impel; when she approaches, then beam, O my
> eyes, with the light of happiness. . . .

> Pity the unease of one who at one moment abandons
> all hope, and at another lulls himself with
> fond illusions. . . .

> The love that consumes me is as pure as the
> visages of the elect. . . .

> One evening we found ourselves peradventure
> in a place where was none to keep watch over
> us, and no slanderer was near that might
> wrong us by his calumnies.

> I laid my face against the ground that it
> might be as a footstool to my lady. She said:
> Rejoice, for you may set your lips upon my veil!

> But my heart would not consent: for she
> entrusted to the nobility of my feelings
> the care of her honor.

> And we passed that night as I would have
> desired. Me seemed I owned the kingdoms of
> the earth, and that time obeyed my
> bidding as a slave.[17]

No Provençal poet of the twelfth century, it may be affirmed, ever approached the heights of spiritual sublimation which inspired Muslim poetry. The troubadours borrowed from the latter much of its terminology,[18] but we should not be justified in regarding the principles whence derived the poetry of Moorish Spain and those on which rested the conventions of courtly love as identical. The feudal society of Languedoc and the Islamic world exhibited differences which could not fail to be reflected in the characters of their respective poetical inspirations.

The contrast between the two societies was, however, much less pronounced than we might be led to suppose. In the Middle Ages, Europe and the Islamic world resembled each other more closely than at any subsequent period. The setting and aspects of daily life in many a *kasbah* of the Atlas recall vividly, even to this day, those of a French medieval castle.[19] The harem system was not, in the early days of Islam, what it subsequently became. Down to the present time, among the Berbers, women pay little heed to it, and the veil is seldom worn. The conquerors of Spain brought with them but a few female companions, and peopled their palaces with Spanish women. These retained a large measure of their independence of manner and were encouraged to do so. They were in general much more highly cultivated than their sisters in Christian lands; they received the same education as the men, and often in classes including both sexes. Learned women were even to be found who took to the study of philosophy and mathematics, and sometimes visited the East in order to attend the lectures of noted professors. Others, the wives and daughters of viziers and caliphs, occupied posts in government departments. The transcription of manuscripts was a feminine occupation; hundreds of women were, in one quarter of Cordova, employed on the fabrication of books. The manuscripts of a certain Fatima were renowned for their beauty.[20] A number of women are mentioned as distinguished for their poetical talents. The wives of emirs and viziers frequently took part in literary gatherings, and shed the inspiration of their wit and cultivated taste upon those assemblies. The princess Walhada, daughter of Muhammad II, (reigned 1008-1010) and Aisha bint-Ahmed are named with particular commendation as composers of verse and patronesses of the poets.[21]

While no sharp contrast existed in the Middle Ages between the West and the Orient, Christendom and Islam, as appears today, when the one world has become transformed by gigantic revolutions and the other has remained, but for the deterioration of profound decay, unchanged in essential character, it would be idle to ignore the differences between feudal Provence and Moorish Spain. The fact is on that account the more remarkable that so specific and intimate a manifestation as the poetical expression of passion should nevertheless have assumed, in the two, forms so closely similar, and lends added probability to the inference that this concordance is attributable to the influence exerted by the older upon the younger of those lyrical developments. So much at first sight. From those general grounds, let us now turn to the closer consideration of concrete facts.

The lyrical poetry of Moorish Spain contrasts by its form no less than by its contents with traditional Arabic poetry. The latter had fallen into a pedantry which would put academical purism to shame. Tied down to metrical rules and to a form of

construction (*ilm al-qāfiya*) of incredible rigidity, it was moreover composed in a hieratic language (*shi'r*) that had ceased to
be current even in Muhammad's time, and was governed by a
syntax and system of inflections that had long been discarded in
current speech. Casting off the trammels of that traditional
pedantry, the poets of Andalusia effected a remarkable transformation. This literary revolution rested upon one important
circumstance: ancient Arabic poetry had not been sung, that of
Moorish Spain was. It became, in the proper connotation of the
term, lyrical.

The Koran discounted music. The Imam Malik, whose judgment in the matter was accounted authoritative, condemned
melody and song as frivolities unbefitting the character of a true
believer. "The Arabs," says Ibn Khaldūn, "practiced at first no
other art than that of verse."[22] However, the great vogue which
music acquired overcame, though not without a struggle, the
formalist tradition, and induced it to yield to the taste awakened
by the new art. The Arabs improved upon the musical instruments which they had taken over in Iran, Syria and the Maghreb.
They invented the bow, thereby transforming the stringed instruments of Persia into the *rabab,* the ancestor of the violin; they
introduced innumerable modifications into the lute (*al'ūd*) and
into the *ganūn,* a kind of psaltery.[23] Modern music is a result of
the evolution of musical instruments. But for the harpsichord,
which grew by slow stages out of the *ganūn,* the Cremona violins,
perfected forms of the Arabian *rabab,* the genius of Bach and
Mozart would have remained mute, and we should have remained deaf to the harmonies which delight us. Accustomed as
is the modern ear to rich sonorous combinations, complex chords,
and the magical effects of polyphony and counterpoint, we find
it difficult to appreciate the thin rills of monodic melody which
were the sole form of musical expression known to the Middle
Ages. Our ears may, on the other hand, have lost something of
the sure sense of rhythm which our forefathers possessed, as do

likewise Orientals to the present day. Their simple and merely cadenced music, however, afforded as much pleasure to a world that had hitherto known nothing beyond the tinkling of the four strings of a primitive harp and the tootling notes of a flute, as we derive from our own music. It was in Spain, where since the time of Martial the women of Cadiz danced to the sound of Andalusian castanets,[24] that the music achieved its most notable advances and attained its most widespread popularity.

The adaptation of Arabic poetry to song was brought about by substituting short lines for the long lines in which were composed the traditional poems, the *qaṣīdas,* of the Arabs, and the couplets with which they were fond of enamelling their writings and speeches. Those lines, each of which formed a complete whole, were divided into two equal segments by a caesura, or middle pause, which was heavily stressed. The hands, even the feet, were used to mark the beat. With Oriental poetry, as with Oriental music, rhythm is everything. Quantities being only lightly marked, rhyme was used as a further means of stressing the cadence. The complicated rules of prosody in traditional Arabic poetry bear no relation to those governing Greek and Latin verse, in which accent was pronounced, and owing to the uniformity of inflections, rhyme would have produced a banal and monotonous effect. It was the Arabs who introduced rhyme into Europe. All the lines of their *qaṣīdas* were built upon one rhyme, which never varied throughout the composition. The caesuras were also occasionally indicated by interior rhymes.[25]

By dividing its lines into their constituent half-lines, a classical couplet yields a quatrain or strophe (*baīt*) which admits of being sung. But in order to stress the fall of the melodic phrase which likewise marks the close of the subject-matter of the strophe, the last line of the cad strophe was distinguished by a different rhyme, called *asmat*. This rhyme, repeated at the end of each strophe, thus produced the effect of a refrain, though Arabic poetry was not acquainted with the use of the true refrain.

A couplet of short lines ending with this thematic rhyme usually introduced or concluded the song. In the former case it was called *marqaz;* in the latter, *kharga.* This form of strophe presents, then, the following schematic arrangement:

____A	____A		*marqaz*
____B	____B	____B	*1st baīt*
	____A		*asmat*
____C	____C	____C	*2nd baīt*
	____A		*asmat*

This ordonnance of rhymes—*aa bbba ccca,* etc.—is known among the Arabs as *murabba'.* It is by far the most prevalent structure in stanzic Arabic poetry, though it is susceptible of numerous variations.[26] In its literary form in the traditional tongue, the song composed on this model was known by the name of *muwashshaha,* from the expression denoting a particular form of girdle held in place by a shoulder-strap (*wisha*) which was worn by women. In the songs composed in current speech the same arrangement of rhymes was simply called a "song," *zajal* (plural, *azajal*). Insofar as the structure of the strophe is concerned, there is no difference between the *muwashshaha* and the *zajal.*[27] Both were composed with a view to being sung to the accompaniment of instrumental music.[28]

This strophic structure was fully developed in Spain as far back as the beginning of the tenth century. Its popular form goes back to an even remoter time.[29] In the eleventh century its vogue amongst all classes of the mixed population of Andalusia, Arabian, Mozarabian and Romance, was general, and extended as far as Egypt and the countries of the Near East.[30] The *Sessions* of the poet Harīrī (1054-1122), a work which, after the Koran, has had in the course of eight centuries, more readers than any others in the Muslim world, are lavishly spangled with *murabba'* strophes. Harīrī's German translator, Friederich Rückert, gives some excellent imitations of them, of which the following is an example:

> *O Abu-Seid, wie lange*
> *willst du noch sein die Schlange*
> *stets lauernd neuem Fange*
> *und wechselnd Haut um Haut?*
>
> *Macht dir mit Gottes Schutze*
> *der Prediger's Wort zu Nutze;*
> *ihn unter die Kaputze*
> *zu schaun ist unterlaubt.*[31]

And here is a *zajal* of Moorish Spain translated into Spanish by M. J. Valera, who also retains the meter and the distribution of rhyme of the original:

> *En balde es tanto afanar,*
> *amigos, para pescar.*
>
> *En las redes bien quisiera*
> *prender la trucha ligera;*
> *mas esta niña hechicera*
> *es quien nos debe pescar.*
>
> *Los peces tienen recelos*
> *y burlan redes y anzuelos;*
> *pero en sus dulces ojuelos*
> *van nuestras almas a dar.*[32]

The transliteration of an Andalusian *zajal,* accompanied by a translation, is given in the notes.[33]

With this metrical form of Hispano-Moorish song, let us now compare one or two of the very small number of extant examples of popular Provençal songs dating from the twelfth century:

> *Coindeta sui, si cum n'ai greu cossire,*
> *per mon marit, quar ne.l voil ne.l desire.*

Qu'eu be.us dirai per son que aissi drusa;
qu'ar pauca son, jovenetta e tosa,
e degr' aver marit dont fos joiosa,
ab cui toz temps pogues jogar e rire.[34]

And again:

Quant le gilos er fora, bels ami
vene vos a mi.

Balada cointa e gaia
faz, cui pes ne cui plaia
pel dolz cant que m'apaia
que audi seir e de matin.[35]

The *murabba'* form of the Andalusian *zajal* is invariably adhered to in the Provençal *aubade* or *alba*, a genre current among the people:

Quan lo rossinhols escria
ab sa par la nuege e.l dia,
yeu suy ab ma bell'amia
jos la flor,

Tro la gaita de la tor
escria: drutz, al levar!
qu'ieu vey l'alba e.l jorn clar.[36]

Even when a courtly troubadour composes in this manner, the form of the stanza, and the popular style of the song, are usually retained. The following example is probably by Gaucelm Faidit. It begins:

En un vergier sotz fuella d'albespi
tenc la dompna son amic costa si,
tro la gaita crida que l'alba vi.
Oy Deus, Oy Deus, de l'alba! Tan tost ve!

Plagues a Deus ja la noitz non falhis,
ni.l meus amics lonh de mi no.s partis,
ni la gaita jorn ni alba no vis!
Oy Deus, Oy Deus, de l'alba! Tan tost ve![37]

Cardinal Bembo, who had in his youth made a long sojourn
in Provence, wrote in the sixteenth century: "This form was very
commonly used by Provençal versifiers . . . in the ballads, so
called because the song was accompanied, in these compositions,
by a dance, the last rhyme of the two lines sung by the 'crown,'
that is to say, by all the voices taking part together, was repeated
in the last line of the solo part."[38] The learned Venetian Cardinal, who had such a precise knowledge of the structure of the
popular Provençal ballad, was doubtless in a better position than
we are to estimate the wide range of its popularity. This
anonymous poetry, designated as "popular," was indubitably, in
the main, the production of itinerant singers and jongleurs,
whose business it was to enliven with such diversions the festivities and gatherings of all classes of the population.

Let us now pass on to a consideration of the poetry of the
troubadours properly so-called. The oldest that we know, so far
from being a man of the people, was the most powerful noble-
man in France, Count Guilhem VII of Poitiers, Duke of Aquitaine, ninth of the name. The following strophes conclude one
of his most pleasing songs:

Tot ai guerpit cant amar sueill,
cavalaria et orgueill;
e pos Dieu platz, tot o accueill,
e prec li que.m reteng' am si.

Toz mos amics prec a la mort
que vengan tut a m onren fort
qu'eu ai avut joi e deport
loing e pres et e mon aizi.

Aissi guerpisc joi e deport
e vair e gris e sembeli.

Gone now's all I have loved best,
pastimes bold and pleasures quest.
Be done God's will! and may I rest
in the mercy of his hands.

Friends, when I am passed away,
show me honor, all you may.
We've both had high times, revels gay,
both abroad and on my lands.

Gone's joy now and the life gay,
brave trim, revels, merry bands.[39]

As in the examples of popular Provençal poetry just quoted,
the strophic structure and the distribution of rhymes will be seen
to be punctually identical with those of the Andalusian *zajal*. The
distich forming the *marqaz* in the latter is relegated, in the Provençal example, to the end of the composition, and forms a
kharga, coda or *envoy*.

This rhyme pattern, *aa, bbba, ccca* or *bbba, ccca, aa,* is indeed
unique. In its complete form, that is consisting of a crown, the
rhyme of which is repeated after each monorhymed tercet, it is
one of the rarest patterns known. It is rarely encountered in
any of the European literatures outside of those of Spain and
Provence, and when it is, Provençal poetry undoubtedly provided
the model. In the trouvère poetry of northern France, which
developed out of full-blown Provençal "courtly" poetry, it is
not so prevalent as among the troubadours. In England, though
the pattern is prominent in a whole class of lyrical poetry, it
occurs but once in Chaucer, who drew his inspiration from
French rather than directly from Provençal sources. There are
two or three examples in Old English, dating from the twelfth
century, which may be found in the Harleian collection.[40] The
pattern is found in a piece doubtfully attributed to Sir Philip

Sidney; it does not occur in Spenser and is only occasionally found scattered among the works of sixteenth-century poets. Shakespeare uses it in Bottom's song in Midsummer Night's Dream:

> The raging rocks
> and shivering shocks
> shall break the locks
>   of prison gates;
> and Phibbus' car
> shall shine from far
> and make and mar
>   the foolish Fates.

He also uses it in some short pieces expressly composed for music. This was generally regarded as the special province for the employment of that verse arrangement in English poetry.

But, on the other hand, numerous examples of the *murabba'* form are found widely distributed in poetry of a popular character and whose derivation from the Provençal models stands above dispute. What was long regarded as the oldest extant specimen of verse in the Italian language, the "Contrasto" by d'Aleano (cited in note 38), follows that pattern. It occurs among the rare specimens of popular songs of the twelfth and thirteenth centuries, and even in narrative pieces in the style of the French *chansons d'histoire,* such as the fine account of the struggle between Guelfs and Ghibellines in Bologna:

> *Del guasto de Bologna si comenza,*
> *como perdé la forza e la potenza*
> *e lo gran senno con la provedenza*
> *ch'aver solea.*

But it is generally modified by a variation of the rhymes within the body of the strophe.

Under the head of popular poetry must be counted that of the Franciscan poets, whose close connection with popular Provençal poetry is well known. St. Francis, whose wayward years were spent in companies of young men particularly addicted to Provençal songs, excelled in this field, and at one time, it is said, had some thought of becoming a jongleur. He urged the practice of poetry upon his disciples. "We are," he said, "the jongleurs of God. For, as servants of the Lord, are we not in truth jongleurs whose vocation is to uplift the hearts of men, and to lead them to spiritual joy?"[41] With Jacopone da Todi (1250-1304), the best known and most copious of the Franciscan poets, the *murabbaʿ* form is by far the favorite and most abundantly employed. He used it not only in numerous short songs and carols,[42] but also in canticles, running to thirty or forty stanzas, all in the *murabbaʿ* form such as a piece on the passion[43] or another on the curious theme of the advantages of ill health.[44]

Towards the latter part of the thirteenth century the Church, which had hitherto cried anathema on the jongleurs and all their works, bethought herself of enrolling them in her service for the production of miracle plays and of religious carols expressly intended to appeal to the populace. Those compositions were accordingly in the popular style. Many were in the Provençal language, but they were also produced in French and likewise in English. Thus it happens that the lyrics of that period which have been preserved in English monasteries are composed in the popular Provençal style, and have no affinity to any popular poetry which may have existed in England. The greater number of those religious ditties and carols are in pure *murabbaʿ* form, as in the following examples from a manuscript in the Bodleian library:

> A man was the first gilt,
> and therefore he was spilt.
> The profecy was never fulfilt,
>   till on the Cristmes day.[45]

His body was wrapped all in woe,
hand and foote he may not go.
Thy son, Lady, that thou lovest so
naked is nailed upon a tree.[46]

Lyrics on amatory or other themes, as well as compositions of jongleurs attached to monasteries, commonly follow the popular Provençal pattern, e.g.:

Her fair eye piercing
my poor heart bleeding,
and I abiding
    in hope of meed;

But thus have I long
entwined this song,
with paines full strong,
    and cannot speed.[47]

Similar Church carols and canticles in rhymed Latin are far less ancient than was at one time supposed. Rhymed Latin tercets postdate troubadour poetry by about a century. Far from having served as a model to popular ditties, as has been suggested, they are much more likely derived from them.[48] According to Durandus de St. Porcain, the *Salve Regina* was composed in Spain by Pedro de Monsoro, bishop of Compostela.[49] The *Stabat Mater* was composed by the Provençalizing Franciscan, Jacopone da Todi, who was mentioned above.

The wide range in European poetry of a popular style indisputably derived from the Provençal, and conforming to the pattern which marks the popular and the most ancient poetry in Provence, again goes to show that that pattern was much more general there than the scanty fragments that have come down to us would warrant our supposing. But at the same time, that strophic form is scarcely found in European lyrical poetry produced independently of direct Provençal imitation. In view of this, its coincidence with that of popular Moorish poetry cannot with any probability be imputed to chance.

That the poetry of the troubadours was related to popular poetry is extremely probable, but we are unacquainted with any such poetry anterior to the age of the troubadours. A. Jeanroy has shown that no fragment of popular Provençal poetry known to us can be transferred to an earlier date than the end of the twelfth century.[50] He has made some ingenious conjectures on this subject. Starting from the hypothesis of "a lyrical poetry in the North of France anterior to its southern imitation," he has searched the most ancient Italian, German and Portuguese poetry for traces of that conjectural French poetry, under the conviction, as he declares, "that everything coming from France enjoyed at that time superlative prestige," and it is his opinion that we may, on the strength of that prestige, perceive in foreign poetical productions "the imitation of a type of French poetry at present lost."[51]

With reference to the verses of the Count of Poitiers, Jeanroy writes: "They represent a variety of the strophic form in which the concluding line of the couplet is indicated by a different rhyme, the same throughout the poem, which takes the place of an ancient refrain."[52] But we know that in Hispano-Moorish poetry the *asmat* rhyme marked the end of a quatrain formed out of a distich, and does not represent a refrain, a device which the Arabs did not use. Nor is there any example of a refrain in the poetry of the troubadours, apart from the five or six stanzas of Marcabru where the recurrent line consists of a single word, a form also found in Moorish poetry. Jeanroy further advances the supposition that the refrains of popular French poetry are "relics of poems of which the greater part has been lost." "They were at first," he says, "no more than a series of meaningless syllables intended to stress the rhyme," such as *mironton, mironton, mirontaine*, but some of them "appear to suggest situations which are left incompletely specified, and introduce characters which must have at one time played a more important and definite part."[53]

But the Arab author, Ibn Sanā' al-Mūlk, speaking of the poetry of Moorish Spain, goes into the following particulars: "It is accounted an imperative rule that the poet, breaking off from the subject matter of the lyric, should pass on to the *kharga* (the nearest equivalent of the Romance refrain) without any transition, and that he should represent it as being uttered by characters who speak in their own names, or, if they remain silent, are connected with a theme other than that of the poem. The *kharga* is frequently couched in childish language or in a foreign tongue. In any case it is a customary convention that it should produce the effect of a meaningless jargon."[54] "The Provençal poets," M. Jeanroy states, "give the two lines of the refrain the same rhyme in order that they should form a complete whole."[55] But it is not the Provençal poets who do this, for their *codas* are often equipped with different rhymes as in the example just quoted. It is the poets of Moorish Spain who almost invariably practice that usage, and did so for almost two centuries before ever a troubadour pricked his first song in Provence.

Out of eleven songs by Count Guilhem de Poitiers which we possess, six, the 4th, 5th, 6th, 7th, 8th and 11th in Jeanroy's edition, follow very closely the *zajal* model. Two others, the 9th and 10th, differ from it only by slight variations. "All the pieces except one, the 10th," says Jeanroy, "are variations of the form *aaab ab*."[56] And commenting on the prevalence of this rhyme-scheme in Provençal poetry, he observes that "it represents, no doubt, some traditional form to which it was obligatory to conform."[57] The three remaining pieces, which, it is agreed, are the oldest, are cast in an entirely different mold. They consist of some twenty rhymes ending with the same rhyme. This is the regular form of the *chanson de geste, chanson d'histoire,* or *chanson de toile.* It is also the form of the ancient Arabic *qaṣīda,* and there is ground for thinking that, in its rhymed form, the *chanson de geste* derived originally from the Arabic *qaṣīda*. Be that as it may, it was current before the time of the Count of Poitiers and was sung in the gatherings of warrior nobles. Not only do those first songs of Guilhem de Poitiers bear no relation, in their structural form, to any of his subsequent productions, but their pattern does not occur in the works of any later Provençal troubadour (except in a *sestina* of Arnaud Daniel, where, so far from being derivative, it is a novelty and *bravura*). Apart from these three pieces, all the poems of Count Guilhem which we possess agree very closely in their form with the verse structures employed in current Hispano-Moorish poetry.

It is further to be noted that Count Guilhem is singular among the troubadours in the closeness and uniformity with which his productions follow the Hispano-Moorish song pattern. Cercamon and Marcabru, the nearest to him in date, also approach him more than do the later troubadours in this respect. One out of the six pieces which we have from Cercamon has the rhyme-scheme *aaaab*. The much more numerous surviving compositions of Marcabru—they comprise some forty pieces—include two, the 6th and the 23rd of Dejeanne's edition, conforming exactly to the *murabba'* pattern, and also the following variations: (I) *aaabaaac*, (II) *aaaab ccccb*, (XVIII) *aaababa*, (XXV) *aabccccb*, (XXIX) *aaabaab*, (XXX) *aaaabbab*, (XLIV) *aaaabcbc*, among many others which in their rhythm are even more closely related to the Moorish *zajal* model.[58] The form *aaab* occurs in the works of numerous troubadours. Thus Peire Vidal, notable for the variety of his rhymes, has a piece in the following form:

> *Mos corps s'alegr' e s'esjau*
> *per lo gentil temps suau*
> *e pel castel de Fanjau*
> *qu.em ressembla Paradis....*[59]

and Bernard de Ventadorn ends his stanzas with a *murabba'*:

Tan ai al cor d'amor,
de joi e de doussor,
per que.l gels me sembla flor
  e la neus verdura.[60]

Similar rhyme patterns are found in the poems of Gaucelm Faidit, Bertram de Born, Folquet de Romans, the Monk of Montauban, Peire Cardenal, Arnaud Plagues, Nicolet, Guilhem Rainols and Magrut.[61] The only song by King Alfonso II of Aragon which we possess is couched in the *murabba'* form:

Per mantas guizas m'es datz
joys e deport e solatz;
que per vergiers e per pratz,
e per fuelhas e per flors...[62]

But, speaking generally, the most ancient troubadour productions are those which show the closest and most constant adherence to the Andalusian model. Those of later date, while employing rhyme-schemes which have manifestly that pattern for their starting point, deviate from it by numerous technical variations.

Popular taste is far less keen to lust after new things than are courtly fashions. Popular poetry thus usually preserves its form almost unchanged. The correspondence of that form with that of the most ancient troubadour poetry proper, bears out the assumption of an original connection between the two. But the acceptance of that connection scarcely brings us any nearer to a final resolution of the matter, for we are still left confronted with the question of the origin of that popular poetry itself, and with the remarkable fact that it presented on both sides of the Pyrenees an identical structure which is not found elsewhere.

As already indicated, there existed since the tenth century in Moorish Spain, as later in Provence, two different trends in poetical composition, the one learned and literary, the other popular in character. The Muslims were at that period engaged in debating, like the Italians in the thirteenth century, whether the use of the vernacular tongue in poetry was legitimate. They were, in general, of the opinion that the hieratic tongue alone was beseeming the dignity of poetic diction. This view, however, did not prevent cultivated Moors from expressing the pleasure they derived from the vernacular songs which constituted the repertory of both court and street entertainers. They testify with a profusion of Oriental hyperbole to the raptures into which they are lifted by these songs: they are "the pearls of the universe; they are more exquisite than the perfumes of India."[63]

But despite that enthusiasm, the cultivated classes bowed before the pronouncement of their grammarians, who disallowed the claim of such compositions to being regarded as a literary art. Ibn Bassam (d. 1147), after telling us that Mūqadam Ibn Mū'afa al-Qabri composed *azajal* in the ninth and tenth centuries, states further:

> He used in these compositions short lines similar to the hemistichs of the Arabic metrical system. These productions are however unstudied in their style and written without regard for the rules of Arabic prosody. They are couched in the vernacular and even in the *agami* ("foreign," *i.e., rūmi*) idiom. The name given to the *rūmi* phrases introduced in them is *marqaz*. Being thus indited without any division into hemistichs, and in short lines, those compositions are lacking in scholarly and polished elegance.[64]

And 'Abd al-Walid al-Marrakishi, the historian of the Almohades, after bestowing high praise on the *azajal* composed in the vernacular by the noted physician Abu-Bakr Ibn Zuhr (Abenzoar, 1114-1224) delivers himself of the following curious and enlightening remark: "I should have liked to quote some of the strophes that occur to my recollection, were it not contrary to literary usage to cite such compositions in works of a serious character intended for the perusal of scholars."[65] From as early as the tenth century, not a few men of letters indulged in the composition of vernacular *azajal*. Ibn 'Abd Rabbihi (860-939), a poet attached to the court of the Caliph 'Abd ar-Rahmān III, and Yūsuf Ibn Harūn ar-Ramādi, whom we hear of as having accompanied his master, Al-Manṣūr, to Barcelona in 996, are particularly mentioned for the pleasantness of their *azajal*. Nevertheless, in Moorish Spain as in the Christian world, poetry of a popular character was not considered worthy of being set down and preserved in writing.

About the first years of the twelfth century, however, a song-book of *azajal* was published by Abū Bakr Muḥammad Ibn 'Abd al-Malik Ibn Quzmān of Cordova (1078-1160), for some time vizier to Al-Mitabid, Aftiside Emir of Badajos.[66] The *Diwān* of Ibn Quzmān, which comprise 149 *azajal*, has come down to us and places at our disposal an invaluable document concerning the popular poetry of Moorish Spain.[67] Unfortunately, we have no equivalent of it with respect to the popular poetry of the same period in Christian Europe.

The *Diwān* is composed in the vernacular, and the author discusses in a preface the much debated question of language.[68] "As regards the grammatical conventions of the hieratic language," he writes, "no greater mistake can be committed than to apply them to the composition of a song"; and he proceeds to cite strophes by poets who attempted "to clothe the tenor of everyday converse in the grammatical garb of a *qaṣīda*," showing that the employment of the archaic inflections in short lines results in cacophony. "For that reason I have stripped my language of all inflections and archaic peculiarities of the *shi'r*." He praises the poet Shaikh Ahtal Ibn Numāra for having followed the same practice. "My only hesitation in consigning this collection of *azajal* to writing," Ibn Quzmān adds, "arises from the fact that I deprive myself by so doing, of the advantage I might have derived from the public delivery of these poems," a remark which calls attention to an additional cause of the scarcity of popular songs in written records.

The subject matter of the songs of Ibn Quzmān offers considerable diversity, and the language varies according to the theme. Seven genres of *zajal* were recognized: (1) the love-poem, or *ghazal;* (2) the spring-song, or *neharye;* (3) the drinking-song, or *khamrye;* (4) licentious verses, or *baleik;* (5) satires, or *farki;* (6) colloquies in slang speech, or *mozeiledge;* (7) moral and sententious pieces, or *mokeffer.*[69] Most of these types figure in the *azajal* of Ibn Quzmān's *Diwān.* Thus, one piece begins, in the manner of the troubadours, by a reference to the spring: "The earth puts on the hues of greenery, the flowers of the camomile open out their petals; the whole world becomes decked with a carpet of flowers" (*zajal* 79). In another *zajal,* a pious *alfaquis* reproves the poet for his addiction to pleasure and exhorts him to penitence: "Listen to me and repent of your sins," says the holy man. "I shall repent me," replies the poet, "when the gardens shall have ceased to beam with smiles of joy, and when the breezes shall no longer be laden with the perfumes of musk" (*zaj.* 148). Another song recalls a Provençal *aubade.* Reference is made to the night watchman; the sky grows pale; the lovers grieve; they bid each other farewell in a last embrace (*zaj.* 141). The songs in which the love-theme predominates number about thirty. Several appear to be addressed to men, but it should be borne in mind that it is a current Arab usage to disguise references to a woman by the use of the masculine gender.[70]

Ibn Quzmān refers with derision to those poets who affect to subtilize passion to an impalpable ideal, and who "will depart from this life without ever having enjoyed it." His conception of love, like that of the troubadours, proceeds on the assumption that passion can attain its full impetuosity only in extra-marital relations (*zaj.* 123). "Love is a heavy burden," he says. "What heart were stout enough to bear its load, did not beauty quicken the spirit and multiply its power? . . . The very victims of love are grateful for their sufferings and sing the praises of the power that anguishes them . . . Love takes its origin from sight. Let my eyes meet a pair of charming eyes that are replete with sorcery, and I am forthwith deprived of calm and reason. The shafts from those eyes hold at their mercy my pierced heart" (*zaj.* 117). "O joy of love! In thee is life, in thee is death! Since my eyes met thine, I am like to die, and no pang equals what I endure" (*zaj.* 115). "Mighty God! My love burns more ardently than a live ember . . . but the more bitter is my condition, the sweeter it is to me . . . My life ebbs, but my love does not pass away. The whole world ages from day to day; and my love does not age" (*zaj.* 132). A dozen *azajal* are wine-songs. "Life were intolerable to me without good wine; I shall beseech the Prophet to intercede for me with Allah, so that I may be allowed a due ration of good vintage" (*zaj.* 40). Elsewhere the poet expresses the wish that he might be buried in a vineyard, wrapped in twining shoots (*zaj.* 90).

Ibn Quzmān's songs abound in personal and egotistic touches. He boasts unblushingly and, trumpeting his own work, proclaims that his songs are the most beautiful ever composed (*azaj.* 15, 61, 65, 71, 134). That ostentatious vainglory appears to have been a recognized pose, as with quack vendors of nostrum, among song-makers, both in Spain and in Provence. Rambaut d'Orange proclaims that "never was wrought so excellent a song by man or woman, in this age or the last."[71] Despite his many gibes at pious *alfaquis,* the mirthful Andalusian troubadour bethinks himself, as he feels the years creep on, of turning to care for the welfare of his soul. His whims of repentance and reform lead him to contemplate procuring the charge of *imam* in a mosque (*zaj.* 147). We learn from a piece, which calls to mind Villon, that the poet once got into serious trouble with the police (*chorta*); he was imprisoned and severely mishandled, until rescued by the intervention of one of his admirers, Siyar al-

Mūhammad. The *Diwān* includes political sirventes. *Zajal* 47 refers to the battle of Frage, in which King Alfonso I of Aragon, a kinsman of Count Guilhem de Poitiers, fell at the hand of the Almoravid Emir, Ibn Ghania.

Like the oldest *azajal,* those of Ibn Quzmān are not only composed in the vernacular, but contain words and expressions belonging to the Romance idiom, with which he appears to have been quite familiar.[72] Moorish Spain was, in fact, bilingual. In addition to the official Arabic, a Romance dialect was widely spoken. In the streets and in the harems, peopled largely with Spanish women, Romance, more or less larded with Arabic, was current. *Cadis* and other officials were expected to be conversant with both languages so as to be able to communicate with all classes of the mixed population, and to take down the depositions of witnesses. The Romance tongue spoken in the Christian kingdoms differed in but trifling respects from the speech of Catalonia and Provence. When, later, Castile expanded southward, the Arabo-Romance vernacular of Andalusia became the foundation of the Castilian tongue.[73]

Of the 149 *azajal* of Ibn Quzmān, the greater number (ninety-two) conform in all points to the *murabba'* pattern. The remainder present common variations. The most frequent consists in a reduplication of the tercet strophe (*aaabbbc*). In twenty-seven instances the two rhymes of the *marqaz* are repeated after the tercet (*aa bbaa cccaa*). The forms *aaa bbb aaa ccc* (*azaj.* 77, 149); *abc ddd* (*azaj.* 32, 57); and *ab ccc* (*zaj.* 58) also occur.

The *Diwān* of Ibn Quzmān introduced no innovation into Moorish lyrical poetry, and its publication did not bring about any notable extension of the favor and popularity which the songs had enjoyed for over two centuries among all classes. The only effect it produced was to break the obduracy of certain circles of grammarians and to bring about, in their despite, the lifting of the interdict they had pronounced against vernacular poetry. Men of letters felt freer than before to apply themselves, without loss of dignity, to the composition of *azajal*. In Aragon, Abū-Bakr Ibn Malik distinguished himself particularly in this lyrical form, which came to replace almost entirely the *muwashshaha* couched in the traditional language.[74] Those details concern the history of Arabic literature; they do not bear on the latter's influence on Romance poetry. It is indeed quite unlikely that this influence worked along literary lines. Songs do not circulate through the medium of books, and those who sang them troubled themselves little about the disputes of pedagogues.

The importance for us of the *Diwān* of Ibn Quzmān lies in the advantage it has procured for us of laying open to our examination the popular songs of Moorish Spain in the eleventh and twelfth centuries. The learned Ribera can scarcely be taxed with overstatement when he declares: "The key to the mystery which has hitherto surrounded the origins of the lyrical structural forms of the civilized world has been given to us by the Andalusian song as we have learned to know it thanks to the song-book of Ibn Quzmān."[75]

It is of particular interest to enquire into the working of that influence upon the poetry of Count Guilhem de Poitiers, the oldest troubadour, specimens of whose productions have survived. It has generally been assumed that he was not the first. Indeed it seems improbable that this war-like prince, who led an active and checkered life, should have played the part of an almost revolutionary innovator in literature. His ripe technique, firmly established in its characteristic traits and showing no sign of experimental groping, indicates moreover that we have to do with a mature poetic tradition of long standing. Those considerations have caused all historians to place the beginning of troubadour poetry at least as far back as the closing years of the eleventh century, although we possess no evidence of the existence of such a poetry in Provence before the first decades of the twelfth century. It may be, nevertheless, that the Count de Poitiers is much more closely connected with the inception of troubadour poetry than has been generally supposed, and that he was indeed, in a very definite sense, the first troubadour. Dante expressly asserts that "many years have not passed since the introduction of this vernacular poetry . . . We find, in fact, no poetical composition in the *langue d'oc* dating farther back than a hundred and fifty years."[76] Since Dante wrote those words about the year 1292, they prove that he did not know any more than we do, either directly or through the tradition of his time, of any Provençal poetry anterior in date to that of Guilhem de Poitiers.

Not only are we unacquainted with any predecessor of Guilhem de Poitiers, but he has neither a known contemporary nor an immediate successor. Between the date of his death and that of the literary activity of the jongleurs Cercamon and Marcabru, a lacuna of at least eight years is interposed. The position occupied by Count Guilhem as a poet is, then, a singularly isolated one. Even when the penury of documentary evidence dating from the eleventh century is allowed for, it is hard to believe that no hint whatsoever, no illusion, no legend having any reference to predecessors or contemporaries, if any existed, should have reached subsequent generations. And since, on the other hand, it remains wholly inadmissible to attribute the Athenic birth of an entirely new poetical form, furbished at all points, to the unaided invention of a warlike dilettante, it can only be concluded that the development and adoption of that style is to be assigned to persons too obscure, and addressing themselves to audiences too unwitting in such matters, to have attracted general attention.

That poetical form must therefore have been current in Languedoc or in Spain, or both, among the numerous itinerant songmakers who frequented both countries. This anonymous lyrical poetry fell upon the ears of audiences who, however greatly they might enjoy it, were nowise interested in its cultivation. The nobles, even though they dabbled in the recital of songs, were habituated to martial and Bacchic descants, for the most part unrhymed and of quite another cast. The French clerks looked upon profane and frivolous songs with contempt and condemnation, and would no more have thought of indulging in such pastimes than of consigning those futilities to precious parchment fit to serve for the transcription of lives of saints. The Count of Poitiers, Duke of Aquitaine, a prince more powerful than the King of France, and sufficiently aristocratic in his superiority to opinion to be democratic in his tastes, may well have been the first person of importance to lend the luster of his name to these trifles, and to call attention to them in the circles of the nobility of Aquitaine and Languedoc.[77]

Guilhem de Poitiers, moreover, was placed in a singularly favorable position to appreciate the fact that what in Languedoc passed for inconsiderable popular diversions fit only for the entertainment of hinds and churls, was elsewhere an art held in the highest esteem among persons of choice and cultivated taste, and was accounted one of the chief ornaments of princely courts and gatherings. He was throughout his life in close relation with Spain. His father, Guilhem (Guy-Geoffroy) VI of Poitiers and VIII of Aquitaine, is chiefly known for the expedition which he undertook in 1064, in alliance with King Sancho-Ramiro of Aragon, and which was brought to a successful conclusion by the capture of the rich Moorish alcazar of Barbastro, an exploit which was extremely remunerative in booty and captives. An Arab author mentions that the latter included many accomplished Moorish female singers.[78] Guilhem the younger was only fifteen when he succeeded his father who, according to his own desire, was buried in Spain, at Santiago da Compostela. When Sancho-Ramiro was killed in 1094, before Huesca, Guilhem IX married Philippa, the Aragonese king's young widow. He went to fetch her himself, and spent at least the summer and autumn of that year in Spain.[79]

The family of the Count of Poitiers was already connected with the Spanish kingdoms by marriage; one of the Count's sisters had married Pedro of Aragon, another had married Alfonso VI of Castile, the conqueror of Toledo. At the time of this last expedition Guilhem was too young to join the many gentlemen of Limousin, including his most intimate friend, Hugues de Lusignan, who took part in it; but later on he missed no opportunity of associating with his Spanish brother-in-law. After spending some years in Toulouse (of which he gained possession in 1098) during the absence of Raimon de Saint-Gilles in the Holy Land, and again in 1114, during the minority of Count Alphonse-Jourdain, Guilhem de Poitiers went in 1115 to Spain. He took part in a raid by King Alfonso I of Aragon in Andalusia, carrying a daring thrust as far as Granada and the neighborhood of Cordova, and bringing back with him to Aragon several thousands of Mozarabian families. He again took the road to Spain in 1119 as an ally of the King of Aragon.

There is general consensus that Guilhem's literary activities should be assigned to the first years of the twelfth century. According to Ordericus Vitalis, Count Guilhem, on his return in 1102 from the crusade, "sang before the princes and the great assemblies of the Christians, of the miseries of his captivity among the Saracens, using rhymed verse jovially modulated."[80] Whatever interpretation we may place on the evidence, it brings to mind songs which differ considerably from the poems we know of the Count of Poitiers with the exception of the three oldest, but which, like the latter, are in the style of the *chansons de geste* or *chansons d'histoire* current in the circles of warlike princes. "Most of the warriors," as Gaston Paris remarks, "were themselves able to recite rude verse."[81] The Count de Poitiers, then, having been in the habit of composing such songs, changed his style completely and abruptly. Discarding the *chanson de geste* form, he thereafter struck out a new and entirely different verse form and one which from his first using of it was completely defined in every particular of its technical structure. That change is so remarkable and pronounced that it calls for an explanation, but it has not received a satisfactory one.

The facts noted above allow us to conjecture with a certain amount of precision the circumstances which brought about that modification in Guilhem de Poitiers' poetical style, and at the same time they throw light on the origin of troubadour poetry. That poetry was, as the Romance school maintains, in a large measure a development of popular poetry, but its evolution to maturity did not take place in Gascony or in Provence, but in Spain, under the dominant influence of Andalusian poetry. By long usage it had already been brought to a high degree of technical development by the time that it came to be diffused in Provence in a popular style. Mainly, or perhaps solely, in consequence of the example set by the Count of Poitiers, that poetical form, from being popular, became adopted in princely circles and displaced entirely in those circles the rude songs they had been wont to use. The new model, once erected to the rank of courtly poetry, was trimmed by the jongleurs and troubadours to the intent of their changed audience, who gave themselves to bringing their songs in tune with courtly taste and to embroidering upon them at pleasure. They are fully entitled to the merit of having made this poetry, whose inspiration and technique had been supplied by the Hispano-Mauresque songs, into the model which was to exercise a permanent influence on the lyrical literature of Europe.

Later in the thirteenth century, and more particularly at the time of Alfonso the Wise, the Spanish poets set themselves to imitate the technical virtuosity of the Provençals. The influence of those styles, the one upon the other, thus came to operate reciprocally, Provençal poetry, which had owed its original inspiration to the poetry of Andalusia and Aragon, contributing in turn to the rise of Castilian verse. It is worth noting, however, that the original form of the Moorish *zajal* persisted in Spain after it had disappeared or become transformed almost everywhere else in cultivated poetry. Thus, Juan Ruiz, generally known under the designation of Archpriest of Hita, the most distinguished versifier of medieval Spain, composed pure *azajal* as late as the fourteenth century. The following is a sample:

Mis ojos non verán lus
pues perdido hé á crus.

Crus crusada, panadera
tomé por entendera,
tomé senda por carrera
como andalús.

Coydando quela avría,
dixelo a Ferrand Garcia
que troxiese la pletesía
e fuese pleytés e dus.[82]

This form is still found in popular songs. It is interesting to note that Calderon, in the seventeenth century, introduces a perfect *zajal* in his play, *Amar despues de la muerte.*

Aunque en triste cautivero
de Alà por justo misterio
llore el africano imperio
su miseria ley esquiva
¡Su ley viva!

Viva la memoria extraña
de aquella glorioso hazaña
que en la libertad de España
a España tuvo cautiva,
¡Su ley viva![83]

Calderon, moreover, places this Andalusian *zajal* in the mouths of a Moor and a Moorish chorus, implying that he was well aware of the Moorish origin of this particular form of versification.

To ask by what paths the song of Moorish Spain made its way into Languedoc is to overlook the political geography of these regions at the time. The native lands of the troubadours were not, in the twelfth century, either in a political or cultural sense a part of France, but a part of Spain. The Provençal lords, each fighting for his own hand, had striven above all, during the ninth and tenth centuries to efface the last traces of the nominal suzerainty which the Carolingian dynasty had attempted to establish over them. They brought far more ardor to this task than to that of getting rid of the roving Saracen bands, remnants of two centuries of Muslim occupation and invasion, which, from the security of their *kasrs* in the Monte des Maures and from the coastal coves, held up the trade with Italy. The rulers of Catalonia and Aragon were little attracted for their part to adventures in Moorish Spain and were much more concerned with extending their domains north of the Pyrenees. The House of Toulouse, founded by a certain Boson, had been supreme in Languedoc ever since the beginning of the tenth century. These Counts, who had a genius for contracting advantageous marriages, absorbed successively Velay, Gevauden, Vizarais and the diocese of Uzès into their territories. Through the marriage of Raimon Bérenger, cousin of the King of Aragon, to Douce, heiress to Gilbert de Milhau, these domains, much more extensive than those of the King of France, passed in 1112 to the Catalan dynasty of the Bérenger family. Catalonia itself, together with its dependencies, was reunited in 1137 to the Crown of Aragon, through the marriage of Raimon Bérenger IV to his cousin Petronilla. Alfonso II, son of Raimon, the great patron of the troubadours, assumed the titles of King of Aragon, Count of Provence and of Roussillon, his father having exercised the prerogatives of the countships as Prince of Aragon.

Even before the formal confirmation of this amalgamation, all the Provençal lords, by their interests opposed to France, had recognized the suzerainty of Spain. In 1134 Raimon Bérenger; Roger, Count of Foix, who had married the sister of the Queen of Castile; Alphonse-Jourdain, Count of Toulouse and of Saint-Gilles, brother of King Alfonso; Armegol, Count of Urgel; Mir, Count of Pallas and a number of other lords, travelled to Saragossa with a view to bringing about a settlement of the dispute between the King of Aragon and the King of Castile, who claimed certain of the former's rights. "All these princes and lords," says Prudencio de Sandoval, "acknowledged the king as their feudal lord and swore obedience to him. The King of Castile," the chronicler goes on, "proceeded to treat them with great liberality. To the Count of Barcelona he gave the town of Saragossa and various lordships, as well as a gold vase weighing thirty marks; to the Count of Toulouse he presented several valuable horses and a quantity of precious jewelry; to all the great lords of Gascony, of the lands as far as the Rhone, and to Guillaume de Montpelier he gave articles of gold and silver and also horses."[84] Alfonso II of Aragon performed personally the duties and exercised the rights of his sovereignty over the county of Toulouse, before he delegated them to his brothers and sons. The domains of Provence remained an appanage of the kingdom of Aragon until the annexation of Languedoc to France in 1229, after the Albigensian crusade.

On the eve of this consummation, a troubadour sent his jongleur to the king: "Hie thee, Hugonet," he tells him, "strately and with all despatch unto the noble King of Aragon and sing unto him a new sirventes. Tell him that the sufferance he shows while the French do him great wrong and occupy his lands calls upon him much dispraise."

> *Vai, Hugonet, ses bistensa*
> *al franc rey aragones,*

chanta'l noel sirventes,
e di'l trop fai gran suffrensa
si qu'hom lo ten a falhensa
que sai dizon que Frances
an sei terra en tenensa
tan longamen que s'estensa.[85]

Writing from the heart of what we now call Provence, Folquet de Marseille says: "Our King of Aragon will never deceive, I ween, the hope that every gallant heart places in him."

e nostre reys d'Arago
qu'ieu no crey saubes falhir
a nulh home que.y an ab cor e valen.[86]

The Provençal war-cry was "*Reial!*" (Realm!)[87]

There was no kind of boundary separating Provence and Aragon. It might be said far more truly than in the time of Louis XIV that the Pyrenees did not exist. Language and literature were in every respect identical in both regions. "The new style of poetry was cultivated in the valley of the Ebro just as it was on the banks of the Durance and the Rhone."[88] Practically all the troubadours frequented the Spanish courts with as much assiduity as they did those of Provence. Consequently, to propose a discussion of the connection between Provençal and Spanish poetry would be almost as though one were to enquire into the influences of French literature on the Provençal writers, André Chénier or Alphonse Daudet.

In Spain itself no boundaries existed. Under the Caliphate, the Christian principalities were part of the Muslim dominions, and acknowledged their dependence on the suzerain, whom they furnished with mercenary troops. The name *Frontera* was later given to the plain stretching from Cordova and Seville to Jaen,[89] a sort of vague intermediate land where Christians and Muslims met on their errands. Nor did a barrier of irreducible hostility exist between races and religions, such as we are in the habit of imagining. A profoundly erroneous idea has arisen, in consequence of the fictions related at a later period, in regard to the relations between Christians and Moors in the peninsula. Has not the expedition undertaken by Charlemagne at the request of Suleiman al-Arabi against the Basques and Aragonese, and celebrated at the time of St. Bernard in the famous song of Roland, been represented as an epic struggle between the Cross and the Crescent? Religious legend even managed to transform Diez de Bivar, the *condottiere* or brigand who fought for seven whole years at the head of his Muslim bands on behalf of the Emirs Beni-Hūd of Saragossa, pillaging churches and mosques indiscriminately, into a hero of the faith. The Spaniards commemorate to this day the mythical battle of Cavadonga, which is supposed to have taken place at a time when the half-legendary King Pelayo was apparently enjoying at Cordova the hospitality of the Emir of the Faithful. The fanaticism introduced into Spain by foreigners is antedated by the adoption of these colorful stories.

Alfonso VI (1065-1109), an ambitious prince, married Constance, daughter of Duke Robert of Burgundy. Her retinue comprised a multitude of Cistercian monks. Bernard of Cluny concluded a treaty with the Pope after having become the first Archbishop of Toledo and settling his monks in the bishoprics of Burgos, Salamanca and Segovia. Up to that time, the Spanish Christians, who had been for the most part Arians under the Visigoths, had followed the Mozarabian ritual. Isidore of Seville, the father of the Spanish Church, whose connections with Rome were of the slenderest, used towards the Muslims, under whose rule he lived, the same tolerance that they showed to the Christians. The French monks were determined to change all that. The Spaniards rose up in revolt. Alfonso "the Battler" deposed Archbishop Bernard, attempted to eject the Cistercians from the country and broke off relations with the Pope. Those measures aroused the fury of his wife, Urraca, also a Burgundian, and her frenzy ran so high that she raised an army and waged a long war against her own husband. Women and Burgundians have been, down to the time of Isabel the Catholic and later, the promoters and mainstay of the Catholic Church in Spain.

Nothing of that fanaticism existed in the course of the three centuries during which the two peoples, Christian and Muslim, lived side by side. The question of religion did not enter into the policy of the Spanish rulers; they made no claim to be defenders of the faith. "No instance is known to us before the twelfth century," says Altamira, "of an expedition undertaken by the Christians against the Muslims exclusively." Even after the Christian kingdoms had begun to expand, the Christian kings were nowise concerned to expel the Moors from the peninsula. The most to which their ambition aspired was to extend their power "over the two religions." Thus the more they fought against the Emirs, as they fought among themselves, in order to enlarge their dominions, the more sedulous were they of cultivating the good will of the Muslim population. Peire Vidal reflects this manner of thinking when he dreams of imperial power over *li rei e l'amiran,* "the kings and the emirs."[90]

It was, as a rule, at the request of the Emirs and often with the assistance of Saracen troops that the Spanish princes conducted their campaigns. Thus, Ramiro of Aragon attacked Navarre at the head of a Muslim army furnished by the Emirs of Saragossa, Huesca and Tudela.[91] Al'Mutamid of Seville offered Raimon Bérenger II the sum of 10,000 dinars in return for assistance against Abū 'Abd ar-Raḥmān Ibn Tāḥir, king of Murcia. The Aragonese tendered regularly their services to the Emirs as mercenaries. Al-Mansur, who used Christian armies to win his most resounding victories, pillaged the shrine of Compostela with the aid of Aragonese troops. Numerous other instances of this type could be given. The victories gained were usually mutually recognized by treaties which set up a nominal suzerainty and exacted the payment of tribute. As masters of the fertile lands of Andalusia, the caliphs were not greatly interested in occupying the stony regions of Asturia and Castile. The Christian kingdoms, which had long paid them tribute and furnished them with mercenaries, were regarded by their Muslim suzerains with benevolent indulgence.

When, during the first days of the *reconquista*, the situation became reversed, the Emirs who owed feudal allegiance to the kings sat in the Cortes of Castile (established in 1020). Occasionally, disputes over territory would be decided by the results of chess games. Hospitality was regularly exchanged; on all ceremonial occasions the Emirs travelled to the Spanish courts attended by their retinues. Bonds of friendship commonly united them with the Christian princes. Alfonso VI, being persecuted by his brother, took refuge for a long period with Al-Ma'mūn, Emir of Toledo, and their mutual regard led to the conclusion of a pact of non-aggression which was faithfully observed until the deaths of the Muslim prince and his successor. Al-Ma'mūn lent King Alfonso the assistance of his troops in order to restore him to his throne; 'Abd ar-Rahmān rendered similar aid to Sancho I of Leon, to enable him to regain possession of his estates. Sancho, Queen Theuda and her son travelled to Andalusia in order to consult the great physicians of Cordova.[92] A Christian prince would entrust the education of his sons to learned Muslims and would send the former to an Emir's court.[93] Mixed marriages were of regular occurrence in all classes, whether plebeian, noble or royal.[94]

The twelfth century, the period when Provençal poetry flourished, was also the century of the *reconquista*. That reconquest owed, indeed, a good deal more to the decline of Muslim power and the discussions among the Emirs than to the zeal and energy of the Christian potentates. The latter, engrossed in their disputes over the possession of their petty kingdoms—Leon, Castile, Navarre, Aragon, "the Spains," as they were called—by turns reunited under the power of one of their number and again divided, in accordance with the disastrous feudal custom then prevalent; they had no notion of attacking the Moors. After the fall of the Western Caliphate at the end of the tenth century the Muslim Emirs who had carved principalities, or *taïfas*, for themselves out of the ruins, turned, like the Christian princes, against each other. Enjoying in their alcazars the luxury with which the caliphs had surrounded themselves and giving themselves up, above all, to poetry, according to the historians, they nevertheless lived in the dread of losing all. The most powerful of them, Mūhammad Ibn Abad al-Mu'tamid, king of Seville, in alliance with the Emirs of Granada and Badajoz, being faced with the threat of invasion by the *taïfas* of the north, who owed feudal allegiance to the Christians, called in to their assistance hordes of Berber tribes which had just founded the empire and city of Marrakech in Africa. These warriors of the Sahara had in the first instance come from distant Senegal. Black blood ran in their veins. They fought with their faces veiled and used long notched shields. Filled with fanaticism by a religious reformer, they advanced to the conquest of a new empire to the sound of Sudanese drums. They called themselves the "Saints," *Al-Murābiṭūn*, a name which was distorted in the Spanish dialect into "Almoravides." Under their Emir, Yūsuf Ibn Tāshfīn, they inflicted a bloody defeat on the Christians at Zalaca in 1086. But glutted with pillage, enervated by luxury and orgy, and detested by all, the Almoravides were unable to maintain their power.

The Christian princes, acceding, not without a good deal of asking, to the solicitations of the revolted Mozarabians, took advantage of the anarchy to enlarge their dominions at the expense of the *taïfas*, without, however, laying aside their domestic quarrels. Alfonso I of Aragon (1104-1134), surnamed the "Battler," scoured the peninsula with his roving bands. But lacking the means of consolidating his successes, and hard pressed by a coalition of Emirs, he was obliged to seek alliances. It was at

this juncture that the battler called in the aid of the Count of
Poitiers. The latter was the hero, in 1115, of an expedition
which carried the Limousinian and Aragonese bands to the out-
skirts of Cordova and Granada, causing such anxiety in Andalusia
that the "Prayer of Fear" was recited in all the mosques. The ten
thousand Mozarabians who returned with the Count of Poitiers
helped to populate the wastes of Aragon.[95] The alliance with the
King of Aragon was renewed in 1118; Bernard-Aton, Viscount
of Béziers, the most powerful vassal of the Count of Toulouse,
and several other lords of Provence joined Guilhem de Poitiers
in the expedition which resulted in the capture of Saragossa.[96]

Rather than submit to the yoke of the barbarous Almoravides,
the Emirs of Andalusia, at whose call the invaders had come,
sought alliance with the Christians. But the latter, by reason of
their disputes and jealousies, were almost as powerless as the
Emirs.

The troubadours bewail the painful situation. Peire Vidal
vents his dismay:

> *Als quatre reis d'Espanh' estai mout mal*
> *quar no volon aver patz entre lor;*
> *car autremen son ilh de gran valor,*
> *adreg e franc e cortes e leial.*[97]

The four kings of Spain stand in ill straits, / since peace
among themselves they cannot keep. / Right valorous lords,
and just, / courteous and forthright are they there withal.

Marcabru similarly deplores that the conduct of the princes
beyond the mountains encouraged the Almoravides:

> *Als Almoravis fai conort*
> *par las poestatz d'outra. l port.*[98]

And he offers up pious wishes for union among the kings:

Ab la valor de Portugal
e del rei Navar atretal
ab sol que Barcalona. s vir
ves Toleta l'emperial,
segur poirem cridar: "Reial!"
e paiana gen desconfir.

Si non fosson tant gran li riu
als Almorivas for' esquiu:
e pogram lor e ben plevir
e s'atendon lo recaliu
e de Castella. l seignoriu
Cordoa.il farem magrezir[99]

With the aid of doughty Portugal, and the King of
Navarre as well, if the Count of Barcelona will bend his
view toward the erstwhile metropolis, Toledo, so might we
thereunto win and storm its walls to the outcry of 'Realm!'
and be done with the Pagan kind. Were not the streams in
swell, the Almoravides would be in dire straits. But if their
leisure dwell to take the field unto summer-tide and the King
of Castile come, it might well hap that we contrive, and so
do that they of Cordova might needs draws in their belts.

Meanwhile a new Berber wave broke over the Maghreb, and
the invading host, invited, like the Almoravides before them, by
the Emirs, crossed the straits. The Al-Mūwahhidi or "Unitar-
ians," whom the Spaniards called the Almohades, were Masmuda
tribes from the Higher Atlas, and had for centuries been in relation with the Kharijite capital of Sijilmassa. They were not
savages like the Almoravide nomads; but inflamed by the preaching of their Mahdi, Mūhammad Ibn Tūmart, they were fraught
with religious zeal. The flower of the chivalry of Calatrava and
Santiago fell on the battle-field of Alarcos (1176), and King
Alfonso VIII barely escaped with his life.

'Abd al Mu'min, the Almohad Emir, proved himself generous. He granted the Spanish king a truce of ten years and set thousands of knights at liberty unransomed. This did not, however, prevent Jewish traders from selling Christian slaves in every market of Andalusia on the morrow of the battle.[100] It may be added that, to judge from the conduct of other Emirs on similar occasions, the lot of the war captives was not particularly hard. Al-Maqqari, referring to the reign of Al-Hakim II, speaks of hundreds of slaves "dressed after the Provençal fashion," who were employed in the avocations they had been wont to exercise at home. Some served their masters in the capacities of secretaries and librarians, others even filled administrative posts, and all were treated on a footing of trust and amity.[101] It was at this period that the slave Habid composed poetry which was held in high esteem,[102] and there would be nothing improbable in Provençal prisoners of war having followed his example.

The triumph of Islam drew lamentations from Peire d'Auvergne. "The Almohades have the better of us"—*Almohades nos superan*—he moans. But the contentions between the Christians knew no lull even in the hour of defeat. With the Almohades at their heels, Aragonese and Castilians fought among themselves. The poet from Auvergne gives voice to the bitterness and impotent aspirations of the vanquished: "Could we but contrive accord, we might hurl them back to Morocco"—*tro a Maroc faran lai*. "But by the Christians' own fault, we are held up to the jeers of the Masmuda"—*par las christians faillis, quar Masmut nos fan sobranas*.[103] And Gavaudan the Elder delivers himself in the same strain: "The Moroccans and their marabouts blatter yonder and cast scorn at us, crying: 'Franks, make way! Provence is ours and all the land as far as the heart of Puy!'"

Marroquenas, marabetis
pauzon a mons per mieg los pratz,
mest lor gabons: "Franc, faiz nos loc!
entro Puey totz los meias."[104]

The Almohades succumbed in their turn to the luxury and civilization of Andalusia. Within a bare few years they had waxed corrupt to the point that they produced poets and patrons of artists and philosophers. The very victor of Alarcos commemorated his triumph by the construction of the exquisite Giralda tower at Seville, twin sister to the Kutabia of Marrakech. His son, Abū Ya'qub Yūsuf, was given to book learning and chose his friends among the scholars and poets. Ibn Tufaïl, a renowned philosopher, presented to him a brilliant student of Aristotle, named Ibn Roschd, belonging to a wealthy family of jurists. In the course of their conversation, the Almohad prince expressed a wish that a commentary might be composed to elucidate the works of the Stagirite. Thus did a Berber from the Higher Atlas endow medieval Europe with Averroes.[105]

The flow of tribute and booty, of luxury and culture, as well as the accession of numerous Arab and Mozarabian subjects after the capture of Toledo and Saragossa, produced much the same effect on the Spanish rulers as the conquest of Andalusia on the Berber invaders. The Beni-Alfonso—thus do the Arab historians designate the Spanish princes—had been, before the epoch of the reconquest, even ruder than the barons on the other side of the Pyrenees. They had no coinage; they could not read; they called the clerks' gospel a library; for the least calculation or measurement of land they had to have recourse to an Arab.[106] But no sooner had the Spanish princes crossed the Tagus and extended their power over the Muslim lands than they blossomed out into oriental splendor. The Courts of Castile and Aragon were thereafter accounted the most brilliant in Christendom. They were the Mecca of the poets. According to the jongleur-troubadour Cercamon, the Court of Alfonso VII (1126-1157) was the meeting place of courtly youth, for "he had conquered joy"—*Anfons qu'a joi conquis.*[107] Peire Vidal expresses himself in almost identical terms—*"N'Anfons per cui Jovens es Joies."*[108] Perdigon exalts the magnificence of the Court.[109] According to the author of the *Libro de Alixandre*, "a whole nation of jongleresses," that is, female dancers and musicians, was to be found there, as well as "Jongleurs of all countries and of diverse sorts."[110] The Moorish Emirs did not fail to honor with their presence the festivities to which the Spanish monarchs were addicted.[111]

Alfonso of Castile, having reunited the crowns of Castile and Leon, revived an old Visigoth usage, and arrogated to himself the egregious title of *Imperator totius Hispaniae.* The coronation was celebrated amid much pomp, in the cathedral of Santa Maria de Regla at Leon, in the presence of a brilliant gathering which included the King of Navarre, the Counts of Barcelona, Toulouse, Foix and Commiges, the Lord of Montpelier and the Emir of Rueda, Al-Motansir Jafar-Abdullah, the last scion of the Saragossa dynasty of the Ibn Hūd and King Alfonso's friend and faithful ally. "All these lords," says Sandoval, "did him homage for their dominions. . . . They took part in many great festivities and pleasant diversions."[112] On making his solemn entry into Toledo in 1139, the "emperor" was received by "the entire population of the town, Christians as well as Saracens and Jews, to the sound of drums, viols and rotas and all manner of musicians who sang, each in his own language, the praises of the emperor."[113]

Those splendors were renewed on the occasion of the visit of the King of France. Louis VII, after divorcing Aliénor of Aquitaine, who could not endure the King's sanctimonious disposition and meanness, had just married Constance, the daughter of Alfonso of Castile. The latter went to meet his son-in-law at Burgos at the head of a brilliant company of lords, and received him "with such pomp and magnificence that the King of France was passing amazed at the spectacle of so much glory." After a visit to the sanctuary of Compostela, the Court repaired to Toledo, where "festivities took place at which all the lords, both Christian and Arab, who were vassals of the emperor were present, and the King of France, when he had admired the splendor

of this noble court, said in the hearing of all that the like magnificence was not to be found in all the world, and that he had
never seen a display equal to it."[114] Señor Menéndez Pidal thinks
that the troubadours Marcabru and Alégret attended those festivities in the train of the Court of Toulouse, brother of Queen
Berengela.[115]

Father Mariana, who has a bent for scandal, says that the real
reason for King Louis's journey was his desire to investigate the
rumor which had reached him to the effect that Princess Constance was illegitimate.[116] Whether or not the imputation was
founded, it is a far from improbable one, in view of the standard
obtaining at the Spanish Court during this period. The troubadour Arnaud de Marsan boasts of having gained the love of
another of the daughters of King Alfonso:

E filha N'Alfos
ai mal grat del gilos
conquis a gran onor
e gazanhey s'amor.[117]

The King-Emperor set the example of oriental polygamy. In addition to six more or less legitimate wives, one of whom, Princess
Zaïda, was the daughter of the poet-king Al-Mu'tamid of Seville,
and had brought him as her dowry the provinces of Ciudad Real
and Cuenca, his harem included a number of concubines and a
"multitude" of female singers and dancers. The historians, it can
cause no surprise, are agreed in declaring the Spanish Courts to
be more than half Moorish. They owed, in fact, everything they
had to Muslim civilization.

The *reconquista,* at least in the first stages, so far from breaking off or embittering the relations between the two peoples,
actually extended them and made them more intimate. The Spanish kings encouraged the Muslim population to remain within
the newly conquered territories and guaranteed to all classes the

continued enjoyment of their lands and goods. We possess the texts of the capitulations. Justice was administered by the Muslims' own *cadis* and order was maintained by their *alguazils*; they attended without let to their trades and avocations, and were allowed to keep special butchers' shops that they might observe their customs. The new subjects of the kings were free to practice their religion, and the muezzin's call to prayer from the heights of the minarets of Toledo and Saragossa mingled with the sound of the Christian bells. Such were the privileges accorded to Muslims in the Christian kingdoms at this date that numbers of them migrated from the Almohad *taïfas* and placed themselves under the protection of the kings.[118] The "emperor" prided himself on making no distinction between his Christian subjects and those of Islamic faith, and his favorite title was that of "king of the men of both religions."

In Aragon the Muslims enjoyed even more privileges than in Castile and were consequently to be found in larger numbers. Alfonso II (1162-1198), son-in-law of the King-Emperor, rivalled him in oriental magnificence. Moreover, the King of Aragon, whose grandfather had not been able to sign his name except in Arabic, was not only the most lavish among the patrons of the troubadours, but was himself a poet. The chronicles distinguish him from the other "Beni-Alfonsos" by the description *"el que trobo,"* and his courtiers pushed flattery to the extent of declaring that he was the best troubadour of the age, an exaggeration which is scarcely supported by his only surviving poem, a love-song of somewhat mediocre quality. But he was certainly a munificent patron of literature. Arnaud Daniel says: "I have never, for my own part, left the Court of Aragon without wishing, the next day, to return with a single bound":

> C'anc non estei jorn d' Arago que.l saut
> no.i volgues ir.[119]

King Alfonso, moreover, was not lacking in taste and discernment. Peire Vidal was his favorite poet,[120] and he considered that the songs of his friend, Guiraut de Bornelh, "were fit to be married to the sirventes of Bertram de Born"—*donet per molhers los chansons d'En Giraud de Bornelh a sos sirventes.*[121] Guiraut had occasion to compare the courtly manners of the Arabized Courts of Castile and Aragon with those of Navarre, which had kept clear of influences arising from the *reconquista* and was "destitute of all courtesy"—*cort corta de tota cortesia.*[122]

> He had just left the good King Alfonso of Castile, who had made him a present of a superb grey palfrey and many other gifts . . . But the King of Navarre got wind of Guiraut's good fortune and stripped him of all when the minstrel passed through his lands. Guiraut was relieved of all his money, and the King appropriated the grey palfrey for himself.[123]

As for Bertram de Born, who had at first stood in great favor with the King of Aragon, he quarrelled with the latter in the end, suspecting the King of having given Henry II of England assistance when that monarch was besieging Bertram's own castle of Hautefort. In two sirventes, the quick-tempered knight broke into abuse of the King of Aragon. The latter had also a bone to pick with Gaucelm Faidit concerning a lady for whose favors the troubadour was his rival.[124] The morals of the Aragonese Court were in fact no less frivolous than those of the Court of Castile. Guilhem de Bergadan gives us a picture of the King as a very Don Juan: he was continually coveting his neighbors' wives.[125] Guiraut de Luc accuses him of having violated nuns— *las monjas qu'empreignetz a Valbona.*[126]

A list of the troubadours who visited the Spanish Courts would comprise all the most famous names we know. Such were: Count Guilhem de Poitiers; the first jongleurs-troubadours, Cercamon,

Marcabru and Alégret, Guiraut de Calanson[127]; Peire d'Auvergne, also regarded as one of the founders of Provençal poetry; Guiraut de Bornelh, the "master troubadour," who seems to have spent a great part of his life in Spain; Guilhem de Cabestanh;[128] the Rabelaisian monk, Peire de Vic, better known under the designation of the Monk of Montauban, to whom the King of Aragon presented the priory of Villefranche de Conflans; Arnaud Daniel; Peire Vidal, who in the opinion of many is Arnaud's rival for the first place among the troubadours; Peire Roger, Canon of Clermont; Arnaud de Mareulh, whose intrigue with the Countess of Béziers, Lady of the Manor of Burlatz, was given a favorable turn by the intercession of King Alfonso II; Gaucelm Faidit, the lover of Marie de Ventadorn; Rambaut de Vaqueiras (Vaucluse), the "Noble Knight." I omit the troubadours of a later epoch, such as Guiraut Riquier, Peire Cardenal, Folquet de Marseille, Raimon de Miraval, Uc de Saint-Cir, Bertram d'Alamanon, Aimeric de Pegulh and all those who fled in a body before the Inquisition and found refuge in Spain.

Several of the troubadours known to us were, indeed, Spaniards. Guiraut de Cabrera, friend of the Viscount Eble de Ventadorn, one of the first to protect troubadours, was a Spaniard; he quoted Guillaume de Poitiers, Marcabru and Rudel. He was, therefore, associated with the beginnings of Provençal poetry. Guillaume de Bergadan belongs to the same period; Guillaume de Tudèle, the chief author of the *Song of the Crusade,* was from Navarre. Arnaud the Catalan and Guilhem Cercera were Spanish knights. Hugo de Mataplana was a member of one of the most illustrious families of Catalonia. He fought beside Guilhem de Cabestanh, Raimon Vidal and many Provençal lords at the battle of Las Navas de Tolosa, which broke Muslim power in Spain forever. A year later, in 1213, he died of wounds received at the battle of Muret, which put an end to Provençal civilization.[129] Thus perished, almost at the same moment, the culture of Moorish Spain and that of Provence, to which it had given birth.

It was not, obviously, by troubadours already versed in their art that its diffusion from Spain was effected. Even the oldest, the Count of Poitiers, and the courtly jongleurs, Cercamon, Marcabru, Alégret, had forerunners. In fact, the Spanish courts, before they became the meeting-place of the troubadours, had been frequented by a more ancient and no less nomadic class of songsters. From as early as the sixth century, every Gothic court was the resort of minstrels, *scôps,* gleemen, or by whatever name they might be known. The kings of Spain had their court-singers; one of these, known as Pala, is repeatedly mentioned in the chronicles.[130] He certainly was not the first of his kind.

The term "jongleur" (Sp. and Prov. *juglar*), French in its usage, does not appear in Spain before the twelfth century, the first mention of it occurring in a chronicle of the year 1116 from Sahagun, a Burgundian foundation.[131] Another term, Provençal in form, was current: *segrier, segrer,* or *segrel.* [132] Guiraut Riquier, nettled at being referred to as a jongleur, as any mountebank, begs that he might be designated as a *segrier,* or *trobador segrier.*[133] The word has completely baffled lexicographers. Ribera suggested that it might be a contracted form of some such term as *zegelero,* which would mean "a singer of *azajal.*"[134] Since, in Romance languages, all words are syncopated, the internal syllables being omitted as often as not, Ribera's suggestion would do no more than restitute the suppressed middle syllable in accordance with linguistic probability. In the Romance of Northern Italy, we come upon the forms *jujar, juiar, zuiar, sublar,* for jongleur. But as an occupational patronymic, in which capacity *juglar* was frequently used in Provence,[135] the form *ziegler* occurs, and, as it happens, applied to poets.[136] The use of the old Spanish term *segrier,* interpreted as "singer of *azajal,*" may thus have extended beyond the Alps, at the opposite extremity of the Provençal region.

Minstrels were more numerous in Moorish Spain and more highly regarded than in any other country. Popular minstrels,

or *ahdabi,* abounded in towns and countryside, *ruwahi,* or court-
poets, in the alcazars. No prosperous citizen would bethink himself of entertaining friends without the concourse of singers.
Tournaments of song were held at Seville, and the winner of the
day was acclaimed as is a favorite *torero* in modern Spain.[137]
The popularity of musical and poetical entertainers was scarcely
less great in Christian than in Muslim Spain. No reference to
festivities or to the splendor of the Spanish courts omits the
mention of singers and musicians. These usually constituted
companies of mixed composition. Thus a troop of 27 jongleurs
at the Court of King Sancho IV comprised 13 Moorish singers,
12 Christians, and 2 Jews.[138] Moorish musicians and singers were
employed in Spanish churches even as late as the fourteenth century.[139]

Arab music is generally held to contain echos of Byzantine and
Persian music, and Jewish music probably played a much more
considerable part in its origin than is recognized. But accents
are also to be caught in Moorish music and in that of the troubadour songs distinctly recalling Spanish music, that music which
has at all periods exerted so capital an influence on the development of Western music. One of the most pleasant troubadour
measures that we know is that of Marcabru's song of the crusade: *"Pax in nomine Domini! Fetz Marcabru los mots e.l so
Aujatz!"* The melody is, in Ribera's opinion, a pure Aragonese
jota.[140]

The troubadours attached as much importance to the music of
their songs as to the words. "A song without music is a mill without water," says one of them.[141] However much we may debate
the relation of that music to that of Moorish Spain—both of
which are far from well-known to us—the question did not present itself to contemporary poets; they frankly referred to the
music of their songs as "Saracen." In the tale of *Galeran,* a young
woman is instructed in the musical art:

Si liu apprint ses bons parrains
lais et sons, et baler des mains,
toutes notes sarrasinoises,
chansons gascoignes et françoises.[142]

In Spain, and more particularly in Aragon, the words of the songs which accompanied the dances so much in favor, were composed in Gallician Romance, but were modelled on the songs of Andalusia, and regarded as Saracen. Similarly a large portion of the popular songs of Provence, known as ballads, rondels, virelays, were accompanied by dances. Those dances were known, as far away as England, as Moorish dances—morris-dances.

So widespread was the renown of Moorish musicians that we hear of their exercising their art as far away as Northern France and England.[143] Indeed it would seem that Moorish jongleurs, and particularly "jongleresses," were quite commonly to be met with in Christian Europe. In a *chanson d'histoire* translated and edited in Venice, under the title *Bove d'Ancona,* the following incident is related. The beautiful and highly accomplished Druxiana, the wife of Bove d'Ancona, who had been absent for a long time at the wars, heard from *"nobili contatori"* and *"zublar"* that he was back. But as he still did not appear, she resolved to set out and seek him, disguised as a *zublara,* a "jongleresse." In order the better to look the part, she rubbed herself with herbs till she appeared "dark as a Moorish woman."

The pious Peire Cardenal exclaims: "Would that, while retaining the Christian faith, I could command the language of the Saracens; have both the law of Christ and the deft art of the pagans!"

Dig volh aver de Sarrasà
e fes e lei crestia
e subtileza de paga.[144]

He evidently was well aware of the source of the *dig* (words) no less than of the *son* (music) of the Provençal songs. Peire Cardenal was assuredly not alone in that respect; the casual manner of his reference to the art he envies implies a current and accepted recognition. That the Provençal song-makers, who designated their music, the instruments on which it was played, and the dances which frequently accompanied it, as Saracen or Moorish, should have at all times been similarly conscious of the source of the lyric contents of their art is more than probable. We are nowhere expressly told so. But then neither are we anywhere told by the Provençals a word as to sources of questions concerning the history of their art upon which we should have liked to have had their views. Literary history, so abundantly discussed in Moorish Spain, was not among the branches of literature cultivated in Provence. Silence on the subject is complete, and no negative conclusion can be drawn from it in any particular instance.

The art of the jongleur suddenly took on, in Provence, an enormous expansion during the closing years of the eleventh century and the early years of the twelfth. It is during the same period that the Spanish courts assumed, after the capture of Toledo in 1086 and of Saragossa in 1118, the splendor and sumptuous tastes for which they became famous. The coincidence is not fortuitous.

With the transformation of their art, the numbers of jongleurs multiplied manifold, and their activities became greatly extended. The author of an article in one of the older numbers of the *Histoire littéraire de la France* thus quaintly expresses his ideas on the beginnings of lyrical art in Provence: "The Provençal poets," he says, "who had revived the art of the ancient Gallic bards, multiplied enormously in number, and discovered the secret of adding the charm of instrumental music to those of rhyme and cadence."[145] Those naive words touch the truth at one point. The calling of the itinerant singer, who had existed from time immemorial, suddenly took on unprecedented numerical expansion and a new importance, as, equipped with the new rhyme and structural forms, and the musical instruments imported from Spain, his songs became truly lyrical.

The practitioners of the art flocked to where they found its most prodigal patronage: to the semi-Arabic courts of Spain. We find the mention of their names more often associated with the courts of Aragon and Castile than with those of Toulouse or Limoges. In a land which rang both day and night with music and song, the jongleurs from over the hills mingled with the heterogeneous and polyglot troops of their Spanish colleagues among whom Moorish singers appear to have predominated. A miniature in a manuscript at the Escorial pictures two jongleurs, the one a Moor, the other dressed "in the Provençal fashion," singing together a duet or a tenson, affording thus a graphic illustration of the relations between the singers of the two nations.[146]

In love, as he was, with his art, the jongleur neglected no opportunity of improving it and of adopting novelties. "He took over another people's knowledge with avidity," says Uc de Saint-Cyr, speaking of Marcabru, "and willingly imparted it to others."[147] The troubadours were great imitators; plagiarism was in honor among them. Cercamon copies the Count of Poitiers, Marcabru imitates Cercamon and Peire d'Auvergne, and Arnaud Daniel helps himself to Marcabru. If in the polyglot gatherings of the courts of Spain, songs were at times worded in a tongue which the Provençals did not understand, bilingual Moorish minstrels, Mozarabians, Jews, Mudehars were at their elbows, ready to explain the words and themes, and eager to devise of professional matters with their Provençal colleagues.[148] These certainly did not lack facilities for benefiting from the greatly perfected form which their art had long since attained in Moorish Spain.

If there be a "legend" connected with the relation of Moor-

ish to Provençal literary culture, it is the monkish legend of an
"abyss" between the two, a legend charged with virus so fierce
that it stultified the judgment and learning of Renan. Renan
himself remarks that literature diffused in the Middle Ages with
a rapidity which astonishes us and which we are not always able
to account for. "Many a work composed in Morocco or in Cairo,"
he observes, "became known in Paris or Cologne in less time than
it takes today for an important German book to cross the
Rhine."[149] Songs are wafted on swifter wings and farther afield
than books. But there is in this instance no occasion for wonder.
The spread of songs in Aragon, from the Spanish to the Provençal portions of those domains, does not call for the invocation of
a miracle. Aragon was particularly noted for the popularity there
of Hispano-Mauresque lyrical poetry, and some of the favorite
composers of *azajal* were Aragonese. The Moorish lyrical style
with which the wandering jongleurs who trooped back and forth
between the several parts of the kingdom became acquainted,
completely renewed their uncouth original repertoire. It imposed
itself in Languedoc on even the most popular forms of entertainment provided by the professional song-makers. However
conservative, rude and uncultivated popular taste might be, it
could not but yield to the charm of the new music.

Nor was it indeed necessary to cross the Pyrenees to become
familiar with the Andalusian style. Singers, male and female, of
Moorish songs were almost as common in Provence as Provençal jongleurs in Spain. Toulouse, where one brushed in the streets
against traders from Seville and Valencia; Narbonne; Béziers
where Spanish Jews were engaged in the diffusion of Moorish
culture; Montpellier,[150] where there existed a whole Moorish
colony of refugees from Almohavid misrule, echoed with the
sound of Moorish song and music. There is no mystery about a
process of diffusion which ascertainable facts show to have been
inevitable. What indeed would require a great deal of explaining
is that any Provençal jongleur should have remained unac-

quainted with the lyrical productions of Moorish Spain. With Count Guilhem of Poitiers, the cultivation of that poetry became extended to Provençal and Limousinian manorial circles. But prior to that aristocratic adoption, it had already for some time been spread by popular jongleurs among the people.

Amour Courtois

The songs of Count Guilhem de Poitiers contain no token of
the "courtly" manner which is a distinctive trait of troubadour
poetry.[1] Their broad joviality would sort with the taste of the
guard-room much better than with that of elegant gatherings
presided over by the ladies. And in this respect, no less than by
their form, they resembled the *azajal* of Ibn Qūzman. The
Count's son and successor, Guilhem X of Aquitaine, surnamed
the *Toulousain,* continued to song-makers the favor shown them
by his father. His daughter, the illustrious Aliénor, was as yet
too young to second him in his role of a Maecenas; she was but
fifteen when she was married to the King of France, whose court,
thronged with monks, did not hold songs in much favor. But the
passion with which she applied herself to poetry throughout a
long life—she attained the age of eighty—bears witness to the
deep impression the "Toulousain's" Court must have made upon
her.

When Guilhem X died, the jongleur Cercamon expressed
himself with a poet's exaggeration, as though all the luster of
poetry had gone out from the world with his patron. His hopes
turned once more to the Court of Castile and also to that of Eble
II, Lord of Ventadorn, a noble manor, whose imposing ruins

look down to this day over the moorland of Corrèze, and which, according to Froissart was one of the strongest castles in all the world. There was much rivalry, under a surface of friendly inter-course, between the Viscounts of Ventadorn and the Dukes of Aquitaine.

The Eble family, founded by Archambaud, Viscount of Comborn and Ventadorn, considered that they possessed claims to the duchy. Furthermore, Viscount Eble II prided himself on rivalling Count Guilhem in pomp and elegance, accounting him somewhat niggardly for so great a lord. To that rivalry was added professional jealousy, for Viscount Eble was himself a poet. The epithet *cantor* is applied to him in all the genealogies, and he "cultivated," says Prior Jaufré of Vigeois, "the art of light verse even in his old age."[2] Those tastes became hereditary in the family. Eble III, son of the *cantor*, appears to have presided, like his father, over a sort of school of jongleurs at Ventadorn. Cercamon maintained relations with the elder of those princes; Marcabru studied, his biographer tells us, for a considerable time with Cercamon. With the two elder troubadours were closely associated Alégret, Peire d'Auvergne, Bernard Marti and Jaufré Rudel. Whether those poets took advantage of the instruction imparted at the school of Ventadorn, it is not possible to say. At any rate the lords of Ventadorn, it appears, started on their careers a whole group of jongleurs, who attached themselves to their Court. Finally, the Lord Eble III, having noticed the poetical disposition shown by his baker's young-son, Bernard, had him carefully tutored in the art of poetry. The Provençal style as-sumed thenceforth the "courtly" character of which it became the model.

There existed then a particular association between the de-velopment of the "courtly" style and the Limoges country. The poetical vocabulary of the troubadours, enriched from every re-gional source, was currently spoken of as the *lengue lemosina,* although Jeanroy candidly admits it bears no particular mark of

Limousinian dialectical peculiarities. It is those circumstances that gave the Parisian theorists occasion to conceive the daring scheme of inverting the obvious, and of deriving the poetry of the South from that of the North, the troubadours from the trouvères or some conjectural predecessors of the latter. The Limoges country was not the cradle of Provençal poetry, but it was the seminary of its subsequent adaption to the entertainment of noble audiences. Following the example set by the Count of Poitiers, whose talent did not particularly draw its inspiration from the spires of his native land, his neighbors, the nobles of Limousin, were the first to adopt the novel fashion introduced by him. Jongleurs from every region of Languedoc naturally betook themselves to where they found their most fervent patrons. The "instruction" imparted in the schools of Niort and Ventadorn was, we may surmise, largely directed to bringing the popular poetry into line with the chivalric spirit accounted distinctive of the "gentle" and well-born, as by study of the chivalric romances and, maybe, of scraps from Ovid. That Limousinian development of early "courtly" art goes to confirm the importance of the personal part played by Guilhem de Poitiers in launching the whole poetic movement.

Cercamon's love-songs are of the pathetic order. The lover pines, deploring the severity of the lady of his thoughts. This was, to be sure, a commonplace current in the love-poetry of Moorish Spain. Like the troubadours, the Andalusian poets declared themselves "victims of the fair"—*ṣarī 'al-ghawāni*. These are not yet the punctilious distinctions of courtly love. Marcabru, on the other hand, devoted considerable attention to those distinctions between love and "villainy." In a fourteenth-century manuscript at the *Bibliothèque Nationale* (fr. 22545), Marcabru's poems are prefaced with the following note: *"Aissi comensa les so de Marcabru que fo lo premier trobador que fos"*—here begin the songs of Marcabru, who was the first troubadour that was.[3] That strange statement is remarkable in many ways. It can scarcely be supposed that its author had never heard of Guilhem de Poitiers as a poet. Can it be that he regarded the count's songs, composed in the "popular" style, as not properly belonging to courtly troubadour poetry? (Jaufré Rudel, of the Ventadorn school, flatly declares that Count Guilhem de Poitiers "could not write a song"—*No sap cantar*).[4] Marcabru was the first to lay stress on the opposition between *fin amors*, "refined," or more correctly "perfect" love, and gross amatory vulgarity; although he was, for some reason that is not quite clear, vehemently hostile to the ideas and teachings of the Eble school.[5] But Marcabru does not enter into the subtleties of the style, nor does he illustrate them in his poetry. The "courtly" manner attains at a bound its full development with Bernard de Ventadorn.

The characteristic features of that style were impressed upon troubadour poetry by the conditions obtaining in the manorial society which adopted the lyrical fashion introduced by the Count of Poitiers. The tide of wealth and luxury which had transformed the courts of the kings of Spain after their domains had become extended over Moorish territories, had reached the South of France. Provence was far more richly endowed with natural wealth than the lands of Castile and Aragon, and had just been launched upon a career of far-spread commercial expansion. A port had been established at Aigues-Mortes for the direct supply of the products of Spain and Syria; the Counts of Toulouse had contracted treaties with the great commercial republics of Italy, Genoa, Pisa, as well as with the Emir Ibn Mardanish of Valencia. The wealth of the East poured into Provence and Languedoc, and was disposed of in the markets of Toulouse and of Beaucaire, which latter could be reached up the Rhone by caravels from Valencia and Almeria. The outward aspect of the Provençal nobility and its manner of life had undergone a notable transformation.

The luxurious tastes and frivolous pleasures of that society have sometimes been set down to a somewhat effeminate natural

disposition and to the leisure resulting from the peaceful conditions supposed to have prevailed in Provence. That view involves
a good deal of exaggeration. In Provence, as elsewhere at that
period, local wars on a small scale were almost unceasing. The
Church specifically deplored them; it instituted "truces of God"
which were not observed.[6] Each feudal lord sought to become
independent of his suzerain. The counts of Toulouse had disputes with the kings of Aragon, and were often called upon to
defend their rights against other claimants. The lords of the Des
Baux family never ceased putting forward imperial and matri-
monial titles, contesting those of the Bérengers. The Plantagenets
and the dukes of Aquitaine also advanced territorial claims.
Henry II of England came, in 1159, to besiege Toulouse, but was
repulsed; Richard Coeur de Lion waged war in Languedoc; he
laid siege to the troubadour-knight Bertram de Born's castle of
Hautefort. Count Raimon Bérenger IV led 100,000 men from
Provence to the crusades, and during his absence Guilhem IX of
Poitiers fought against the men of Toulouse. In short, one sometimes comes to wonder how these noble lords managed to find
time for poetry.

But the luxury and elegance of the southern nobles made them
appear effeminate in the sight of the uncouth northern barons,
bearded, unkempt, and indifferently clean of their persons. A
French chronicler tells his astonishment at first meeting a company of Provençal lords, richly attired, mounted on Arab steeds
and carrying damascened arms. The northerner remarks that
"they shaved their faces, and wore their hair parted," which
foppery, he sourly comments "caused them to look like mum-
mers."[7] The southern lords were lavish and ostentatious; they
could never get used to the stinginess of the French. At an assembly convened by King Henry II at Beaucaire in 1174 to
arbitrate a dispute between the King of Aragon and the Count
of Toulouse, the latter gave a certain lord, the Baron d'Agoult,
a present of 100,000 sous to distribute among his knights. An-

other lord, Bertram de Raimbaux, had a field ploughed by twelve yokes of oxen and sowed in it 30,000 sous; a third, Guillaume the stout, of Hartelos, who had brought 300 knights to the assembly, caused a meal to be cooked for them over a fire of wax candles. The Countess of Urgel wore a crown of gold and precious stones valued at 40,000 sous. A swarm of jongleurs lent the charm of their descants to those diplomatic assizes.[8] "All these people," remarks M. Andraud, somewhat censoriously, "lived above all for their own pleasure; such was the ideal that they pursued and to which they sacrificed everything."[9]

The position which women occupied in Provençal society differed considerably from that of their Spanish sisters. In the Courts of Catholic Spain, women's conventual seclusion was far in excess of any relic which might survive of the segregation of the Islamic harem. The ladies of Provençal manors were not Burgundian princesses surrounded by monks. They were usually rich heiresses and played the chief part in the social circles over which they presided. It needed no courtly theories and troubadours' praise to establish their position; they were already semi-divinized. The means of elegance at their disposal, the opulence of the "Provençal fashions," the oriental perfumes and cosmetics with which they did not disdain to enhance the advantages of their persons, excited the envy of the ladies of the north. If the songs of the troubadours were mainly addressed to the women, the reason was that the latter were to a great extent the protectors and inspirers of the poets' art, which some of them actually practiced. If they did not understand Latin, they were well-versed in matters of love—of "courtly" love, that is, such as was thought beseeming for a lady of high lineage whose marriage had been nothing more than a diplomatic act resting almost exclusively on political motives.

The phrase, "Courts of Love" has obtained a hold on the imagination of a public which, concerning the nursling days of European literature, knows scarcely any other particular detail.

The romanticized account of the matter given by Master Jehan de Nostradamus need not be taken seriously. Nothing could be at wider variance with courtly principles than to pass judgment on individual cases or even to refer in such a connection to any person by name. But it would, nevertheless, be fully in the spirit of twelfth-century gallantry to bestow such an appellation on fashionable gatherings enlivened by tuneful flattery of the poets and jongleurs, and presided over by ladies who were quite prepared to voice their judgments on the verses descanted and on the "questions of love" therein raised. It was in the *"salons"* of these bluestockings born before their time that "courtly" poetry originated, at the house of Aliénor of Aquitaine at Poitiers, at Ventadorn in the home of Azelaïs, daughter of the lord Guillaume de Montpelier, under the presiding patronage of Bertrane, the Lady of Signe, of Rostangue, Lady of the Manor of Pierrefeu, of Phanette de Gentelme, Lady of Romanin, of Hermesende, Lady of Posquieres, of Beatrice, Countess of Die, of Alalète, Lady of the Manor of Ongle, of Adalazie, Viscountess of Avignon, of Mabille, Viscountess of Ieres, of Staphanie, wife of Raimon des Baux and daughter of Gilbert, Count of Provence, of Jausserande, Lady of Claustral, of Ermengarde, Countess of Narbonne and of Bertrane d'Orgon.

Like the ladies, the poet-princes who shared their tastes and pastimes were, in their character of patrons of the new poetry, anxious above all that its aristocratic refinement should place it clearly above the level of the rude ditties current among knaves and churls. The "courtly" or "aulic" character of the poetry of the troubadours was deliberately imposed upon it.

The ideas of self-styled chivalry—spread in all directions by the verse romances, the orders of knighthood, and the preaching, the "propaganda," as we should say, of the crusades against the Saracens of both the Holy Land and Spain—had fired the imagination of feudal society. We shall not stay to discuss what those ideas owed to the very foemen against whom they spurred the Christian knights. The barbarous crusaders received from the knights of Islam many a lesson in magnanimity and honorable dealing.[10] Be that as it may, the ideal, if not the practice, of those chivalrous virtues was then at the height of its vogue. In order to harmonize with the modish tastes of manorial society, the songs of the jongleurs, popular in their origin, had to indue the garb of chivalric language, of chivalric honor, with regard to which the ladies were particularly insistent.

Honor and "gallantry" in the erotic sense have in all ages gone hand in hand in the ideals of "noble" classes. The epithet and what it stood for, like the whole notion of chivalry, in romance or in the "orders," were above all an expression of aristocratic pride and exclusiveness, studious of underlining the differences which divided the privileged caste, the "worshipful," "gentle" and "well-born," from the run of common humanity. Stendhal speaks in terms less than respectful of "the absurd prejudice which went by the name of honor in Madame de Sévigné's time, and which mainly consisted in dedicating one's life to the service of the master under whom one chanced to have been born and in winning the favor of the ladies. A man could not prove his true worth, in sixteenth-century France, otherwise than by courage in the field or in duels. And since women are particularly fascinated by physical courage and audacity, they were the supreme arbiters of a man's merits. Thus grew the spirit of 'gallantry.' "[11] Much the same conditions obtained in twelfth-century Provence. Venus and Mars have at all epochs been intimately associated; "gallantry" and "courtly" manners had reference to the spheres particular to both those tutelary divinities of warriors and lovers.

Associated with martial valor and the spirit of "gallantry," in the traditional chivalric ideal, which was from its inception linked with the customs and fantasies of pagan times, was likewise the gift of music and poetry. The ideal knight was a poet. Gawaine "of the hundred loves" charmed the ladies with his songs; Tristan was a poet and a musician. The ingenious hidalgo,

Don Quixote de la Mancha, an irrefutable authority on the chivalrous code, was well aware that "all, or nearly all, the knights
errant of times of yore were great troubadours"—*todos o lo mas
caballeros andantes de la etad passada eran gran trobadores.*"[12]

The bard, the *skôp* of pagan times was *ex officio* noble, a "free-
man." In like manner the troubadour poet was, in theory, supposed to be a belted knight.[13] But like most of the rules of the
chivalric code, this was little more than a conventional fiction.
The age of knightly and monastic orders took delight in drawing
up rules and codes, without concerning itself overmuch with
their relevance in the circumstances actually obtaining, and still
less was the demonstration of those rules their practice in life. As
with the modern election candidate, the publication of principles
was what chiefly mattered. Once declared and accepted their
application might go whistle. The whole of the ideas which constituted those ideal codes appertained essentially, like the knight
errants and the peers of the Table Round, to a realm of a poetic,
and it may be added, a politic, fiction.

The poetic gift, conventionally regarded as an inborn attribute
of men of "gentle" blood, was nevertheless one which, by long
tradition as well as by appeal to their tastes and habits, the noble
classes thought it fitting to display. It acquired a new importance
with the rise of courtly Provençal poetry. In the twelfth century,
lords, kings and emperors were proud of parading their poetic
talents. Among the names that have come down to us, some
twenty-three reigning princes are included. Almost all the Provençal lords plumed themselves on their skill in poetry. Besides
the Dukes of Aquitania and the Lords of Ventadorn, the Counts
of Toulouse, the Beaux family, Lords of Marseilles, Boniface,
Lord of Castellane, the Blacatz, Lamanor, and Adhemar families
were known as troubadours. "Indeed it appears," says Master
Gaufridi, "that every man of high lineage or great wealth considered it an obligation to show himself an adept in the gay
science, and able to rhyme a couplet to a graceful musical ac-

companiment. The accomplishment was regarded as a token of noble birth and good education."[14] But it must be recognized that scarcely one of those poets has left a lyric that rises above the level of mediocre doggerel. Few indeed of their poetical effusions have survived, and had Provençal poetry depended for its reputation upon the talents of those noble practitioners, it would have had little enough to show, either in the way of quantity or quality.

From the very outset, the troubadours who raised Provençal song to the high summit of its influence were jongleurs of low birth. Cercamon was a vagabond, known by that appellation alone; Marcabru was a foundling "left at a rich man's door"; Perdigon was the son of a fisherman; Bernard de Ventadorn was the son of a hind and a kitchen wench; Guiraut de Bornelh was a jongleur of low birth. Not a few troubadours were poor knights, who availed themselves of the convention that a poet's status was a noble one to attach themselves in that capacity to the service of some powerful lord and thus cloak their penury without forfeiting their rank.

Instances have occurred of a jongleur being knighted, and even, like Perdigon and Rambaud de Vaneiras, given lands in fee.[15] But these are rare exceptions. "Nearly all the Provençal poets whose works we read," says an old Provençal lexicographer, "were jongleurs." And after excepting the princes and great lords already named, who were "men of wealth and power and disposed of independent means," the anonymous glossarist goes on to say: "All others earned their living by their poetry." That, to be sure, was in itself a notable achievement which has seldom been repeated by poets of a later period! But the position of the poet was nevertheless a completely dependent one. In short, aristocratic claims and conventions notwithstanding, troubadour poetry was from first to last, in its origin, development and practice, essentially an art of jongleurs of humble extraction.

The term *trobador* (inventor), a fairly close equivalent of "poet" (maker, composer), honored the noble dilettante in his poetic character. But it rightly applied with equal propriety to the itinerant jongleur who invented and composed his songs. Critics have labored to establish, each in a different manner, a precise distinction between the troubadour and the jongleur as separate personalities. But it is idle to seek precise distinctions where none existed. The terms overlapped. The princely troubadour was not, of course, a jongleur; but the jongleur who composed his songs was a troubadour.

The term "jongleur" (in Latin, *joculator*) was in use as early as the sixth century to designate any sort of professional entertainer, acrobat, buffoon, bear-leader. It had no particular reference to song or music. The word had notoriously disreputable associations, both on account of the violent anathemas with which jongleurs were visited by the Church,[16] and by reason of the rabble of mountebanks, vagrants and rapscallions which it included.

> *Qual mestiers es plus aontos,*
> *D'eser joglar o laire?*

asks a later troubadour. "Which is the more shameful calling, to be a jongleur or a thief?" Autolycus might have supplied an apt answer. We may recall the irritation of Guiraut Riquier at the aspersion cast on a gifted poet by his being referred to as a jongleur, and thus placed in the same category as the sword-swallower and the man with the monkey. The lack of a special term for a jongleur who was a troubadour certainly led to confusion, but the long established usage persisted.

From the moment, however, that he plucked the chords of his lute and lifted his voice in song, the courtly jongleur-troubadour stepped into the part of the ideal minstrel-knight. It was in that character that he paid his poetic homage. It was not the itinerant jongleur who sang of "gentle" and "refined" love, who boldly loved the liege-lady, but the ideal poet-knight. The impersonation was, as admitted, like the convention of the play-actor, or of the novelist who relates fictitious inventions as though they were true facts. But, as in drama or story, the convention though known to be fictitious was required as an integral parcel of the poet's art to be "convincing."

The part of that poetic, one might almost say dramatic, fiction in all that has reference to that art should be more clearly borne in mind than has generally been the case. The character of troubadour poetry cannot be rightly appreciated unless it is placed in the setting which framed its presentation. The song was a manner of operatic monody in which the jongleur-troubadour who sang it before an elegant audience occupied the place of the fashionable tenor. We should therefore be chary of attaching greater weight to the stylized passion he was under the obligation of displaying, than to the stage-love tunefully bestowed by the Italian tenor upon a prima donna graced with a lengthy career and Junonic presence. Bernard de Ventadorn celebrates in lascivious terms the personal charms of Aliénor of Aquitaine at a time when the latter was well on in her fifties.

Many modern interpreters of the troubadours follow the example of the authors of the Provençal biographies in taking literally the poet's lyrical effusions and drawing from them a chronicle of their amatory intrigues. But the passion sung by the hard-working artist bears in truth but slight relation to his actual life. The fiction went by the name of "well-dight saying of praise," and if the poet had any particular lady in view, she was as often as not his gracious patroness. Poetry, in this form, was not the effusion of a lorn soul's intimate emotions or the musings of a recluse, but a public entertainment, and the *libretto* of the performance, which our scholars con word by word, was not composed in view of being read. We deplore the monotony of the theme, and the troubadours themselves were at times conscious of this fault.[17] But the ladies would have no other. A song which did not treat of love would have moved them to disdain and indignation, as would, in another age, an Italian opera or a novel devoid of love interest.

If the sentiments expressed appear to us artificial, the intention and the setting of its presentation were in fact avowedly artificial. The lady represented as the object of the poet's passionate inspiration often did not even exist. She is never named; at most she is referred to by some fanciful appellation, or *senhal*. The amusement offered by this drawing-room entertainment was enhanced by the riddle which, like a *roman à clef*, it propounded. One of the connotations of the term "slanderer" (*luzengier;* "losengere" in Caxton's English), so conspicuous in troubadour dialectics, had reference, there can be little doubt, to the solutions put forward concerning the identity of the lady in question. The *senhal* was used to rebut the guesses put forward by the audience, even should they happen to be grounded. The conventions of chivalry, like the pedantic rules of courtly love, were poetical fictions, and were in large measure consciously and admittedly such.

Whatever might be the actual social condition of the poet, the courtly convention decreed that the exercise of poetic talent should be a knightly vocation. The vagrant poets of low birth compare themselves with Tristan, Lancelot, or Percival. Allusions to the subjects of the epic abound in their compositions.[18] The service offered by the minstrel-knight as a love-token to his lady, is equated with that by which he might have earned a claim to her favors in battle and in joust.[19] As Petrarch put it, "their voice stood them in stead of sword and stave, of helm and shield":

> . . . *a sui la lingua*
> *langia e spada fu sempre, e targia ed elmo.*[20]

The "knight," or the impersonator of the knightly part, who performed such service, proclaimed himself his mistress' liegeman; he owed her loyalty and homage, while she, for her part, having once formally accepted her appointed bard, was held bound to keep true plight with him and to induct him in the fief-tenancy to which he had a legitimate title.[21] The love relationship followed the pattern of the reciprocal obligations of the liege knight towards his suzerain, or towards the lady whose colors he wore in battle or list. Those poetical conventions were essentially stage-conventions. Yet for all their artificial character, they harmonized as a whole, if not in detail, with the spirit of the social circles they were designed to entertain. If the poetic passion was in large part fictitious, its seductive intention was real enough. Both men and women liked to let themselves be deceived by the fictions which at times deceive our critics and historians. Fantasy was invited to effectuate itself in actual life.

Poetic chivalry, being an aristocratic privilege, bestowed upon men and women of "gentle" birth a measure of chartered license in their relations. Such an acknowledged and statutory freedom, far from betokening a growing laxity of morals, or as a theologian would say a "corruption," introduced, on the contrary, a measure of restraint in the far more undisciplined license of old-time barbarism. But, for all that, the ruling classes availed themselves, under cover of those highly artificial conventions, of the right to indulge their ancient use and wont without overmuch concern for a rigid interpretation of Christian sexual ethics. "Gallantry," as it came to be called in the French seventeenth and eighteenth centuries, "courtesy," "druerie," as it was termed in the twelfth, rested primarily on the privileged immunity claimed by the ruling and leisured classes.

As late as the time of Dante and Petrarch, and even much later, literary tradition was to be at pains to assert that only a "gentle" heart, a "courtly" soul, a person of worship and lineage, was capable of experiencing the delicate emotions and the exalted raptures which the elegant diction of the poets was concerned with setting forth. The troubadours, accordingly, never weary of dwelling upon the subtle distinctions to be drawn between the delicacy of courtly emotions befitting well-born persons and the grossness of "villainy" which betokens the coarser fiber of boorish and plebian minds. Prudery in a woman, jealousy on the part of a husband were regarded as the marks of a low and vulgar disposition and of an inexcusable lack of conversance with the usages of polite society.

The whole ritual of poetic service was largely aimed at bringing out those distinctions. The flight of the poet's inspiration was accordingly circumscribed within the framework of rigid prescriptions, from which he might not deviate without laying himself under the intolerable reproach of bad taste. The merits of a composition were assessed by reference to the fidelity shown in the observance of consecrated principles and the closeness of its conformity to accepted models. Manifestations of originality were thus confined to the dexterity evinced in modulating adroit variations upon the prescribed themes. Subject, sentiments, "conceits," all that went into the composition of a poem, were dictated by the rigid canons of art.

A conventional pedantry no less meticulous governed, in the realm of poetic fiction, the relations of the courtly lover and his lady. It laid down the behavior to which they should conform, the emotions which they were expected to experience. Each individual sigh and heart-beat, the "cruelty" of the fair one, the "despair" of the lover, the concession of "favors" to be doled out on a guarded scale, were foreseen in the erotic code, any departure from which counted as a breach of courtesy. The various situations which may arise in the unfolding of a love-intrigue, and the problems they might raise, provided the subject matter of disquisitions and set disputes closely patterned on the scholastic debates of theologians. Knotty points were referred to recognized authorities whose pronouncements were used in codifying the corpus of erotic jurisprudence.

The society of the castles of Languedoc devoted to those de-

bates on "questions of love" their fastidious leisures with much
the same fervor which, in a later age, the guests of the Hôtel
Rambouillet and of Mlle. Scudery's salon were to apply to the
pursuit of wit and good taste. Such were the gatherings which
gave themselves or were given the name of "Courts of Love."
Their actual staging is of small importance; it is of much greater
interest to note the amplitude, the formality, the incredible seri-
ousness which characterized those whimsical debates on psychology in the twelfth century.

The phenomenon has no parallel in classical literature; still
less can it be traced to barbarian precedents. To our taste the
whole thing lapses into the grotesque. No subject could, in our
eyes, be less suited to theoretical debate, conducted with sober
solemnity and without the slightest embarrassment, than erotic
sentimentality in its mannered and affected form, as understood
by the dialecticians of the twelfth century.

Novelists and psychologists have since written a great deal
on the subject of love; sexual problems, as presented from the
point of view of the psychologist, the psychiatrist, the physiolo-
gist and the sociologist, are responsible for a vast literature. But
light, sentimental and romantic love is hardly ever treated in the
spirit of objective science or abstract metaphysics. "Most psychologists," observes Ribot, "have been very sparing of details in
this connection and one could name a number of voluminous
treatises which do not even refer to it."[22]

Though the fops and bluestockings of the seventeenth century
found entertainment in mapping out the contours of the "*Pays
du Tendre*," the amusement was but a pretext for a quipping
exercise of wit. It might lend itself to ridicule, but it raised no
problem. The amatory dialectic of the twelfth century was extravagant in quite a different manner and appears at the first
glance to bear no relation to any feature of its ambience. That a
whole society, still not very far removed from the ages of barbarism, should come to be smitten with a passion for debates of

the scholastic type on the details of a profoundly artificial psychology of love, that it should have devoted itself to the pursuit of this manner of pseudo-science with the gravity of so many doctors of theology, is a phenomenon singular enough to call for some explanation.

The conventions of courtly love were, deliberately or not, the expression of the opposition between two converse orders of sexual morality. The pagan societies of barbaric times, like primitive societies, were unacquainted with the merits of continence and chastity. Marriage was a contract based on economic and political considerations, in which calculation entered in far larger measure than sentiment. It was often polygamous or provisional. Neither prenuptial purity nor conjugal fidelity were in those days prescribed by current ethics. Not to go beyond the lands which were to become the home of poesy, we find the first Christian witnesses declaring that "the whole of Aquitania is no better than a huge brothel." They denounced in particular, in this connection, the moral disorder prevalent throughout the great estates, the "villas" which were to become the manorial castles of a later epoch.[23]

It was long before any considerable change was brought about by the Christian religion in the morality of the barbarian chiefs and, later, in that of the powerful nobility, towards whom the Church generally showed itself very indulgent. Nevertheless, as time went by and the power of the Church grew greater, the violent contrast between the inveterate use and wont of the ruling classes and the principles of Christian morals could not but become more apparent. Feudal society, while jealous of maintaining its privileges, did not care to offer an open challenge to religious susceptibilities. The nobles owed it to their own dignity not to expose themselves to the strictures of commoners and priestlings. By bringing aristocratic usage into association with claims to cultivated taste and a refined emotional sensibility; by representing amorous relations as subject to fine distinctions passing, by their subtlety, the comprehension of the vulgar throng; by adopting heroic and knightly principles appropriate to the manifestation of lofty ideals and emotions, courtly and chivalric theories came to constitute a manner of apologetics serving to shield the time-honored way of life to which the privileged ruling class was accustomed. Love proclaimed itself noble that it might not be declared scandalous.

In a society which professed the principles of Christian morality those conventions performed the function, one might say, of a protective coloring by means of which its bearer mimicked its environment. They enabled the favored caste to denounce license, coarseness and disorder in language practically identical with that used by Christian morality, and to guard against the imputation of discreditable conduct, while they simultaneously went their wonted pace. The pedantic subtleties of "scholastic" conceits served to take the wind out of the sails of cavilling and censorious ignorance. The *trobar clus* helped the ends of disguise. "The refinements and obscurities of abstruse conceptions in the poetry of Arnaud Daniel and Guiraut de Bornelh," a critic remarks, "derived from a desire to counterfeit depth and abstraction of thought."[24] But the gossamer of those dialectical veils was not spun in view of metaphysical abstractions, and the interest they aroused in a world intent on pleasure was far from being a purely intellectual one. "The dialecticians of love," as another commentator puts it, "pronounce judgment on a point of courtly casuistry in the current style of debate, and with a gravity that may call forth a smile, but shows nevertheless to what extent this solemnity in the pursuit of a frivolous pastime, factitious though it was in a sense, interwove with the interests of actual life."[25]

The scholasticism of love, like that of the theologians, derived in its form from Islamic sources. It was from the first connected with the lyrical style borrowed from Moorish Spain,

which anticipated by two centuries the language of the "Courts
of Love." The terminology of Sufi mysticism fell in admirably
with the purpose the Provençal jongleurs were called upon to
advance. But however conscientiously they might seek to become
acquainted with the ideas behind the lyrical manner of their
models, these contained elements which they would not have
been able to understand and which, could they have done so,
they would not have cared to adopt. In Sufi poetry, sentimentality
had its roots in an idealization which was not fictitious and conventional. It rested on genuine convictions and aspirations. That
religious inspiration was rejected, it is true, by the larger number
of Andalusian minstrels, who nevertheless retained its form and
formulae from purely decorative motives.[26]

The Provençal disciples of those poets adopted much the same
course. Unable to make anything of doctrines of chastity and
purity, they set themselves to reproduce such of the refined—the
Arabs said "noble"—sentiments of Hispano-Moorish lyrics as
were best calculated to impart a choice elegance to their art. They
appropriated the language of that religious poetry without concerning themselves about the springs that inspired it. Thus the
troubadours in search of mystery and esotericism had but to
borrow the manner and language of Hispano-Mauresque poetry.
There they found ready to their hand the "courtly" style and the
trobar clus. Thus also did troubadour poetry come to lend itself
to a misinterpretation which it in part invited, since it appeared
to flaunt an idealism which was in fact foreign to it, but which
its diction, with but some shades of modification, enabled later
interpreters to ascribe to it.

The lyric love which these conventions aimed at idealizing or,
as the Freudians would say, sublimating, referred exclusively
to extra-marital relations. The homage of the troubadours was
without exception addressed to married women.[27] That condition, for which there existed, moreover, reasons of social ex-
pediency, is abundantly underlined by the poetical casuists who

expound the difference between "delicate" and "honorable" love on the one hand, and on the other the brutish intercourse which went by the name of "villainy" and which they likened to the coupling of dogs. Any woman requiring the duty of fidelity from her husband was charged with conducting herself "like a commoner." Any husband manifesting jealousy stood under the self-conviction of "discourtesy" and "dishonorable conduct."

Raimon Vidal addresses a humble supplication to King Alfonso II of Aragon, beseeching him to curb the scandal arising in his realm by the jealousy of husbands: "Generous King and thou Queen upon whom virtue and beauty wait, forbid unto all the married men of your estates to entertain feelings of jealousy. Women are withal endowed with so much cunning and power that they can, whenever they list, give the color of truth to a lie, and the color of a lie to truth.[28] The poet-knight Mataplana, one of the most noble of Spanish grandees of the old school, composed a sirventes directed against Raimon de Miraval, upbraiding him for his indelicate and dishonorable conduct, the said Raimon having had, it appears, a dispute with his wife in regard to her lovers.

> He hath done great shame and disworship [says Mataplana] against the rules of courtesy, which he had hitherto professed to use and honour. So it be he ever did sue the straight trace of courtly honour, his sentiments have suffered much change, for that he hath comported himself in such wise that it will be hard for him to excuse himself from the appel of villainy. . . . A husband who delighteth in youth should approve himself debonair, so that his neighbors may in their turn show themselves gracious unto him. After suffering the blot of so gross unbeseemingness, he now assays to bring about an accord with his wife. An he would in troth have her return to him, it will behove him to approve himself more generous, and to allow her to entertain a belami after her own heart. So soon as he has made his accord with her,

joy will once more grace his house, if so it be that he is not distrained from seeing it frequented by wooers for her bountyes. An he fill those obligations, he will be returned to the favour of such as, like ourselves, are affected to the use of honour and courtesy.[29]

"Courtesy," "honor," "refined love" (*fin amor*), whereby the delicate sentiments of which only a "gentle" heart is capable were exalted above vulgar grossness and "villainy," were, from the point of view of Christian standards, flagrantly immoral in principle and practice. Yet that scandalous sexual code and its poetical exaltation came to be the source out of which issued in time a literary treatment of amatory themes, thus spiritualized into a mystic idealism severed from all carnal associations. The forms, the manner, the language and vocabulary of the troubadours continued to be employed in that "Platonic" inversion of all the conceptions of the "courtly" love they had sung. The primary condition even of that love, that it had reference exclusively to illicit love for a married woman, persisted in the literary tradition.

Following the example of the Provençal troubadours, the most representative poet of the Italian Renaissance, the universally acknowledged singer of idealized love, Petrarch, was to celebrate in a long series of lyrics his love, real or fictitious, for a married woman. Romantic idealized and disincarnated love, as in the courtly poetry of the troubadours and the chivalric versions of pagan sagas, remained, despite the utmost spiritualization, an adulterous passion. Commenting on the tale of Tristan, Gaston Paris refers to his own feeling of regret over the immorality of the barbaric bard, who appears to have deliberately set himself the task of "glorifying adultery."[30] If Messer Petrarch, worthy titular canon of the Church, could celebrate a passion as adulterous as that of Tristan without giving cause to scandal, that is because a profound change had in the meantime come about in the treatment of the theme.

From an artistic point of view, we may prefer the poignant emotions which come into play in the drama of Tristan and Iseult to the suave, elegant and sugary conceits which lend luster to the long-drawn literary passion of the Italian poet. But the latter bears, from the moral point of view, a well-nigh irreproachable appearance. If it is in fact no less adulterous than the love of Tristan, passion is idealized and subtilized to such a degree and so completely detached from all carnal suggestion in its literary presentation, that only a singularly mawkish moral pedant could find scandal in it. In the interval of time which separates the barbaric saga from the standard of poetic treatment set by the foremost representative of the Italian Renaissance in that field, the expressions of love had undergone a spiritualizing change. This notable metamorphosis took place in relation to the poetry of the troubadours and to the tradition it had established. It is therefore of particular interest to examine the causes which led, in Provence, to that notable transformation.

Conception of Love

WHILE the part of the troubadours in the development of European literatures has failed in general to be appraised at its due measure, their contribution to morals has afforded occasion for much edification. A view, in truth very ancient, credits them with having initiated a "new conception of love." Passion, known to pagan antiquity in its sensual aspect only, is supposed to have been raised by the poets of Provence to the level of an ennobling sentiment detached from the flesh, and the ideal of woman, deified by their poetic worship, is said to have inspired them with a cult which blended with that of the Holy Virgin. This theme has been developed at large with all the enthusiasm and eloquence it is calculated to inspire. A certain Emil Lucka of Vienna has devoted to those lofty conceptions and their elucidation with the aid of metaphysical theories on the "development of the Ego," a number of works, one of which appeared in English under the title, *The Evolution of Love*. "The first expression of true love," writes this author, "makes its appearance through spontaneous inspiration, and without the aid of philosophical concepts, in the works of the troubadours. To the greatest of them, Bernard of Ventadorn, is due the honor of having been the first to celebrate chaste love. If ever a champion of civilization deserved a monument, it is this poet"[1]. As one example among a large number of similar declarations, I cite the remarks of M. Louis Gillet on the subject in his admirable study of Dante:

> They [the troubadours] had done something extraordinary, While addressing an audience of women, they had invented the cult of women. It was an immensely far-reaching revolution. Those archaic poets, whom no one now reads, . . . wrote their works for a posterity of centuries and carved deep in our souls the fundamental feature of our civilisation . . . By modeling the forms of love on those of knightly service and homage and by giving it a special ritual and language . . . they brought about a change so unprecedented that its effects have been incalculable. It was a genuine act of moral creation, the most original in the Middle Ages, a kind of love entirely detached from all idea of generation and the reproduction of species. Woman became a religion.[2]

M. Gillet cannot, of course, be reproached for according credence to an opinion universally current in regard to those poets "whom no one now reads."

Strange as it may appear in the light of those confident assurances, there does not exist in the whole of troubadour poetry, from its inception down to its sudden extinction in the cataclysm which overtook the country of its birth, a trace of that "new conception of love" so freely ascribed to the troubadours. In the opinion of several authorities, the impression derived from a perusal of that literature is anything but edifying from a moral point of view. Dr. Weinhold writes: "This literature is completely lacking in delicacy and modesty of any sort. There is not a feeling of respect and deference towards women which it does not brutally trample under foot."[3] M. Pierre Andraud admits that troubadour poetry is inspired only by "a moral unconcern which is not without grace and elegance, but can scarcely be accounted noble."[4] Severe as are those judgments, there can be no question, throughout the period when the poetry of the troubadours flourished, of the idealization commonly attributed to them. After the annihilation, in 1209, of the society which brought about the development of that literature, the activity of a few poets of Languedoc continued for a while on a much reduced scale, and in a form almost unrecognizable under the aspects of disintegration and decay. Prior to that date, nothing is to be found in the poetry of the troubadours that suggests a platonic idealization of passion.

It assuredly is not with reference to Count Guilhem of Poitiers that we may speak of chastity and spiritualization. William of Malmesbury calls him *fatuus et lubricus*.[5] The author of the life of Bernard de Tiron declares that Count Guilhem was notorious as "the enemy of all chastity and female virtue."[6] A gay dog if ever there was one, a deuce of a fellow, the worthy Count flaunts in his lucubrations an impudicity which embarrasses his editors. He sings, as do all his successors, the praises of love; but his paean has not a touch of the ethereal. Far from it. The pleasure which, to the merry Count's way of thinking, passes all others is wholly and undisguisedly carnal.

> *Adonc esta ben c'om s'aisi*
> *d'acho don hom a plus talan*[7]
>
> It is but right that each shall joy
> In that which all men most desire.

"Not only is love not represented as platonic, but the expression of sensual desire assumes extremely crude, sometimes almost brutal forms."[8] That is the least that can be said. Let the reader judge for himself.

One of these canticles in praise of chivalrous love ends with the following stanza:

Qu'ieu ai nom "maiestre certa":
ja m'amigu' anueg no m'aura
que no.m vuelh' aver l'endema;
qu'ieu suy d'aquest mestier, so.m va,
    Tan ensenhatz
que be.n sai guazanhar mon pa
    en totz mercatz.[9]

Klept am I 'Master infallible'; never had leman mine my company one night, but fain would have it on the morrow. In that trade am I so much well-approved that I could thereby dorst trow earn my bread on any mart.

One of the pieces of the noble troubadour furnished Boccaccio with the motif of one of his broadest tales.[10] It concludes with the following verse:

Tant las fotei com auziretz:
cen e quatre vint et ueit vetz,
q'a pauc no.i rompei mos corretz
    e mos arnes;
e no.us puesc dir la malaveg,
    tan gran m'en pres.[11]

I tupped them as ye shall rate; one hundred fourscore times and eight, so girth and gear did wellnigh burst; nor can I tell you the languor great that got me erst.

Cercamon and his pupil Marcabru, likewise accounted "archaic" in the succession of troubadour poets, composed their works, it is thought, between 1136 and 1145. "Their style," observes Jeanroy, "has not yet attained the stage of refinement which was soon to permit the veiling of the most ardent sensuality under the cloak of vague phrases."[12] In contrast with Count Guilhem, Cercamon sings of love's sorrows and melancholy moods; but he is none the more ethereal on that account.

Quan totz lo segles brunezis,
delai on ylh es si resplan.
Dieu prejarai qu'ancar l'ades
o que la vej'anar jazer.[13]

What time the whole world waxeth dark, a light shines there
as she abodes; lief God I had dipped her in love's toils! Or
but espied when as for bed she dights her and despoils!

Qu'eu non puesc lonjamen estar
de sai vius ni de lai guerir,
si josta mi despoliada
non lo puese baizar e tenir
dins cambra encortinada.[14]

Here I cannot dwell, ne from thence endure, without I strain
her fast and kiss, naked to my side, in curtained rowme.

Saint Salvaire, fai m'albergan
lai el renh on mi donz estai,
ab la genzor, si q'en baizan
sien nostre coven verai
e qe.m do zo que m'a promes;
pueis al jorn s'en ira conques,
si be l'es mal al gelos brau.[15]

Send God the saviour I may hoste there as my gentle lady
wones; and may she lap me in her fold, and yield the thing
she hath fore gaged; apert let her forth uncoyed, eft shot
the bolt, and ill betide her jealous dolt.

Marcabru (or Marcabrun, or Marc Brun), who is very unlike
the elegiac Cercamon, is in many respects an interesting poet.
He has been pronounced a misogynist. Five centuries before
King Francis I, he proclaimed that woman oft does change and
"ben es fols qui si fia"—who so trusts her a mighty fool is he.[16]
But his challenge is of wider range; he hits with scourge all

forms of egoism, deceit, and insincerity, whether in women, or in great lords or commoners, and his revolt imparts to this archaic poet a modern flavor. Unlike the greater number of his colleagues, Marcabru delights in railing upon love: "Famine, plague nor war do more wreck in this world than doeth love."

> *Fams ni mortaldatz ni guerra*
> *no fai tan de mal en terra*
> *quon amors qu' ab enguan serra*
> *Escoutatz!*
> *quan vos veira en la berra*
> *no.n sera os heulhs mulhatz.*[17]

We shall have occasion to return to Marcabru; suffice it here to establish that his language and sentiments savor of anything but idealization.

> *Denan mei n'i passon trei al passador*
> *no sai mot tro'l quartz la fot e.l quinz lai cor.*
>
>> *Del deslei*
>> *que me fai*
>> *li fauc drei*
>> *e.il m'autrei*
>> *mas sotz mei*
>> *aplat sei*
>> *qu'ela.m lass'e.m lia.*[18]

Three wend afore me down the vestibule; a fourth is at his fling; I say not any word, whenas a fifth hyes running in hot haste; I remit her brothelness, so she liggen moot, her length to my behof, flat on her toute.

The love-songs of Bernard of Ventadorn (1148-1195) are declared by some to be the best of the kind in Provençal literature, and even in the whole of medieval poetry, an opinion which may be debatable but is not extravagant. Other troubadours exhibit a more brilliant virtuosity, but the songs of Bernard of Ventadorn are distinguished by a sincerity and simplicity, which are, at any rate, nicely calculated. They are as tender and gentle as a song by Robert Burns. They do not contain, however, the least allusion to the chaste form of love which Herr Lucka chooses to ascribe to Bernard's invention. "The love that Bernard of Ventadorn proclaimed as the most precious thing in the world," writes his principal editor, "rests quite frankly on sensual desire. The language with which he clothes his feelings is more or less delicate; often he is rather coarse, though his manner has nothing of the crudity of diction employed by Guilhem de Poitou."[19] Let the following serve as examples:

> *Amors, e que.m farai?*
> *Si guerrai ja ab te?*
> *Ara cint qu'e.n morrai*
> *del dezirer que.m ve,*
> *silh bela lai on jai*
> *no m'aizis pres de se*
> *qu'en la manei e bai*
> *et estrenha vas me*
> *so cors blanc, gras et le.*[20]

Sweet heart, what shall I make? Am I then never to have hap of thee? Of my desire unto my Lady lief, me thinks I'm like to die; but if she leed me to her bower, whereas I may cull and kiss, and compass her white, and sleek, and silk-smooth form.

That expression of love's ideal aim, which becomes a set formula of the troubadour repertory, is repeated with but slight variation in the songs of Bernard de Ventadorn:

> *Deus, que.l mon chapdela*
> *si.lh platz, m'en lais jauzir!*[21]

Please God, who the world ruleth, I mote of her have joy.

Res de no.n es a dire
ab sol c'aya tan d'ardit
c'una noih la os despolha
me mezes, en loc aizit
e.m fezes del bratz latz al col.[22]

Troth hath she all things good, saving that her lacks the
sprite to bring me to meet ite anight; and sans bedeck, set the
sweet halter of her arms about my neck.

No panegryric of spiritualized love is complete without a
reference to Jaufré Rudel, Prince of Baia (1140-1170) and his
long-range passion for the Countess of Tripoli, the "Distant
Princess." She was, be it noted, the daughter of his good neigh-
bor and patron, Count Raimon IV of Toulouse, to whom doubtless this celebrated conceit, intended as a compliment in the taste
of the time, was addressed. One of the lays in which it is set
forth contains the following lines:

Dieus que fetz tot quant ve ni vai
e formet sest'amor de lonh
mi don poder, que cor ieu n'ai,
qu'ieu veya sest'amor de lonh,
verayamen, en luoc aizis.

Ver ditz qui m'apella lechay,
ni deziron d'amor de lonh;
que nulhs autres joys tan no.m play,
cum jauzimens d'amor de lonh.
Mas so qu'ieu vuelh m'es atahis.[23]

Please God, who all things did create, and framed my Lady-
far-away, I sight my Lady-far-away with wordly eyes, as
lists my heart, in flesh and deed, and stead parted steed.
Sooth redeth he who entwighteth me with lecherie, nor
deems me sate with distant druerie, for that on lustihead
none am faster bent than joy to have of my Lady-far-away.
Alack a-me! that I list may never be!

Elsewhere, rehearsing a less mystical interlude, his tone is even more sensual:

> *Et s'amors mi revert a mau*
> *car ieu l'am tant e liei non cau:*
> *tost veirai jeu si per sufrir*
> *n'atendrai mon bon jauzimen.*

> *D'aquest' amor suy cossiros*
> *vellan e pueys sompnhan dormen,*
> *quar lai ay joy meravelhos,*
> *per qu'ieu la jausitz jauzen;*
> *mas sa beutatz no.m val nien.*

> *"Amicx, fa s'elha, gilos brau*
> *en comensat tal batestau*
> *que sera greus a departir,*
> *tro qu'abdui en siam jauzen."*[24]

Of this my love are bred my grame and woe! Such fondness mine, and not a whit recks she! But full soon shall I wot an my long durance win to hap of her . . . Desire doth vex me or I wake or sleep; lulled then in dreams, oft am I wondrous fain, for I have joy of her passing great, receiving and rendering love's delice . . . But of her goodly self small comfort have I gotten . . . Friend, quoth she, the jealous churls such pother raise that hard't will be to quell them so we may desport.

Bertram de Born, Lord of Hauteford (1180-1205), was better known as a singer of battles—*Bertramun de Bornio arma poetasse*, as Dante says[25]—than as a composer of love-songs. Sir Bertram, who was closely involved in the intrigues and struggles which preluded the Hundred Years' War, resided for a considerable time at the English Court of Normandy. He thought it shabby and intolerably dull: "We of Limoges," he says, "prefer folly before wisdom and are of our disposition gay and fond of

lavish living and laughter."[26] Accordingly, disgusted with the
stinginess and the glum temper of the men of the North, he
sought compensation in addressing his attentions to the Duchess
Matilda, daughter of King Henry II and wife of Henry the Lion,
Duke of Saxony. Bertram calls her *"Saïssa,"* the Saxon, and celebrates her charms in the following terms:

> *A mo Meils-de-Be deman*
> *son adrech, nuou cors prezan,*
> *de que par a la veguda*
> *la fassa bo tener nuda.*[27]

Best-of-best I ply with love's request, her lithe body enfold-
ing. To rede from what sees eye, good't were, ween I, naked
to hold her and behold.

Or again:

> *Ren en beutat no gualia*
> *ni.n fai nula fantaumia*
>   *Lo joios,*
> *joves, gens cors amoros,*
> *e genza, qui la deslia,*
> *et on hom plus n'ostaria*
>   *guarnizos,*
> *seria.n plus enveios,*
> *que la noch fai parer dia*
> *la gola, e qui.n vezia*
>   *plus en jos*
> *totz lo mons en genzaria.*[28]

Nought unto her fair form in loveliness is peer; nor is this
fancy mere; who so disparts her dress, belied is not his guess;
show forth bedazzling fruits of youthsomeness; and the more
raiment's doffed, the more flames lust aloft; shene of her
bosom's turns to noonday night; and somewhat downward
to enquire the universal world setteth afire.

Guilhem de Cabestanh (1162-1197) is, if one may risk the syncretism, the classic troubadour. Rightly does Stendahl choose the gallant knight for the paradigm of his kind. Cabestanh celebrates with deferential delicacy his tender devotion to his lady, reiterating the hackneyed formulae of courtly love. The details of his life are overshadowed by the poetic legend with which his name is associated; an incensed husband killed him, it is said, and gave his wife her lover's heart to eat. The story, common in folklore, provides an appropriate frame for the romantic figure of the troubadour-knight. Yet, however delicate and chivalrous the expression of his sentiments, no doubt may be attached to the nature of the felicity after which he so tenderly sighs. Thus sings the gallant bard:

> *Belha dompna, mielher de las melhors,*
> *cuenda e plazens de cors e de faisso,*
> *Amors me te en sa doussa preyzo:*
> *per vos o dic, que pros m'er et honors*
> *si ja fos mais que Dieus m'espires tan*
> *que.m volcsetz far de vostres bratz sentura;*
> *en tot aitant cum ten lo mons e dura*
> *non es mais res qu'ieu dezir aver tan.*[29]

Fair Lady, alderbest, gracious of form and mien, love doth me thrall detain in his sweet jail. Mine were, I ween, great meed and vaunt, an God thy folded arms for girth did grant; nought list I more while the world dures.

> *Lo doux cossire*
> *que.m don' Amors soven,*
> *dona.m fai dire*
> *de vos maynh ver plazen.*
> *Pessan remire*
> *vostre cors car e gen,*
> *cuy ieu dezire*
> *mais que no fas parven.*[30]

The dear smart where with love full fills my sprite to pleasant discant doth me oft incite. I look in fancy upon thy body's snow and burn with more desire than I list show.

Peire Vidal (1175-1215) is, on account of his originality, animation and variety, the most accessible among the troubadours to the modern reader. Leading a life of adventure in various countries, he shared with lively interest in the political passions of his time, and he was gifted with a feeling for the aspects of nature rare at that period. Peire Vidal is ingenious and versatile, and the matter and manner of his verse form a picturesque blend. In the treatment of amatory themes, he is equally free from excessive affectation and from coarseness; he is tender without being sugary, and scrupulous without falling into pedantry. Vidal is fond of dwelling on the merits of patience and restraint in the love relation, and discourages precipitate haste. His descants thus abound in expressions which, torn from their context, might pass as evidence of reserve. But this does not in the least signify that the happiness he seeks is other than normally sensual, and that he has any other view.

> *De clartat m'a mes en escur*
> *cela per cui vauc dezirans;*
> *e pos Amors vol totz mos dans,*
> *no.m meravilh si mal m'en vai.*
> *Mas be.us dic que tan sofrirai,*
> *tro posca en loc avenir,*
> *qu'ab mos olhs son bel cors remir;*
> *e s'i aura trop al meu par.*[31]

She hath me cast from light into the dusk, she whom I go desiring; and sith that love breeds all my grame, I have no wonder that she does me woe. But wot ye well a sooth I can assure for that I shall thereto endure on till I feed upon her body's meed.

Ai! Don', humilitatz
e pretz e pietatz
vos met' entre mos bratz.[32]

Ah! Lady mine, may the submission and humble behaviors
I use move thy dear ruth thereto that it shall bring me to thy
arms.

Sabetz per que.lh port amor tan coral?
Car anc no vi tan bela ni gensor
ni tan bona, don tenh qu'ai gran ricor,
car sui amics de domna que tan val.
E si ja vei qu'ensems ab mi.s despolh,
melhs m'estara qu'al senhor d'Eissidoth.[33]

Wot you wherefore my heart is possessed with my love to
her alone? 'T is that never was, I wont, lady so fair, so noble
and so sweet, Her friend to be is most wealth to own. Beeth
she and I rise bedight to meet the amorous rite, more hap I'd
deem my part than I were Sir Richard of the Lion Heart.

E.lh baizei a lairo
la boca e.l mento.
So n'ai agut e no mas re,
e sui tot morts, si.l plus rete.[34]

On her mouth and chin I've laid a kiss. More have I not had
of her, and shall die iwiss or I reach the rest.

Abrazar e cremar
me fai com focs carbo.[35]

She stirs and fans me to a brenning coal.

Peire Vidal also utters his sensuality under the light disguise of
a topographical *double entendre,* a procedure not uncommon at
that period:

Color fresć a ab cabelh saur
et anc non obret de pinsel.
Mas Mongalhart e Daurabel
li platz qu'a sos obs retenha.
Beljoc no ven ne empenha,
e mi fai Montamat tener
e Bon Repaus per melhs jazer,
e per m'amor platz l'Ostals Rics.[36]

Fresh of hue and fair of hair is she; nor brush to gaud
herself withal. But fainly would she hold reserved Mount
Pleasant and Well Adorned; nor does she barter or pledge
Fair Sport. Yet doth she consent me Fort Beloved and Fair
Repose for my softer recline and barters Goodly Mansions
for my love.

Guiraut de Bornelh (1175-1220) was held in such high account by his contemporaries that he was named the "master
troubadour." Dante is doubtless right in considering that reputation excessive, although at first he appeared to endorse the high
estimate. But Guiraut has a fine lyric lilt. One may imagine that
the music and its lively movement went for a good deal in placing
his reputation so high.

Bel companhos, si dormatz o velhatz,
Non dortmatz plus, quel jorn es apropchatz.
. . . .
Bel dos companh, tan soi en ric sojorn
qu'en no volgra mais fos alba ni jorn,
car la gensor que auc nasques de maire
tenc e abras, per qu'en non prezi gaire
        lo fol gelos ni l'alba![37]

Pretty fellows! whether awake or a-sleeping,
sleep no more, for the day's a-peeping.
. . . .

Sweet pretty fellow! I dwell in such delight
I would nor day nor dawn e'er broke the night;
for enarmed I hold the fairest ever born;
and all ado I scorn
of husbands and of morn.

"His conception of love is the same as that of all other troubadours of his time,"[38] and he can be "as classic in his vocabulary
as Guilhem de Poitiers."[39]

Arnaud Daniel (flor. 1180-1200), the best artificer of his
mother tongue—*miglior fabbro del parlar materno*—in Dante's
phrase,[40] uses no disguised language in declaring the tenor of
his emotions:

> *Dieus lo chauzitz,*
> . . . .
> *voilla, sil platz, qu'ieu e midonz jassam*
> *en la chambra on amdui nos mandem*
> *uns rics convens don tan gran joi atendi,*
> *que seu bel cors baisan rizen descobra*
> *en quel remir contra.l lum de la lampa.*[41]

Please God! . . . . We twain shall bed, my lady and I. In
pointed stead, whereto rich tryst convenes to banquet of her
body, catered by wanton hands to hungry eens, that laugh
with glee, Heigh ho! feeding on what they see by lamp's
glow.

> *. . . sieus solatz es dels autres sobriers.*
> *Ai! si no l'ai! Las! tant m'a comors!*
> *Pero l'afans m'es deportz ris e jois*
> *car en pensan sui de lieis lecs e glotz:*
> *Ai dieus, si ja'n serai estiers jauzire!*[42]

Joy of her surmounts all that another has to give. She who
hath smitten me, may she make good the smart she bred by
fill of my desire! Desire itself doth the while pleasure bring;

what time I think upon her, I delight in the desiring. But ah!
God of Mercy! that I nathless had joy of her in other wise!

Dante makes him atone in Purgatory the "hermaphroditic
sin," and that of indulging his appetites "like the beasts."[43]
Arnaud, in fact, does not shrink from using language that goes
beyond any Latin:

> *Dompha, ges Bernartz no s'atill*
> *del corn cornar ses gran dozill*
> *ab quel seire tranc del penill*
> *puois poira cornar ses perill.*[44]

There follow eight stanzas of erotic scatology. Dante's tribute to
him as an unrivalled craftsman in the handling of language and
metres, "whom we have followed"—*et nos eum secuti sumus*[45]—
is nevertheless fully merited. His quality stands brilliantly apart.
Arnaud Daniel likes to pose as a blundering flutterpate.

> *Ieu sui Arnaut qu'amas l'aura*
> *et chatz la lebre ab lo bou*
> *e nadi contra suberna.*[46]

In other words, "I am Arnaud, who reapeth the wind; and waste
my time and swim against the stream." But something more than
a glossary is required to apprehend the verbal fireworks with
which he loves to ply his audience.

Arnaud Daniel swears eternal devotion to one woman after
another.

> *Ans er plus vils aurs non es fers*
> *c'Arnautz desam lieis ont es fermanz necs.*[47]

Gold will be sold at the price of iron ere Arnaud unloves her
whom to his heart is vowed.

But his promises are given with a smile:

> *La lenga.i.s feign, mas lo cors vol.*[48]

The tongue lieth, the heart doth as it listeth.

He scorns the poor-spirited creature who holds that a lover is bound to pine and give himself up to anguish, and that every woman should be a *belle dame sans merci*. Arnaud Daniel's song is tuned to another key:

> *Bona es vida*
> *pos poia la mante,*
> *que tals n'escrida*
> *cui ges no vai tan be;*
> *no sai de re*
> *coreillar m'esacrida,*
> *que per ma fe*
> *de mieills ai ma partida*
>
> *Ges non es croia*
> *cella cui soi amis;*
> *de sai Savoia*
> *plus bella nos noiris:*
> *tals m'abelis*
> *don ieu plus ai de joia*
> *non ac Paris*
> *d'Elena, cel ce Troia.*[49]

> Aye, life is beautiful that's coped with joy!
>   let harsh-luck cry fie!
>   my own plaint defy.
> Ne cruel she whose friend I be, ne coy;
>   ne fairer this side Savoy.
> Fond is my love to her, nor greater joy
>   did Paris have of Helen, her of Troy.

Raimon Jordain prefers a night in the arms of his mistress to his chance of Paradise,[50] and Gaucelm Faidit (1190-1240) is even more lascivious.[51] Others go even farther, and we have to hark back to Martial for parallels of their "conception of love."[52] Of that conception, Arnaud de Mareulh (1170-1200) gives us a precise definition: it is *"voluntatz qu'ai del vostre cors gen"*— the desire I feel for your graceful body.[53] And lest any doubt should linger, Arnaud Daniel himself puts even more precision into the statement; he informs us that he wishes "to be united with her in body, not in soul."

> *Del cors li fos non de l'arma*
> *que.m consentis a celat dins sa chambra.*[54]

To sum up, there exists in the poetic output of any troubadour of the twelfth century no shadow of ambiguity as to the frankly sensual character of the erotic passion which inspires it. Not one can be suspected of entertaining any other conception of love. However affected and pedantic the conventions of courtly intrigue, however obscure the diction of the *trobar clus,* our poets —far from casting a veil, even diaphanous, of mystery over the nature of the felicity, the "joy," after which they sigh—express themselves on this head with a crudeness unparalleled in any other literature. All prudery aside, the directness they display in this respect is disconcerting by its artlessness. The constant recurrence of terms and phrases such as *despolhar, jazer, estrenher, tener nuda, sos cor gras et le,* produces by its monotonous iteration the effect of an incredible penury of imagination and vocabulary, and by depriving the bald expression of sensual desire of any element of invention or surprise, reduces those colorless formulae to the level of the indecencies of naughty schoolboys.[55] Of "sublimation" or "platonic love" no trace soever is to be found throughout the range of this literature.

As noted above, the troubadours love to dwell upon the distinctions, at once captious and obscure, which they draw between courtly love, or *"druerie,"* and the coarse feelings of vulgar minds. Those distinctions lie at the very root of the apologetics of courtly love. No clown, no person whose sensibilities are uncultivated, is able to apprehend the refined emotions that inspire aristocratic gallantry. Arnaud Daniel, frankly sensual as he is, girds at "those lovers whose commerce brings shame upon a woman and degradation to a man." "I have myself renounced the love of a wealthy lady of high estate," he tells us, "that I might not incur the stain of shameful pleasures, whose vulgar grossness is unredeemed by any delicacy or honour. To such pursuers of women, the love I seek is a closed book; despite their claims to elegance and refinement, such lovers destroy all courtesy."[56]

Wherein consist in fine, then, those sacrosanct distinctions, so insistently referred to, yet for the most part wrapped in the obscurities of the *gai saper* and of the *trobar clus*? It happens from time to time, though on but rare occasions, that the poets allow a clear idea of what they mean to pierce through the conventional jargon.

Marcabru is particularly garrulous on that point. Violent as are his invectives against love, his song sometimes mingles with the paeans of Eros intoned by his colleagues and is in no way inferior to them in poetic quality:

> *Ai! fin' amors, fons' de bontat,*
> *c'as tot lo mon illuminat,*
> *merce ti clam!*[57]
>
> O subtile love, fount of all good, that lightest the world, I crave of thee mercy!

Or again:

> *Amors a signifianssa*
> *de maracd' o de sardina,*
> *es de joi cim' e racina,*

c'ab veritat seignoreia
e sa poestatz sobranssa
sobre mouta creatura.[58]

Love virtue hath of smaragdyne and sardonyx: of all joy
is he root and crest; sooth is he most lord of all, who wieldeth
sovereign might over all creatures quick, and all-kind wight.

What then is the love against which Marcabru rails in such
scathing terms? He defines it in unmistakable language: It is
mercenary and interested love. It is the love which those women
practice who flout the rules of *druerie,* and deserve the name with
which he rates them in good round Provençal—*putanas.* The
mercenary motive is in fact the *corpus delicti* of offenses against
love. The corollary of the principle that love justifies all things
is that conduct which is motivated by interest, since it is not the
effect of love, is for that reason unjustifiable.

Hence the insistence upon the rule that a woman should never
take a lover of a higher estate than her own:

E domna fai gran folor
que s'enten en gran ricor.[59]

A dame committeth great folly and disgrace when so a friend
she takes in high place.

"A woman," says a poetess, "should give herself to a lover as
to a friend and not as to a master."[60] Accordingly a noble lady
of manorial rank does not demean herself in taking a lover of
low birth to the extent that she would by yielding to a man of
more exalted social station than her own. "A woman who takes
a great lord as her lover should be regarded as dead," declares
an ancient commentator.[61] Raimon de Miraval cries shame upon
a lady who has been guilty of an impropriety of this kind. "He
who pays the highest price has first claim to the goods," he ex-

claims, "but it was an ill wage the lady drew, for she hath thereby lost her good name."[62]

Furthermore, refined love demands "loyalty." The term must not be understood as having reference to fidelity, for we are expressly told that there is nothing against a woman having several lovers or a man several mistresses.[63] A lover has no more right to be jealous than has a husband, for jealousy is one of the most inexcusable crimes against the spirit of courtesy. Courtly loyalty has reference in particular to the scrupulous observance of secrecy. It is one of the most strictly observed rules of courtly love that a lover shall not disclose the name of his lady, unless it be to some trusted friend who offers to assist him in his intrigue. Thus saith Bernard de Ventadorn:

> D'una ren m'aonda mos senz
> c'anc nulz hom mon joi no m'enquis
> q'eu volentier non l'en mentis,
> qar no.m par bons ensegnamenz,
> anz se foli' ez enfança
> qi d'Amor a benenanja
> q'en vol son cor ad ome descobrir
> se no l'en pod o valer o servir.[64]

Upon one point never did sense forsake me: none ever sought from me the name of her who grants me joy, but I of set purpose lied to him. 'T is contrary to good doctrine, and folly 'tis one's heart to ope when it lucks me well with one—saving only to such a one as is couth of affording help and service.

Accordingly, the lady of the songs is invariably shadowed under the disguise of a pseudonym, *senhal*. A "loyal" lover neglects no precaution to keep her secret, even should he, in order to do so, have to pretend to love another woman, who plays the part of "screen." "No one suffers greater unease than I," exclaims Guilhem de Cabestanh, "for I must needs feign to unlove you, whom I desire beyond any other in the world, and to disavow my love to you."

> *Nulhs hom de mi no sen;*
> *quar vos qu'ieu plus envey*
> *d'autra qu'el mon estey*
> *desautorc e mescrey*
> *e dezam en parvensa*[65]

There is much reference in Provençal poetry to *lauzengiers,* a term which has unnecessarily perplexed critics, for although etymologically it contains the idea of flattery, its use in Provençal is identical with its current use in Italian, where *lusinga, lusingiero* simply means "deception," "deceiver." Deceivers are they who do not respect a lady's secret. The love relationship extracts from both lovers a loyalty that is proof against such deception and that of slanderers who charge lovers with being guilty of the breach of faith.[66]

"Had not my beloved lent ear to false deceivers, I should have been her own, nor ever used guile or unsooth," says Marcabru:

> *Se l'amia non crezi enganador*
> *lauzengier ni mal parlier acusador,*
> *sieu seria, si.m volia, ses bauzi' e ses error.*[67]

He fulminates, as do all the poets, against the churls who neglect or fail to apprehend the principles of courtly love, and who suppose they are being romantic when abandoning themselves to indiscriminate amours. "An they call that *druerie,* they speak unsooth," says he, "for perfect love is joy, but likewise is it unease and measure."

> *. . . benenanssa*
> *es jois, sofrirs e mezura.*[68]

"Measure," *mezura,* that is, "holding back" ("religion held even thieves in measure"—Spenser), is one of the consecrated terms of erotic scholasticism. It is not merely to promiscuous debauchery that "measure," the antonym of which is *leujairia,* is opposed. The term has reference in particular to patience in the pursuit of love's meed. The lover should not be precipitate, he should know how to wait and travel by easy stages to his goal. Peire Vidal is fond of dwelling upon such persevering and measured waiting. He engages in a *tenson* with Blacatz on this "question of love." Blacatz accounts the delaying endurance of Peire Vidal excessive. "As for me," says he, "after that I have done service to my lady for days early and late, I like her to quit my promised guerdon. Willingly do I leave to you your long joyless wait; for my part it is the joy I desire."

> *Et a vos lais lo lonc atendemen*
> *senes jauzir, qu'eu volh la jauzimen.*

Peire Vidal replies:

> *Blacatz, no sui eu ges d'aital faisso,*
> *com vos autres, a cùi d'amor no cal;*
> *gran jornada volh far per bon ostal*
> *ne lonc servir per recebre gen do.*[69]

Blacatz, I am not framed after your sort, who take no pains in love's pursuit. I like to make a long day's travel before I reach a good hostel, and the longer the delay, the more delightful is the meed.

Garin le Brun, a later troubadour, wrote a poem in the form of an internal dialogue, a style much in favor in the Middle Ages, and in Moorish poetry, between *Mezura* and *Leujairia.*[70]

> *Mezura* bids me not be hasty nor lack in patience. "Do not play thy counters all at once, for if thou doeth so, what shall

be left then to proffer"; *Leujairia* says: "What avails long bidding? If thou makest not haste, thou wilt lose thy hap of winning to the goal." *Mezura* tells me: "Go cunningly to thy work if thou wishest to make sure of thy meed." *Leujairia* tweaks me by the nose and says: "When thou holdest the goblet in thy hand, what availeth longer tarrying?" Forsomuch am I torn between *Mezura* and *Leujairia.*

There is nothing in all this that bears any relation to platonic love or chastity. When the subtleties of courtly dialectic are sifted to their meaning, the refined love which the poets defend against coarseness and vulgarity remains no less frankly carnal. Marcabru inveighs, and his tongue is a sharp one, against those men and women whose behavior degrades love, and who heed not lofty sentiments and emotions. After which diatribe, he makes himself snug with his *bon amia,* who, for her part, is never guilty of such unworthy conduct, and therefore merits the refined devotion of an *entendedor,* and he caresses her "while he puts off his clothes."[71]

It may readily be conceived that the expressions used in troubadour poetry to establish the distinctions between "refined" love and gross "villainy" lend themselves to confusion. Editors and commentators have not always been at pains, in their interpretations and translations, to guard against such misunderstandings. The word *fin,* for instance, is sometimes translated by "pure" or even "chaste," and the terms referring to "villainy" are rendered by "sensual love."

The import of words undergoes an evolution in correspondence with the varying conditions and conceptions of successive periods. Many of the terms of the courtly vocabulary originally serving the purpose of idealization, elevation, and refinement have come to acquire the exactly opposite connotation. Thus the word "mistress," having been used relatively to the assimilation of the love bond to the feudal, has come to acquire a pejorative meaning. A similar transformation has changed the intention of the words "leman"—*lief-man,* dear man (or woman); and "paramour"—*par amour.* The term *druerie,* in fourteenth-century English, "drury" or "love drury," was at first a synonym for courtly love. A knight called himself the "dru" (in Provençal, *druz;* in Italian, *drudo;* in Celtic *druth*) of his lady. The word is etymologically related to *"droit," "droiture,"* and to the English "truth," "troth." In the *Roman de Renard,* the loyal vassals of the king are called his *drutz.*[72] The word is even at times employed with reference to divine love.[73] In the *Tristan* of Thomas, the virelay of the song to Iseult runs:

> *Isot me drue, Isot m'amie*
> *en vous ma mort, en vous ma vie.*[74]

Dante gives the word a pejorative connotation, using it in the masculine as the correlative of the coarsest word for "prostitute":

> *T aide è la puttana che rispose*
> *al drudo suo . . . .*[75]

In an old Celtic lexicon the word *druth* is translated "whore." The latter word itself was originally a term of endearment, cognate with the Latin *carus,* dear, beloved.

The vocabulary of the troubadours underwent, over a period of years, modifications in the direction of delicacy. The blunt and ribald aspect of the language becomes mitigated at the same time and it grows richer and more flexible, while the ideas and sentiments denoted continue unchanged. The crudity of the classical word for the carnal act gives place to the term *jauzir* (to enjoy), which is none the less employed in the same definite sense.[76] Later, after the ruin of Provençal civilization, the meaning of almost all the words formerly employed by the troubadours to distinguish courtly from vulgar love came to be used to indicate entirely different distinctions.

But no trace of that ambiguity and amphibology exists in the works of the troubadours prior to the cataclysm which overwhelmed their art under the ruin of their country. The changes which had already taken place in their social position nevertheless might easily have brought about related modifications in ideas and language before that time. The position of the poet had considerably altered at the end of the twelfth century from what it had been at the beginning. His vocation had become more specialized and professional. The pretense that he must be an armed knight had been completely dropped. The noble bard, who had left at first to his jongleurs the care of singing his poems, had come to entrust to them the task of composition as well. The courtly fiction had indeed lost much of its dogmatism before the growing power of the mercantile class. Talent was freely recognized irrespectively of the social level from which it came. The lords of the old school voice their protest against the elevation of persons of low birth to the dignity of the poet's calling. Peire de Mala in a sirvente takes exception to those wretched parasites.[77] The situation is intelligible enough, for "the perpetual complaints made by the troubadours from the end of the twelfth century against the niggardly treatment meted out to them at the hands of great lords prove in what measure their art had become dependent on the latter."[78]

It might at times happen that the troubadour, presuming upon the privileges of poetic talent, usurped the claims of the poet knight, and took seriously the literary passion which the discharge of his calling required him to display. In a society whose morals are not very strict, literary talent confers a certain license where women are concerned. But in many cases it would have been an absurdity and an inexcusable impertinence on the part of the provider of poetic pastimes to lay claim to the favors of the noble Dame who condescended to grant him her protection. The lady, the *drue,* originally celebrated in song by the noble bard, became the gracious patroness of literature, and the most precious favor she could bestow upon the esurient poet would be to feed him.

Nothing would have been more natural under those conditions than a change in the character and expression of the feelings which formed the theme of troubadour poetry. If the love sung by the poets, being anything but platonic to begin with, had become so by the force of circumstances, there would be nothing surprising in the evolution. The remarkable fact is that nothing of the kind occurred. At a time when the social position of the poets had undergone a profound alteration, towards the close of the twelfth century and the beginning of the thirteenth, not even a pretense of spiritual interpretation of passion is to be found in their productions. On the very eve of the disaster which cast the lands of Provençal poetry into an abyss of annihilation, out of which they were never to rise again, that poetry stood at the pinnacle of its fame and brilliance. There was no gradual decay. It was mowed down in full bloom. The last days of its efflorescence were the age of Arnaud Daniel, Peire Vidal, Giraut de Bornelh. It showed no signs of exhaustion or gradual deterioration in its quality. The conception of love upon which it was based remained, too, frankly sensual. The blemishes of decadence do not appear before the year 1209, the date of the proclamation of the crusade against the Albigenses, and then they appeared indeed suddenly. It was after that date, when the poetry of the troubadours had lost every literary quality, that it became moral. The change took place in the corruption and dissolution of the grave.

The Albigenses Crusade

PROVENCE in the twelfth century was the most civilized, in the widest sense, of any country in Christian Europe. It was also one of the richest. Civilization and wealth were still the privilege of the sunlands, the cradle of Western culture. West and East met and mingled, each complementing the other, on the shores of the Mediterranean. The Rhone valley was the great artery which carried the merchandise unloaded in the ports of southern France to the misty north: sumptuous webs, Cordovan leather, weapons tempered at Damascus and Toledo, enamels, African ivory, and spices, to which the Middle Ages were very partial (French cookery, dating from the seventeenth century, has lost the taste, but the provision dealer is still called an *épicier*). From as far back as Carolingian times, the men of the north wondered at the pomp of Provence. Theodulus, Bishop of Orleans, one of the *missi dominici* of Charlemagne, reports his astonishment at the wealth of the inhabitants of Marseilles, and at the rich gifts they offered him:

> One presented me with precious stones and Eastern pearls.
> . . . another brought me handfuls of gold coins with Arabic lettering on them . . . another said to me: "here are Saracen

draperies of richer hue and the most delicately woven there
may be . . ." another presents me with ensamples of Cordovan leather, some as white as snow, others red . . . another
proffers carpets.[1]

The towns of Marseilles, Arles, Avignon, Brignoles and
Grasse, grown rich through trade and at the height of their
prosperity, were free cities governed by their own consuls and
"capitouls." Toulouse, the "rose," the "flower of cities," as it
was called, bore an oriental appearance, with its bazaars in the
Rue de la Pourpointerie, its many fountains adorned with
mosaics, and its baths copied from those of Granada. Its wealth
was said to rival that of Byzantium. The richness of Provençal
land excited the covetousness of the needy, rude and barbarous
populations of the north.[2]

Provence excelled in mental culture no less than in material
prosperity. When the brilliant civilization of the Western
Caliphate suffered devastation at the hands of the Almoravides,
and the schools and libraries of Cordova and Toledo were sacked
by the barbarians, many refugees sought shelter in Provence.
Some of them set up a school of medicine at Montpellier which
became a center for the dissemination of Arabian science; a whole
new city arose to accommodate the students who flocked from
every quarter. At Narbonne the famous brothers Aben-Ezra and
their collaborators set themselves to lecture upon scientific and
philosophical subjects, and to translating the Arabic books. "It
was Provence," says Munk, "which supplied almost all the trans-
lators and commentators of the Arabian philosophers. Averroes
would perhaps have remained unknown to the Christian world
had not his works been acclaimed by the Jews of Provence."[3]

Although the ancient Roman provinces were among the first
of Gaul to receive the faith, the influence of the Church never
went as deep in Languedoc as it did in the Kingdom of the
Franks, where it rested upon the support of a central power that,

in turn, derived from the Church the sanction of its authority. The Languedoc country during a span of three centuries had been occupied by the Arian Visigoths, founders of the kingdom of Toulouse. Arianism was the form of the Christian religion adopted by the great majority of the Germanic peoples. Its distinctive trait was a rigorous monotheism which refused to identify Christ with God and rejected the cult of the saints, whose numbers the Orthodox and Catholic Churches were at pains to multiply. This simplified form of Christianity came near to triumphing over the Orthodox and Roman Churches despite the official decision of the Council of Nicea. It was the conversion of Clovis, for purely political ends, that saved the Catholic Church. It was the Franks who, after having rescued the Roman Church from the Lombards, laid the foundations of its temporal power, extended its sway over Germany, and later imposed it on Spain. In spite of the conversion of the Visigoth King Recarredus in 589, the kingdom of Toulouse remained profoundly averse to Catholicism. The political particularism which characterized the people was intensified by their traditional opposition to the religion of the French.

When the kingdom of Toulouse passed directly from the rule of the Visigoths to that of the Muslims, who controlled it during a period of more than half a century and who brought about important developments in its agriculture, irrigation and industry, the men of Toulouse felt more closely drawn to their new masters than to the common enemy, Catholic France. The difference between the uncompromising monotheism of the Arians and that of Islam was in truth but a slight one. This substantial identity was doubtless one of the causes, and not the least, which kept the relations between Christians and Muslims in Spain free from religious bitterness. In the East, the persecuted Arians and Paulicians sometimes joined the Muslims against the Orthodox and Catholics.[4] The people of Languedoc, who had been withdrawn during a period of close on four centuries from the tutelage of the Roman Church and had been exposed to other influences, manifested little of the fervor which animated the populations of France, the eldest daughter or, as it might more accurately be called, the mother of the Catholic Church, which, as Guillaume de Puy-Laurens puts it, "has always fought the wars of God"—*semper consuevit gerere bella dominica.*[5]

Saint Bernard paints a dark picture of the state of mind prevailing among the populations of southern France:

> The churches are empty, the people have no priests; the priests are not shown the respect which is their due. The Christians deny Christ and their temples resemble synagogues. The sacred character of God's sanctuaries is ignored, and the sacraments are not accounted holy. Feast-days are not observed with due solemnity. Men die in their sins and their souls are carried off, alas, before the awful judgment-seat without their being reconciled with the Lord and provided with the holy sacraments. Children do not learn to know Christ and the grace of baptism is not conferred upon them.[6]

The tale of *Aucassin et Nicolette,* though it has come to us in the language of Picardy, probably derives from a Provençal original, and gives a faithful picture of the disposition of the people of Provence in the twelfth century. "In Paradise what have I to win?" exclaims *li biax, li blons, li gentix, li amorous* Aucassin.

> For in Paradise go none but such folks as I shall tell thee now: Thither go these same old priests, and halt old men and maimed, who all day and night cower continually before the altars, and in the crypts; and such folk as wear amices, and old clouted frocks, and naked folks and shoeless, and covered with sores, perishing of hunger and thirst, and of cold, and of little ease. These be they that go into Paradise; with them have I naught to make. But into Hell would I fain go; for

into Hell fare the goodly clerks, and goodly knights that fall in tourneys and great wars, and stout men-at-arms and all men noble. With these would I liefly go. And thither pass the sweet ladies and courteous that have two lovers, or three, and their lords also thereto. Thither goes the gold, and the silver, and the cloth of vair, and the cloth of gris, and harpers and makers, and the prince of this world. With these I would gladly go, let me but have with me Nicolette, my sweetest lady.[7]

In Provence—from of yore an intermediate borderland between contrasted worlds, whence Latin civilization had looked out upon savage Europe, and whence in turn, in the twelfth century, Europe, from the depths of the barbarism into which it had relapsed, viewed the civilization of victorious Islam, enriched with all the legacies that Christianity had lost—the forces which were contending for the future faced one another. On the one hand, the dawn of a new age was piercing the night of five centuries, and heralding the Renaissance; on the other, the medieval Church, supported by the France of the crusades, of St. Bernard and St. Louis, regarded the gleam of a new day as a menace to its power.

White monks and black monks pounced upon Provence, determined to master the indifference of the people, and to denounce the harborers of heretics and unbelievers. Even a Pope, Urban II, went out of his way to preach to the men of Toulouse. Folquet, Bishop of Toulouse, in conjunction with the Bishops of Foix, Albi and Béziers, addressed a protest to Rome against Provençal impiety. He had at one time practiced the calling of a troubadour, but after an attempt on the virtue of the wife of Barral des Baux, Lord of Marseilles, he had been expelled from the city and had taken orders. A Castilian monk, Dominique de Guzman—*mensongier Castella*, "the liar of Castille," as Peire Cardenal calls him[8]—had founded the order of the Predicant Friars and had flooded the country with them. Rosaries, adopted from the Muslims, were distributed among the people. Finding, however, that persuasion had little effect on their minds, St. Dominic sounded the note of menace.

Many troubadours raised their voices against ecclesiastical tyranny. The Church was not, in the Middle Ages, a purely spiritual power. It was also the dominant force in politics, in economics. In the course of centuries, every form of power and wealth had accumulated in its hands. It held the reins of Europe, gave the law, made and deposed kings, and dictated their politics. The medieval Church disposed of the irresistible lever which in our day is represented by money. It was the greatest landlord in the world, held the best land, profited by every privilege and immunity. When the monks of Cluny arrived in Spain, they comported themselves as though in a conquered country. From their principal seat at Sahagun, they issued decrees forbidding the inhabitants to bake their bread elsewhere than in the convent's ovens; they prohibited the gathering of fuel, the selling of wine till the monks had sold theirs. Similar regulations affected all the necessities of life; the monks claimed absolute priority; no meat, vegetables, cloth, footwear could be bought until the needs of the monastery had been fully met.[9]

Dogmatic issues formed, then, but a relatively small parcel of the causes which set the people against the Church; it was much rather the eternal question of domination by economic power, and all the abuses to which it gives rise. Moral corruption, in the broadest and in every sense, is inseparable from such absolute power. Pope Innocent III denounced the vices and the corruption of the monastic orders, and brought charges against them which few lampoonists would have ventured to advance. "This state of things," he concludes, "affords heresy great encouragement."[10]

Long after the troubadours, Dante and Petrarch were to express themselves in language very similar to that of the Provençal poets, whom indeed they copied in this as in so much else. "The priests have made them a god of gold and silver," Dante said—*Fatto v'avete Iddio d'oro e d'argento.* "Their robes trail over the quarters of their hacks, so that two beasts are in one hide."

> *Copron dei manti loro palafreni*
> *si che due bestie van sott' una pelle.*[11]

And the lover of Laura was to sing:

> *L'avara Babilonia ha colmo'l sacco*
> *d'ire di Dio e di vizi empi e rei,*
> *tanto che scoppia!*[12]

Avaricious Babylon hath her beggar's poke full filled with wrath of God bred of fell vices rank, so that it bursts.

Peire Cardenal, though a puissant and deeply pious lord—he was the first troubadour to indite religious poetry—could not contain his indignation:

> I am in the fashion framed, that I ever did hate injustice and cherished right. Set they who will their hearts upon other treasures; to my deeming is justice precious before every other good. Whereby have I drawn upon myself relentless hate from them who enstyle themselves right-thinking. Let them then hate me! Me it nothing recks.[13]

He caused his jongleurs to sing fiery sirventes against the clergy.

> High felons are they who sell God, and men undo! They colour their perfidy under the cloak of honest seeming, they preach unto men, telling them they are to lead holy lives. But never shall I hold my peace and stand aside from discovering their villainies, for it were impiety to do so; he who shieldeth a robber is no less guilty before God than is the robber. And robbers are they, who over us rule . . .

abounding in covetousness, and spare of kindness, affable of mien, but monstrous of heart. The clerks cannot suffer that any but themselves should wield authority in this world. . . . Kites and vultures are not keener to scent out carrion, than are clerks and Predicant Friars to nose riches to be squeezed . . . Nor is their pope a whit less guilty than they themselves; he would enrich the rich, but of the poor makes no reck. To be the world's universal legatee is the goal of his ambition . . . Yea, and the whole brood of clerks by dint of theft, and hypocrisy, and sermons, by force or felony, by God's help or the devil's that which they seek they get![14]

At Toulouse, Guilhem Figuiera, a man of the people, exploded in invectives against Rome:

> *Roma enganairitz*
> *qu'etz de totz mals guitz*
> *e sima e razitz!*
> *Roma, falsa e tafura*
> *per qu'en vos s'escon*
> *ei.s magra e.is confon*
> *l'engan d'aquest mon.*[15]

Rome! head-fount of evil and of all our ills! False and perfidious Rome, arch-cheat and liar! wherein the world's roguery gather, swarmes and crawls! . . . Thou breedest all wars and woes . . . thou gnawest the flesh and bones of simple folk, and the blind leadest to the pit . . . and tramplest under foot God's commandments . . . Such Rome be thy high deeds! . . . Lamb-like in thy demeanor, wolfish in thy rapacity; thy talons dig so fast what thou holdest that it may never be wrested from thy grip . . . Crowned viper that, with the devil for thy cronies rulest to no other end than lucre . . . And if thy power be not full soon destroyed, it will be all y-do with the world, which lies crushed and cut-throated, and brought by thee to the uttermost brim of undoing. May the Justice of God smite thee down, crime-laden Rome!

Skeptical Provence was the natural refuge of all heretics. From the ninth century, when the Adoptionist heresy spread from Toledo, where it originated, over Languedoc, down to the first foretokenings of Protestantism, medieval heresies were primarily inspired by revolt against the spiritual and material tyranny of the Roman Church. The doctrines and beliefs, often grotesque, which became substituted for the Church's dogmas represent the feeble attempts of the human mind, crushed and ill-equipped for rational effort, to shake off the yoke of that tyranny.

The teachings of the Cathars, a name etymologically equivalent to "Puritans," are imperfectly known to us through contradictory and often manifestly distorted accounts. But modern researches have clearly shown that the heresy of the Cathars, so far from being the doctrine of a petty local sect, was affiliated with similar kernels of resistance scattered throughout Christendom, and deriving in direct continuity from the earliest years of the Church. The Cathars were connected with the Paulicians, disciples of Paul, Bishop of Samosata, and Patriarch of Antioch in the third century, who had aimed at rationalizing to the utmost the dogmatic edifice with which Christian ethics were associated.

Like Arianism, from which it is scarcely to be distinguished, the Paulician teaching survived the opposition of the official Church and the decisions of the Council of Nicaea, and had in fact thereafter grown and extended. The headquarters of the sect were in Constantinople, and branches existed in Thrace, Bulgaria and Dalmatia. Its Bulgarian affiliations gave rise to the designation of *bougres,* applied by the French monks to the Cathars. A number of Paulicians betook themselves to Hungary, Germany and Italy, where they were known as *"publicani"* and *"patarini,"* and whence they spread to Provence and Spain. In 1167 the head of the Paulician Church, Nicetas, after visiting the churches of the Balkans and Dalmatia, held a synod at Toulouse, where he consecrated five bishops, or "Prefects." Sicard Cellerier was appointed Bishop of Albi.[16] The popularity which was enjoyed in Spain toward the close of the tenth century by the doctrines of the "Brothers of Purity," which show a striking similarity to theirs, may, as some think, have had something to do with the expansion at the same epoch of the Catharian movement in Provence.

In spite of the divergence of their beliefs from those of the Orthodox and Roman Churches, the Cathars regarded themselves as Christians. They repudiated the authority of the Old Testament, but they revered the Gospel, interpreting its miraculous elements, such as the Resurrection and the Ascension, in an allegorical sense. They celebrated a form of Christian communion, in which a loaf was symbolically shared, in accordance with the Gospel description of the Lord's Supper. The Cathars, it seems, were believers in Manichaeism, a very ancient conception which postulated two principles, that of Good and that of Evil, but there is no evidence that these were personified. The Cathar faith took much greater account of the moral than of the dogmatic aspect of religion. To follow the way of life set forth in the Gospels was the leading aim of their persuasion; they practiced fraternity, charity, poverty, renunciation and tolerance. They were commonly known in Provence as "the good men."

Their views and example made a great impression on the masses of the people. Goodness and gentleness make more converts among the generality of men than the doctrine of metempsychosis. Any opposition, moreover, to the tyranny of the Church enlisted sympathy. The higher ranks of the clergy challenged revolt by the defiant arrogance of their bearing and luxury. The Papal Legate, Pierre de Castelnau, attired in crimson silks and velvet and belted with rubies, kept the state of a ruling monarch. He was mysteriously assassinated near the Abbey of Saint Gilles. On the other hand, the pretense of humility and poverty of Saint Dominic and his Predicant Friars, which were intended to rival, in the eyes of the people, the virtues of the Cathars, while their pursuit of endowments and inheritances went on apace, deceived no one.

The teaching of the Cathars spread with astonishing rapidity; it became established at Avignon and Lyons, and reached as far as the Alps; it sowed the seed from which the sect of the Vaudois was to spring. The papacy saw in it a threat to the entire edifice of its power. The Bishop of Citeaux declared that if it were not dealt with promptly, there would not be a single believer left in Provence in two or three years' time. One of the first patrons of the "good men" was no other than the troubadour-prince, Guilhem of Poitiers, Duke of Aquitaine. The counts of Toulouse and the lords of Languedoc, without identifying themselves with the sectaries, showed themselves, in general, well disposed towards them. Great ladies like Giraude de Laurac, sister of the powerful Count Aimeric de Montreal, and the two sisters of Raimon Rogier, Viscount of Carcassonne, devoted themselves to charitable works and announced their conversion to the Catharian faith. One of the principal seats of the "good men" was the neighborhood of Albi; hence the designation of "Albigenses" which was applied to them in France.

When Pope Innocent III, who had been educated at the University of Paris, proclaimed the crusade against the Albigenses in 1209, he provided an opportunity for which the covetous feudal barons of the north had long lain in wait. Eudes, Duke of Burgundy, Herve, Count of Nevers, Gaucher, Count of Saint-Pol, Guillaume des Barres and Simon de Montfort divided among themselves, in anticipation, the rich fiefs of Languedoc and insisted upon being promised them before joining the crusade. Armies were levied by the Archbishops of Rheims and Bordeaux, and by the Bishops of Sens, Clairmont, Rouen, Lisieux, Autun, Chartres and others; Theodosius, Archdeacon of Notre-Dame in Paris, assumed the command of the engines of war. This host of more than 500,000 men was reinforced by German horsemen and a horde of *truands* or vagabonds under their "king."

The crusaders hurled themselves upon Béziers, a wealthy and flourishing city of 60,000 inhabitants, which the Count of Toulouse, Raimon "the Old," a man of irresolute and wavering disposition, refused to defend, and they killed all the population regardless of age or sex. "It is thought that no such brutal massacre has ever been planned and perpetrated," says Guillaume de Tudèle. "They slaughtered clerks, women and children so thoroughly that not one, I believe, escaped."[17] "They killed in this town alone fully 60,000 men and more," says Guillaume le Breton, in the High Chronicles of France.[18] Seven thousand persons who sought sanctuary in the church of Sainte-Madeleine were butchered there; six thousand were burnt alive in the Church of Saint-Nazaire. The monks who tolled the knell while the carnage was proceeding, were in turn put to the sword. (Some of the clergy were indeed in sympathy with the Cathars.) "They made a huge slaughter of both catholics and heretics, for they could not distinguish between them," says Saint-Aubin d'Angers. [19] It is from the Cistercian monk, Céssaire d'Heisterbach, that we hold the report of the notorious order issued by his superior, Arnaud, Bishop of Citeaux: "Kill, kill! God will know his own!"[20] The crusaders were promised a remission of several centuries of Purgatory for each ten thousand slain.

"Ye have decked your heads with caps of infamy, you Rome, and you Citeaux, at whose behest the monstrous butchery of Béziers was done," cries Figuiera:

> *Roma del cervel*
> *quar de mal capel*
> *etz vos e Cistel,*
> *qu'a Bezers fesetz faire*
> *mout estranh mazel.*[21]

Carcassonne was defended by the nephew of the Count of Toulouse, Roger de Trancavel, a noted patron of troubadours, and held out for a long time against the assaults of the crusaders. It is said that jongleurs stood on the walls, hurling defiance at the enemy, and singing and playing on their viols. Simon de Montfort had to resort to treachery. He invited Viscount Roger to a parley, had him seized and cast into a "very strait" dungeon cell, where Roger was put to death shortly after. Fifty knights who had accompanied him were hanged; four hundred prisoners were burnt alive. The inhabitants, who had been promised their lives, were all expelled from the city, the men wearing only their breechclouts, the women in their shifts, "carrying with them nothing but their sins." Most of them took refuge in Spain.[22] A troubadour named Guillaume de Béziers, not otherwise known, escaped from the massacre and sang a *planh* on the death of his patron:

> Mort l'an, e anc tan gran otratge
> no vi hom, ni tan gran error
> mais far, ni tan gran estranhatge
> de Dieu et a nostre Senhor
> cum an fag li can renegat
> de fals linhatge de Pilat
> qui l'an mort.[23]

They have slain him, and never was so great wrong yet seen, nor so great a crime, nor a deed so iniquitous against God and Our Lord as was done by those traitors of Pilate's sib, the recreant curs who did him dead.

Smitten with terror, most of the neighboring towns, including Albi, opened their gates to the crusaders without resistance. The French "drive to flight all the men and women of the country and the neighboring towns who were there, all of them naked, their nature without additional cover," reports Guillaume le Breton.[24]

"Each step in the advance of the invading army," says Luchaire, "was marked by a butchery."[25] The ravaged countryside was turned into a desert; more than 300 towns and 200 castles were stormed or burned and all their inhabitants massacred. At Minerve, "many a caitiff heretic of evil brood was burnt and numbers of crazy female heretics, who squalled in the flames."[26] At Lavaur, "there was so great a massacre," says Guillaume de Tudèle, "that I believe it will be spoken of till the end of time." Count Aimeric, Lord of Montreal, a generous patron of the troubadours, was hanged.[27] "Never was yet in Christendom so much baron and of so high estate hanged by the neck, together with so many knights at his side, for of knights alone there were more than four-score, and of the citizens as many as four hundred were burnt."[28] As for the charitable Lady of the Manor, "Dame Giraude was het; she screamed and wept and squalled; they threw her down a well, and cast stones overthwart her."[29]

At Marmande, a town situated on the borders of Guyenne, which attempted to resist, the horrors of Béziers were renewed; "Barons and Ladies, little children and women stripped naked, were put to the sword . . . no living wight escaped." Limbs and entrails "lay strewn about the public places as though blood and gobbets had rained from heaven." The earth and river bank were "reddened." The town was set on fire.[30] At Bram, Simon de Montfort "bote do one hundred men blind and lop their noses, save one who, the noble Dan Simon bade, should have one eye only plucked out, that he might bring the rest to Cabareth."[31] The crusaders fought among themselves over the booty and the women. The camp-followers carried off droves of girls, urging them on with pikes.

In the cloister of Becede, in the Lauraguais country, the deacon, who had shown indulgence to the heretics, was burnt, together with all the friars of the chapter. Pierre de Vaux-Cernai observes: "It was with great joy that our pilgrims again burnt a large number of heretics"—*innumerabiles etiam haereticos pere-*

grini nostri cum ingenti gaudio combusserunt.[32] The Cistercian monks drowned the shrieks of the victims, singing the hymn *Veni Creator spiritus*:

> *Ai Toloza e Proensa*
> *e la terra d'Argensa*
> *Bezers e Carcassey*
> *quo vox vi e quo us vey!*[33]

The troubadour, Bernard de Marjevois, sings:

> Ah! Toulouse and Provence and the Land of Argence, Béziers and Carcassonne, such I but late knew you, and such do I behold you now! . . . The world is put to confusion; the bonds of law are broke; the troth of oaths is fouled. Whereso I wend me do I hear courteous men entreat of *"Sire"* those felon French who no pity ken saving they sight their gain. And you noble clerks, how shall ye be measured the meed that is deserving to you? Your praise surely be multiplied seeing that you have approved yourselves so excellent doctors. What noble ensamples you hold up before the people, what Christian teachings you bestow upon them! Aye! patterns of charity, and no whit covetous are you. So me God help if I speak unsooth!

Peire Cardenal, out of the anguish of his heart, exclaims:

> *Falsedatz e desmezura*
> *an batalha empreza*
> *ab vertat ed ab dreitura;*
> *e vens la falseza.*

> Lies and injustice have joined battle against truth and right; and lies triumph!

On the occasion of negotiations broached by the Pope with a view to the conclusion of an alliance between the Emperor

Frederick II and France, Peire Cardenal is moved to declare: "Italians, Lombards and Germans were passing fools did they accept the men of France and Picardy as allies or as masters; for these attend to nothing but to murder of innocent folk."[34] Guilhem Anelier of Toulouse exclaims: "The clerks and the French have now approved themselves the villainest of all evildoers, and right it is to hate them."[35] And another troubadour, who remains anonymous, proclaims: "The French and the priests wear today the crown of iniquity. And well it befits them! They are withal the most misers and traitors and despicable of this earth. They have foredone the peace of the world by their lies and their rapacity."[36]

The King of Aragon and the Count of Toulouse entered into negotiations with the Pope. Count Raimon, after having done penance at the Abbey of Saint-Gilles for the murder of Pierre de Castelnau, the Papal Legate, who had been killed by one of his squires, travelled to Rome and again made public amends at the Lateran Palace. A shudder of horror ran through the whole of Europe, outside France. The greatest of the German minnesingers, Walther von der Vogelweide, scourged the ferocity of the Church in his passionate lyrics and championed the cause of toleration.

Innocent III was disturbed by the general indignation and tried to curb the zeal of the crusaders. It was rumored that he was seized with fits of horror and haunted by visions of blood and accusing phantoms. But in spite of the Pope and the truce he preclaimed, Simon de Montfort prepared to march on Toulouse. The prelates promised that the great city would suffer the fate of Béziers. The Bishop of Comminges, "a man of admirable sancity," exhorted the crusaders. "On, in the name of Jesus Christ," he told them, "and I stand warrant that whosoever shall lose his life in this glorious war shall obtain, without pains of purgatory, an eternal reward and the martyr's crown."[37] Count Raimon, in the end, determined upon resistance; his suzerain and brother-in-law, King Pedro II of Aragon, joined him with a large army. Peire Cardenal ventured once more to hope:

> *A Tolosa a tal Raimon*
> *lo comte, cui Dieus guia . . .*
> *se defen et de tot lo mon;*
> *que Frances ni clercia*
> *ni les autras gens no l'an fron.*[38]

Now have we in Toulouse a Count Raimon, whom God direct. . . . None, French or clerk, shall overthrow him!

The King of Aragon was killed at the battle of Muret (1213), and Simon de Montfort set siege to Toulouse. But, by a stroke of chance which was recognized as a manifestation of divine justice, he met his death at the hands of a woman, who shattered his skull with a stone hurled from the ramparts.

The young Count Raimon VII, at the head of Spanish troops, reconquered most of the regions which had been occupied by the crusaders. The latter finally left a country wasted by eight years of carnage and pillage and returned home without having achieved the main object of the crusade, which was the annexation of Provence to France. This object was attained by Blanche of Castile, who, with the assistance of Romieu de Villeneuve, the astute minister of Raimon Bérenger VI, arranged the marriage of Marguerite, the eldest daughter of the Count, to the young Louis IX, and that of Beatrice, the youngest of the four Provençal princesses, to Charles of Anjou, the King's brother. Dante wrote:

> *Quattro figlie ebbe, e ciascuna regina,*
> *Ramondo Beringhieri, e cio gli fece*
> *Romeo. . .*
>
> *Ma i Provenzali che fèr contra lui*
> *non hanno riso*

> Four daughters had Raimon Bérenger, and each became a
> Queen; that was the doing of Romeo . . . But the men of
> Provence, who railed against him, had small cause to
> rejoice.[39]

Provence was annexed to France.

A feature which cannot fail to cause surprise in the reading,
but which is found in the most terrible convulsions of history, is
that the course of frivolous life was not entirely brought to a
standstill amid horror and desolation. In the castle of Burlatz,
not far from Castelnaudary, where all the inmates were massacred, the Countess Constance, wife of Raimon Bérenger and
sister of the King of France, and Adelaide, Viscountess of
Taillefer, held what bears all the appearance of a Court of Love.[40]
In the neighborhood of Narbonne, the troubadour Raimon de
Miraval, a knight of limited means, went on composing love-
poetry and paid visits to local lords who continued, it appears, to
lead the heedless life to which they were accustomed.[41] The
region of Narbonne, it is true, was spared by the crusaders. Terri-
fied by the fate of Béziers and Carcassone, the Narbonnes had
entered into negotiations with Montfort and the Papal Legate
and obtained that they should not be attacked, provided they delivered all the Cathars dwelling in their midst. This they did, and
handed over the "good men" naked to the authorities.

The work begun by the crusaders of Arnaud of Citeaux and
Simon de Montfort was completed by the Inquisition. A system of
terrorism, spying and denunciation, which lasted for a century
and a half, extinguished the culture and the wealth of the lands
of southern France even more effectively than had the massacres
and destruction. The Holy Office, instituted at the instigation of
Saint Dominic and of Blanche of Castile, operated at first in a
fashion at once frenzied and hesitant. The high ecclesiastical
authorities, as though panic-stricken by the powers placed in their
hands, tried to curb the excesses of their representatives, whose

fanatical fury roused the local populations to revolt. At Albi in 1234 the Grand Inquisitor was thrown into the river, and at Toulouse in 1236 the Cistercian monks were expelled from the city.

The young Saint Louis regulated and reinforced the organization of the Holy Office by means of the statute *Cupientes* and supplied it with funds out of the royal treasury. He was fond of burning off the noses and lips of any of his subjects who were guilty of having used blasphemous language, and considered that no one except a clerk should dispute with a heretic, otherwise than "with a sword, which he should plunge well into the belly, as far as it will go."[42] Informers were granted immunity. Confessions were wrung from the accused by torture, which was officially instituted in 1252, but had been practiced long before that date. The prisoners who were not handed over to the secular arm, the formula by which condemnation to the stake was pronounced, were immured in "very strait" dungeons. There was not enough room in the prisons; forced labor had to be enlisted to build new ones.[43] The saints having got the better of the "good men," "a precocious civilization which had seemed destined to guide Europe on the paths of culture, was annihilated, and the honor of the Renaissance passed from Provence to Italy."[44]

"So greatly is the world changed that I scarcely recognize it," sighs Bertram d'Alamanon. "Formerly I was wont to make songs and divert myself, engaging in all the occupations befitting a courtly knight, visiting renowned ladies and culling pleasures. But were I to do so to-day, I should expose myself to malevolent strictures."[45] And Guiraut de Bornelh recalls that of yore "minstrels went from one Court to another, richly apparelled and singing the praises of the ladies, while today we are afraid to utter a word and all honour is departed."[46] "Jongleurs are no longer in request," laments Guilhem Anelier. "Gone are the pick of the valiant barons. Where are the Courts, the frequentation

of ladies and the pleasant pastimes, the joy and the gaiety? If
you have a will to company and converse you will be stingily
treated and reduced to penury, for no one thinks of ought but
of keeping what is left him, and anxiety about money banishes
smiles from men's faces.''[47]

Bishops and Dominicans thundered against the impious frivolity of the poets and their shallow glorification of women and
guilty passions, while they illustrated their own views by drag-
ging sick women out of bed and committing them to the flames.[48]
While the Familiars of the Inquisition were rooting out heresy
by fire, and the Archbishop of Narbonne was hunting down the
last of the fugitives in the mountains and burning them alive,
two hundred at a time,[49] the Bishop of Maguelonne was admon-
ishing the poets that they had better give up their "vain ditties."[50]
"The religious authorities regard our art as a sin and are stern
judges of those who engage in it," cries the pious Guiraut
Riquier.

E neis rector
dizon que peccatz es
e tot hom n'es repres
per els mot malamen.[51]

The Papal Legate made noble knights swear never again to
compose verses.[52] The admonitions of the monks, however, were
sometimes couched in the language of the poets. The prior of
Villemeir, a zealous Dominican, published a theological poem
addressed to recalcitrant poets, in which the truths of the Christian religion were expounded. The enunciation of each article of
faith was reinforced, in the text, by the following refrain:

E s'aquest no vols creyre vec te'l foc aizinat que
art tos companhos
Aras uelh que. m respondas en un mot o en dos,
Si cauziras el foc o remanras ab nos.[53]

If you refuse to believe this, turn your eyes to the flames in which your companions are roasting. Answer forthwith, in one word or in two; either you will burn in that fire or you will join us.

Those forcible arguments did not fail in their appeal. In the minds of the poets, inspired by holy terror, they speeded with marvelous effect the transformation in their "conception of love," and imported to poetry a moral elevation worthy of Saint Dominic and Saint Louis. "The theory of love as a sin, which was invented by the Church, pervaded Provençal poetry," says M. Anglade. "Poetry was denounced as a sin by the religious authorities, and underwent, accordingly, a transformation."[54]

The most ardent promoter of that reform, and the most untiring in his endeavor to raise poetry to a higher moral plane, was Guilhem Montanhagol. He had been among the first to take flight when the Inquisition was instituted, and had taken refuge in Spain. Montanhagol had even composed a sirvente against the monks and the French. But he returned sometime later to Provence and, turning his coat to conform with the exigencies of the time, applied himself to the cultivation of the refined tastes which the spectacle of burning stakes had inspired in the minds of the verse-makers. "The poet," reports his editor, "exerted himself to reassure those who, terror-stricken by the prohibitions of the clergy, were giving up the cult of love."[55] "Lovers," declared the defender of this cult, "must continue to serve love, for love is no sin, but a virtue which makes the wicked good and the good better. Chastity itself is born of love and he who truly understands it can never be a bad man."[56] This is the first instance of the use of the word "chastity" in Provençal poetry. Montanhagol develops his thesis with an inexhaustible prolixity. He says:

> I mislike having to hear the morals of our day attacked by ill-disposed persons . . . He who would induce a lady to com-

mit a sin does not truly love her, for no lover could ever desire the dishonor of her he loves. Love could never have ought in view save the honor of her who inspires it, and he who pursues any other end is false to the name of love. Lovers who prove themselves corrupt do not deserve the love of God, but the Lord will, on the other hand, bestow happiness upon those who desire only that which is good and honorable. Sooner or later they will have their reward— at any rate, they will have their guerdon in the other world.[57]

The apologist of reformed love uses a dialectical device which has been much employed in our own day by social historians of morals. Like Father Lafiteau and the influential professors of social ethnology, he asserts that the principles which he upholds have been honored in all ages.[58] If they are not observed as generally at the present time as they formerly used to be, that is a result of modern corruption. "The knights of yore sought from their love no other guerdon but honour, and the ladies who inspired them by their beauty never did ought that they should not have done," he declares. "But nowadays, honour is held in small account, and lovers are, to their shame, guided in their conduct by other principles."[59] Despite his assurances as to the chaste ideals of the poets of former days, Montanhagol admits to the need of some revision and adaption of their style. A new treatment, if not a new conception of love is called for. "The troubadours of the period of heedlessness and frivolity," he says, "did not exhaust their subject-matter to such an extent that we may not compose meritorious songs both virtuous and agreeable."[60]

This momentous change in literary taste was generally adopted "with the sole purpose of mollifying the severity of the clergy." The adaption "was mainly imposed by necessity. If the love-song was to survive at all, it must conform to ecclesiastical requirements. The troubadours could not thenceforth sing of a form of love which did not have the sanction of Christian morality, and was not innocent of evil desires, and perfectly virtuous and chaste."[61]

The principles governing this remarkable reform are set forth in a treatise of prodigious dimensions, containing 27,445 lines of verse, the *Breviaries of Love,* by Master Matfré Ermengaud. The excellence of platonic love is therein demonstrated in the scholastic manner, and is supported by quotations drawn from the troubadours. The largest amount of space is devoted to long chapters bearing the titles: "On the Baseness of Sin" and "On the Vileness of the Flesh."[62] In order to leave no room for doubt as to the purity of his principles, the poet abandons altogether the glorification of love and the praise of women, and sets forth on these subjects opinions of an orthodoxy which is beyond dispute. "Satan," he says, "in his desire to make men suffer, inspires them with an idolatrous love for women. Instead of adoring their Creator, as they should, with fervent love, with all their hearts and with all the strength of their minds, they entertain guilty passions for women, whom they transform into divinities. Know therefore that whosoever adores them very certainly adores Satan and makes a god of that most false demon, Belial."[63]

This new conception of love received full expression in the works of the few poets who survived the ruin of their country, and in particular in the productions of Guiraut Riquier, "the last troubadour." During a period of over twenty years he did poetic homage to Phillippa d'Anduza, wife of the Viscount of Narbonne, celebrating her under the name of "Belh Deport." The delicacy of the feelings expressed by the poet leaves nothing to be desired.

> I deem myself richly rewarded by the inspiration I owe to the love I bear my lady, and I ask no love in return. Adorned with every excellence and every virtue, the lady whom I honour and who begets in me a love which is the deeper sith that the image of her which I carry in my heart has never been stained by an evil thought. Had she ever granted me her

supreme favours, both she and I would have been defiled by the act.[64]

The Provençal troubadours of the thirteenth century, who all, with the exception of Riquier, were utterly insignificant poetasters, vie with one another in displaying the modesty and renunciation of their sentiments. Their self-sacrifice is a passion. The lover makes a point of repudiating the happiness he had formerly been concerned to demand, and of disowning every intention of seeking it.[65] He declares himself sufficiently rewarded with a smile,[66] or a kind look.[67] Poets find extravagant ways of expressing the little which will bestow felicity upon them: the gift of a hair from their lady's pelisse or of a thread from her glove fills them with rapture.[68] The wooer declares that he will be content if his lady deigns to treat him as her slave.[69] If it should be the fair one's good pleasure to see him die, he will consider himself happy in obtaining so agreeable an issue to his martyrdom.[70]

Prostrate at the feet of his lady, the lover grows more and more abject in his abasement; the flow of his tears is unremitting; the pitiless cruelty of his fair enemy waxes ever more remorseless. Conventional affectation attains new heights of incoherence; and no trope or conceit is too extravagant to serve the poet's purpose. Their prolixity swells to a flood; what the troubadours had formerly indicated in four words is expanded into a string of stanzas. The lyrics which were limited in length, in accordance with the Arabian rule, to seven or eight strophes, now expand to long sequences of as many as a hundred stanzas.

A more fundamental change has now taken place: the verses which had been composed to be sung are now intended for reading. *Canzoni*, sonnets, ballads are now such in name only. Poetry and music have parted. Lyrical poetry is henceforth so-called by a figure of speech. It had entered upon a phase of complete decadence and dissolution. "Such is the final term of evolution to which, at the end of the thirteenth century, with Riquier and his contemporaries, troubadour poetry declined. In this form it became scarcely recognisable; yet but little sufficed to transform it."[71]

The Italian troubadours, such as Lanfranc Cigala, Zorzi and Sordello, took their places, in the thirteenth century, among those who survived the decadence and reproduced their manner and conventions. With the zeal of neophytes, they improved upon the extravagances of their teachers. The renowned Sordello of Mantua was a friend of Montanhagol; he surpassed his master. The favor for which he implores his lady is that of granting him no favor at all.[72] He protests: "My sense of honour being without peer, I would rather be her lover in hopeless service, than serve another who might be so indulgent as to invite me to her bed."

> *E quar am de bon pretz ses par*
> *am mais servir lieys en perdo*
> *qu'autra qu'ab sim degnes colgar.*[73]

Sordello's extravagant delicacy astonished even his contemporaries; some had the bad taste to make merry over it.[74] Guilhem de Toulouse declares, in a *tenson* in which he engaged with the Italian poet, that he finds him incomprehensible: "You pretend to despise what everyone else desires."

> *En Sordell, anc entendedor*
> *no sai vi mais d'aital color*
> *com vost iest; qe lh'autr'amador*
> *volon lo baizar el jacer,*
> *e vos metes a no caler*
> *so q'autre drut volon aver.*[75]

And Bertram d'Alamanon laments that his friend Sordello has taken leave of his senses.[76]

The submission of troubadour poetry to ecclesiastical requirements went farther. The aim in view was now to set aside altogether its erotic aspect, and to give it an exclusively religious
character. Love, which, in the songs of the poets, had turned
into a personified abstraction resembling the Eros of the ancients,
now came to be compared to divine love, the Holy Spirit, to
God himself and to Christ. The lady in pursuit of whom the
poetic passion of the troubadours had soared, became transfig-
ured into the Holy Virgin and Queen of Heaven.

"Respect for women rises or falls in proportion to the veneration confessed for the Virgin, the mother of God," writes a
Catholic authority.[77] There is, it must be allowed, some truth in
the contention. The independent character and the high social
position of women in barbarous Europe were associated with an
ardent adoration of the Virgin Mother. But the latter had not
yet become Christian. In the versions of the barbarian tales, she
appears as the fairy or enchantress who allures knights-errant,
casts a spell over them and inspires them with a divine passion.[78]

The cult of the Virgin, which was universal among the barbarous peoples, whether Celtic or Germanic, was at first com-
batted by the Church. But, as has happened with countless ancient
cults and customs, the Christian Church adopted what she could
not suppress. The ancient cult of the Virgin and Holy Mother
was restored by being incorporated in the Christian religion. The
Holy Virgin, celebrated by Saint Bernard and designated "the
great goddess" by Albertus Magnus, had, by the time of the
proto-Renaissance of the twelfth century, replaced the Trinity in
the devotion of the masses. God the Father was terrible and un-
approachable; Christ, gentle and tender as he might be, exercised the prerogative of a judge. The heavenly Queen alone was
in a position to extend unalloyed compassion to sinners.

The Holy Virgin worked more miracles than the whole
heavenly hierarchy and the saints put together. She had resumed
the full exercise of her immemorial functions as the fountain-

head of magical power. It was her privilege to interrupt the order of nature at any moment, and no occasion was too trivial to be accounted beneath her intervention. Among her prerogatives, the Holy Virgin controlled all medicinal and curative resources. A tale was told of a poor monk who found himself in the article of death owing to an ulcer of very suspicious nature, which had eaten out his nose and lips. He was *"hideus et lais et comme mustres; et si a tant plaies et trus qu'il put ainsi comme une sete et cuide chascun qu'il soit etains et que l'ame s'en soit partie"* — hideous and ugly and as a monster; and had so many sores and holes that he stank like a cesspool, and that each one thought he was spent and that his soul had departed from him. Having been abandoned to his fate by his fellow friars, he appealed to the Virgin on the strength of the fervent devotion which he had always shown in her service. Touched by his appeal, the Holy Lady descended in person from heaven and treated the case by applying milk from her breast to the fetid ulcers of the monk.

> *La douce Dame, la piteuse,*
> *trait sa mamelle savoureuse*
> *se li boute dedenz la bouche,*
> *et puis moult doucement li touche*
> *par sa dolor et par ses plaies.*

The divine remedy proved instantly effective, and when his brother friars came with spades to bury him, they found the patient uncommonly animated.[79]

The Holy Virgin always showed a particular indulgence and compassion towards female sinners. Thus it was related that the abbess of a certain convent found herself in a state of great embarrassment, as the indications of the good understanding which existed between her and the chaplain were growing more and more manifest; she was at her wits' end how to cope with the impending disclosure. But the Holy Virgin came to her assistance, acted as midwife and brought her to birth, quite pain-lessly, of a sturdy boy, whom she entrusted to the care of a holy hermit in the neighborhood.[80]

In another convent the portress-nun grew weary of the mo-notonous life she was leading and went off to the town one fine day, after placing her keys on the altar, and entered upon a more varied and vivacious career as a daughter of pleasure. But after spending some time in this mode of life, the one-time nun began to long once more for the peace and tranquillity of her former existence. She returned to the convent, knocked at the door and asked the sister who opened it if she remembered Sister Agatha, which was the name the repentant sinner had borne in religion. The new doorkeeper replied that she remembered quite well Sis-ter Agatha, who had been a very worthy and saintly young woman. Surprised at this answer, Sister Agatha took a closer look at the new doorkeeper and recognized the Holy Virgin, who had replaced her in order that the escapade of her protégée should not be discovered.[81]

The Holy Virgin also comes to the aid of wives who have de-serted the conjugal bed and conceals their absence by taking their places.[82] "We must not suppose," says the Blessed Alphonse de Liguori, "that such prodigies are extraordinary events; they are every day occurrences."[83] On the other hand, the Holy Virgin does not show the same alacrity in coming to the aid of unfaithful husbands, which she evidently could not do by adopting the same expedient. A married woman who was jealous of her husband's mistress prayed to the Holy Virgin to avenge the wrong done to her and do her justice. But Mary answered: "Justice! Chastise-ment! Doest thou seek them from me? No, go to others, for I will not grant what thou asketh; for know that this sinner recites everyday a salutation in my honour, and that by whomsoever it is recited it deprives me of the power of allowing him to suffer or to be chastised for his sins."[84]

A few of the troubadours, such as Peire d'Auvergne and

Folquet de Marseille, had written religious poems, but they made no mention of the Holy Virgin. Peire Cardenal was the first to compose a canticle in honor of Our Lady.[85] Immediately after the institution of the Holy Office, an unprecedented flood of those hymns made its appearance. Peire Guilhem de Luzerna, Albert de Sisteron and Peire Espanhol competed assiduously in their production. Nearly three-quarters of the poetical works of Guiraut Riquier consist of songs in honor of the Virgin.[86] The oldest examples of his work are mere paraphrases of liturgical chants and have no relation to love-poetry.[87]

The troubadours of the decadence took over the formulae and conventions of erotic poetry and applied them to religious poetry by the simple expedient of substituting the name of Our Lady for that of the object of their profane passion. Guiraut Riquier went so far as to reverse this proceeding: he gives the Holy Virgin the name under which he was in the habit of celebrating the Countess of Narbonne.[88] "I formerly sang of love," declares the superannuated poet; "but I did not know, in truth, what love was, for that which I took for love was nothing but vanity and folly. Now love constrains me to give my heart to a lady whom I shall never be able to love and honour as she deserves. May love of her fill my whole being and may I obtain from her the reward for which I hope. I am not jealous of any who may aspire to the love of her I love and I pray, on behalf of all her lovers, that the desires of each one and all may be granted."[89]

The Provençal poets who were writing at the time of the French Inquisition were only too glad to vindicate their orthodoxy at so cheap a cost. The artifice which they used permitted them to exercise their talents in the reproduction of the accepted themes and formulae, and involved little substantial modification in their diction. Nor did it demand any change in their feelings and moral outlook, for poetry had completely ceased to bear any relation to real life. The time had gone by when princely troubadours or patrons of the poets sought to seduce the imagination or to charm luxurious leisures with flights of sensual fancy. The gulf between literature and life had grown deeper than it had ever been, and love-poems, whether addressed to a lady who really existed or to the Holy Virgin, "instead of regaling with the professed recital of highly personal disclosures, contained nothing beyond abstract reflections on the subject of love, and spun a web of insubstantial inventions having no bearing of any kind on real life."[90]

It is needless to suppose that the feelings entertained by master Guiraut Riquier toward the worthy Countess of Narbonne, to whom his poetic homage continued to be addressed for over twenty years, extended farther than the tip of his goose-quill. It is not difficult in the circumstances to "spiritualize" passion. Like the "last troubadour," the troubadours Blacatz and Foulquet de Roman went on pouring forth their laments concerning the "cruelty" of the fair ones after they had passed the ripe age of sixty.[91]

The poets kept one conception of love for use in their literary activities, while patterning their relations with women on quite other notions. Sordello, whose extravagance on the theme of platonic love amazed his contemporaries, was no less renowned for his adventures as a libertine. He abducted at least two married women and was in perpetual danger from the ire of incensed husbands. Bertram d'Alamanon denounces him for changing his mistress more than a hundred times.[92] Sordello himself could put aside, when he chose, all the fine phrases he used when expounding platonic love, and turn with remarkable versatility to compositions in quite another vein. He does not fail to repeat the ancient formula of his predecessors and to declare to his lady of the moment that he will die if he does not "enjoy her graceful form."[93] The stanza which follows is perhaps the most astonishing production that has ever come from the pen of an apostle of chaste and pure love: "I do not wonder," says he, "that husbands are jealous of one so learned as I am in the arts of love, for there is no woman, how prudish soever that is able to withstand the sweet persuasive power of my appeals. Therefore do I not blame him who complains of me and is aggrieved that his wife receives me. But so long as I have my pleasure of her body, I make little reck of her spouse's grievance and complaints."[94]

The Italian troubadours adopted the fashion instituted by the piety and prudence of their Provençal colleagues. Cigala and Zorzi proved themselves hardly less prolific than Riquier in the composition of hymns to the Holy Virgin. Every lyric poet felt he was under the obligation of supplementing his profane works by compositions of this character. As with the other formulae of poetic tradition, the fashion, once started, persisted for a long time. Pulci, in the *Morgante maggiore,* strews with hymns to the Holy Virgin, his parodies of the liturgy; and the "divine" Aretino interlards the obscenities of his pornographic sonnets and of his guide to the prostitutes of Venice with canticles to Our Lady.

The Troubadour Tradition
in Italy and England

BEFORE sinking into the abyss of oblivion, the art of the troubadours had laid its imprint on all lyrical literatures of Europe. The Provençal Muse was silenced in Provence, but a remarkable resurrection of her influence took place, more brilliant to all appearances and more widespread in its effects than that which her first coming had exerted. Italy was the heir of the troubadour heritage, and became, as it were, the executrix of that legacy. To the Italians we owe the survival of most—one might say all—of the texts of the troubadour lyrics which we possess, and but for their preservation in Italy, little more of that literature might have reached us than a vague legend and a few names.

In France, troubadour poetry was not merely allowed to fall into oblivion; it was willfully put aside and buried in complete neglect. That attitude resulted in the first instance from the long-extended repercussions of the passions which had brought about the destruction of Provençal civilization. To that cause, however, another soon became added as a consequence of the scarcely less violent fanaticism with which the dogmas of pseudoclassicism came to be held in France. All artistic production which failed to conform to the alleged canons of classical antiquity was regarded as not only worthless, but offensive and pernicious.

The suppression of medieval art was contemplated as a legitimate aim of good taste. The defacement of medieval churches in the eighteenth century, for instance, was not mainly the work of revolutionary mobs, but of zealots of "classicism," eager to do away with what they labelled "Gothic," that is to say, barbaric. On the threshold of the Renaissance, Joachim du Bellay wrote: "Do not speak to me of all that old rubble of French poetry from the *Jeux Floreaux* of Toulouse and the *Puy* of Rouen, such as rondels, ballads, *chants royaux,* songs and the like groceries which corrupt our linguistic palate and serve no end but to debase our taste and show up our ignorance." Even the philosophic calm of Montaigne was picked to testy petulance by all Romance literature, guilty of not framing itself on "classical," that is, Latin models. Not only does he fret for scorn of the romances of chivalry and "suchlike trash of writings," and cannot contain himself when Ariosto is mentioned by the side of the divine Virgil, but his contempt breaks out against the "new-fangled" Spaniolised and Petrarchistical poets," and he will not hear them named in the same breath with Catullus.

The fervor of good taste did not flame in Italy with such ferocity. The vital debt of Italian poetry to the Provençal was there freely owned from the first. "It is universally recognized and is beyond doubt," wrote Cardinal Bembo, "that the Tuscan language is mainly indebted for its poetry to the poets of Provence, who are our masters. . . . Our tongue itself, which was still uncouth and poor in resources at the time, was refined and enriched by what it borrowed from that foreign store."[1] Italian poets of the thirteenth century composed exclusively in Provençal. Rambertino Buvalelli, of Bologna, who was Podestà of Milan in 1208, and of Genoa in 1220, distinguished himself for his

Provençal verse. Lanfranc Cigala wrote a sirvente about 1245 to the marquis of Monferrato. Bonifazio Calvo wrote a lament on the defeat of the Genoese at Chioggia, and was answered from Venice by Bartolommeo Zorzi. Pietro della Caravana exhorted his Milanese countrymen in Provençal to resist the imperial assailant.

The Romance speech of Italy, north of the Apennines, differed but slightly from the language of the troubadours, and was much closer to it than to Tuscan Italian. To this day a Milanese is able to converse quite intelligibly with an inhabitant of Marseilles, each using his own idiom. Not a few Provençal troubadours made prolonged sojourns in Northern Italy. The court of Count Alberto Malaspina, in Lunigiana, was a noted meeting-place of the Provençal poets. Rambaud de Vaqueiras appears to have spent the greater part of his life in Italy; Peire Vidal, Gaucelm Faidit, Uc de Saint Cyr, Peire Ramon, Aimeric de Perguilhan were frequent visitors to that country. On the other hand, almost all the Italian troubadours, Lanfranc Cigala, Nicoletto, Ferrari, Ugo di Grimaldo, and the most famous and influential among them, Sordello of Mantua, passed extended periods in Provence, and like the Provençal poets, visited the courts of Spain. In the thirteenth century, they almost completely supplanted the Provençal in importance.

The vogue enjoyed in Italy by Provençal lyrics extended to all classes of the population, language placing no bar on its diffusion. It surpassed in popularity the romances of chivalry, which were not accessible in Italian translations until the end of the thirteenth century. It was doubtless in Provençal, and in the prose of Arnaud Daniel, that Francesca de Rimini and Paolo Malatesta read to such fatal purpose "of Launcelot and how love constrained him."[2]

Dante, in the *Convito*, stigmatizes those "froward" Italians who extol the vernacular speech of a foreign country and despise their own,"[3] holding cheap the Italian tongue and praising the Provençal. Yet he himself was for long in doubt as to which to use. In the circles interested in poetry which Dante frequented, one of the burning questions of the day was that *de vulgari eloquio*. Was the vernacular fit for literary use? And if so, should the local dialect be employed or would it be better to adopt some idiom capable of becoming, like Latin, a universal literary language? Dante's tutor, Brunetto Latini, had chosen to write in French. But the majority of poets deemed it most natural to use the one vernacular idiom which had already passed its tests and been illustrated by a mature literary form, to wit, the language of the troubadours.

The first poems composed in the Italian tongue originated in Sicily, at the court of the Emperor Frederick II. That picturesque and learned court, which was more Saracen than Christian, was by far the most cultivated in Europe. It was passionately addicted to the study of the Arabian sciences and philosophy. Michael Scotus brought to it books by the learned men of Cordova, and the treatises of Aristotle and of Averroes. Leonard of Pisa introduced it to algebra and Arabian mathematics. The court of the great emperor, "who was so deserving of honour," *che fú d'onor si degno*[4]—placed as it was, like Provence, under the ban of the Church—offered the most obvious refuge to the exiled poets who fled before the terror of the French Inquisition. Some of their Italian friends took to translating and imitating in their own vernacular the Provençal lyrics. An animating spirit of that movement was the lawyer, Jacopo da Lentino, who had been ambassador to the court of Aragon, as was likewise the imperial falconer, Arrigo Testa. Following his initiative, the chancellor Pier delle Vigne, Percival Doria, Guido and Odo delle Colonne, and the emperor Frederick himself, together with his son, Prince Enzo, distinguished themselves in the imitation of Provençal poetry. Those were the first lispings of the Italian Muse.

The new vernacular poetry was known as "Sicilian," although it was composed in the purest Tuscan, the primacy of which idiom was recognized long before Dante, owing to its closer approach to literary Latinity. Nor was the "Sicilian" manner by any means confined to the court of Palermo. It soon spread to every part of the peninsula, and the term became applied to all Italians versing in the Provençal style. Among these were counted the Sienese poet Folcachieri, Urbicciani of Lucca, the Florentine Dante da Majano, and Chiaro Davanzati. To the youthful Dante Alighieri, no other Italian poetry was known but the "Sicilian." The first verses we have of him are a series of five sonnets in a *tenson*, or exchange of verses, with his namesake of Majano, strangely clumsy, almost infantile toddlings of the Dantesque Muse which betray no token of the future mettle of her pace. Italian did not at first wholly displace Provençal. Many who dabbled in the Sicilian poetry continued at the same time to compose in Provençal. Dante da Majano wrote in both languages.[5] Guittone d'Arezzo says of one of his friends that his Provençal poems are better than those he composed in Italian.[6]

While the "Sicilian" school followed very closely the conventions, conceits and prescribed themes of troubadour poetry, it shows no trace of the doctrines newly introduced into Provence. It is clearly not among the troubadours who had sought refuge in the magnificently heretical court of Frederick II that disciples of Montanhagol are to be looked for. The most distinguished of those exiles was that same Guilhem Figuiera whose vehement denunciations of the tyrants and persecutors had drawn upon him the particular animosity of the clergy. One of the questions put to the inquisitors during the interrogation of a suspect was whether he had read the poems of Figuiera.[7] We find here, then, no word of the "new conception of love" which was being illustrated by the poets who, paying with their orthodoxy the price of immunity, had continued in Provence. There is no reference to the spiritualization of passion or the merits of chastity. On the contrary, critics deplore the sensuality of the Sicilian school.

But a while later, another group of poets composing in the Tuscan tongue made its appearance in Northern Italy, and more particularly at Bologna, the natural gateway between the Romance-speaking North and the more Latin Tuscany. Unlike the Sicilian school, which sprang out of immediate intercourse with the Provençal refugee poets, and which represented unchanged the troubadour tradition, northern Italian versing derived its inspiration from the Italian troubadours, all friends and disciples of Montanhagol and the conforming exponents of ecclesiastical taste.

The manner of the Bolognese school found immediate favor in Tuscany and displaced the Sicilian fashion. The derivation of Tuscan poetry, under that influence, is manifest from the start in the treatment of the erotic theme. Chiaro Davanzati, who had been counted as a distinguished follower of the Sicilians, took to translating Sordello, and composed didactic pieces that might be paraphrases of the edifying *Brevaries of Love* of Matfré Ermengaud. "Love in its true nature and interpretation," declares this predecessor of Dante, "is not a sin. It is unworthy of a poet to covet a woman who is not his wife. All carnal desire is a temptation of the devil. Woe to him who succumbs to it."[8]

The most reputed among the Tuscan poets of the time, Fra Guittone d'Arezzo, who even foreshadowed the Bolognese school and exerted his influence upon its leader, Guido Guinicelli, appears to refer his inspiration to an even more exalted source: his canticles recall the dissertations of the Church fathers on the excellence of chastity. He thus sings the praises of that virtue:

> *Castitate, tu luce e tu bellore!*
> *Ah! quanto amo e commendo*
> *donna che tene casto e corpo e core.*
> *Vivere in carne fuor voler carnale*
>
> *e vita angelicale.*
> *Angeli castità hanno fuor carne,*

ma chi l'have con carne
in tant'e via maggior d'angel di celo.

Umanitate dannoe
e mise ad onte fuor di paradiso
per lei fu Cristo ucciso. . .[9]

Chastity, thou light and beauty of the world! Ah, how I love and commend the woman who keeps her heart and body chaste! To exist in the flesh without feeling the desires of the flesh is to be more virtuous than the angels, for the latter possess chastity without the flesh, but he who possesses at once both flesh and virtue surpasses the angels of heaven. Ah! true virtue, genuine love, thou alone art the virtue of virtues . . .

He recalls that love caused the damnation of humanity, which was on that account expelled from Paradise, "and therefore was Christ slain." He expounds the abject state of lovers who forget God and make a divinity of the woman they love.

Guido Guinicelli (1240-1276) hails Guittone as his master and testifies his admiration in a sonnet. The small group of Florentine poets who gathered around the Bolognese leader was destined to achieve particular importance, for to this group belonged Dante Alighieri. Adopting an expression of Montanhagol, they termed themselves the poets of the *dolce stil nuovo—* "the sweet new style." Dante calls Guinicelli "the supreme Guido"—*maximus Guido*[10]—and names him as the father of Italian poetry:

il padre
mio e degli altri miei miglior, che mai
rime d'amore usâr dolci e leggiadre.[11]

The enunciation of Patristic doctrines notwithstanding, love continued to be the exclusive theme of lyrical poetry. Dante assumes that any other theme is inconsistent with lyrical composition,[12] holding as Gaucelm Faidit had long since laid down "that a song must treat of love, and to introduce any other theme is bad versing."[13] Indeed the Italian poets of the thirteenth century and the early Renaissance often speak as though love and poetry were equivalent terms. When, for instance, Dante and Petrarch call Arnaud Daniel the "master of love," they do not intend to exalt him as a lover, but as a poet. The harmonizing of that association with the Patristic views enounced by Guittone d'Arezzo, however, came to assume, with the poets of the *stil nuovo,* a subtler form than the crude device of assimilating the lady of songs with the Madonna. Guinicelli meets the difficulty in much the same manner, by declaring that he mistook his lady for an angel of God:

> *Donna, Dio me dirà:—Che presumisti?*
> *Sendo l'anima mia a lui davanti;*
> *Lo ciel passasti, e fino a me venisti,*
> *E desti in vano amor, me per sembianti:*
> *Ch'a me convien la laude,*
> *E alla Reina del reame degno,*
> *Per cui cessa ogni fraude.—*
> *Dir li potrò:—Tenea d'Angel sembianza*
> *Che fosse del to regno:*
> *Non mi sie fallo, s'io le posi amanza.*[14]

He assures us of the purity of the love which his lady "who is pure, bears to me, who am also pure":

> *La sua beltà piacente*
> *e il fino amor ch'è puro*
> *in ver me che son puro.*[15]

There is little need for those assurances, for the object of his affections is so disembodied that it is often open to doubt whether the poet is referring to a woman, the Holy Virgin, or the Moon:

La vostra Donna ch'e'n ciel coronata,
ond'e la vostra speme in paradiso,
e tutta santa ormai vostra memoria
contemplando.[16]

The lady who awakened his affections "is crowned in heaven; she is his hope of Paradise. To think upon her is to enter into a state of sanctity." She is, he tells us elsewhere, like the star that measures time and sheds its lustre through the heaven of love:

La bella stella, che il tempo mesura
sembra la Donna che m'ha innamorato
posta nel ciel d'amore.[17]

It was Guido Cavalcanti who founded the group of Guinicelli's Tuscan disciples. Dante calls him his "first friend," and places him in the forefront of "the most famous troubadours of that time"—*famosi trovatore in quello tempo (Vita Nuova)*.

An imitation of the *Roman de la rose,*[18] commonly though dubiously attributed to Cavalcanti, repeats the principles of Patristic sexual ethics by which the Provençal conformists protested their orthodoxy. These run directly counter to those set forth by the scholastics of love in the palmy days of troubadour lyricism. "The lover must above all observe the precepts of religion"; "One must not love the lady of another man," it is therein declared; and in a notice prefixed to the exposition of those sentiments, the reader is requested to blame upon an inadvertence any expression which might appear prejudicial to modesty.[19]

But with the Tuscan poets of the *stil nuovo,* that monkish insistence upon the principles of Patristic morality is superfluous. Those principles are implicit in their amatory poetry. They are, moreover, incorporated in conceptions of far wider range and bearing. The old troubadour conceit about love penetrating through the eyes, for instance, occupies a paramount place in the ideological gist of their poetry; but it becomes invested with implications which soar into the rarefied atmosphere of transcendental metaphysics. Guido Cavalcanti, though many of his *canzoni* are colored with pleasant images, versifies those conceptions in terms whose meaning it is sometimes difficult to penetrate, under the mellifluous purl of linguistic flow.

> *Ven da veduta forma che s'entende*
> *che prende nel possibile intelletto,*
> *come in subietto, loco e dimoranza.*
> *In quella parte mai non è pesanza,*
> *perchè da qualitate non descende;*
> *resplende in sè perpetuo effetto:*
> *non è diletto, ma consideranza*
> *si che non pote là gir simiglianza.*[20]

This example, paraphrased into prose, would run something like this:

> Love originates in the vision of the Lady, whose image, turning into a pure idea by the operation of the active intellect, becomes lodged in both the subjective and active intelligence, where is neither pain nor pleasure, but only the eternal light and contemplation of an image free from all substantial elements.

The treatment of amatory themes, in fact, underwent a remarkable transformation with the poets of the *stil nuovo*. One may indeed truly speak of a new conception of love, and an extraordinary one. Love became above all an object of metaphysical interest. The Provençals had debated "questions of love" in a mock-scholastic manner; but those questions bore on the rules and proprieties of erotic "courtesy." The Italians incorporated in their poetry the subject-matter as well as the manner of scholastic disputations. The poetical treatment of the amatory theme assumes with them the form of "reasoning about love"— *ragionar d'amore*. The nature of love constitutes the gist of their concern. Was it a "substance" or an "accident"? In the exchange of sonnets which took the place of the Provençal *tensons*, even the Sicilians, such as Pier delle Vigne and Jacopo Mostacci, were drawn into an expression of their views on that scholastic quiddity.[21]

The effects of that approach upon the form of early Tuscan poetry were not to its advantage. Abstraction is bad in prose; in poetry it is intolerable. However artificial and affected may have been the matter of Provençal song, it was concrete. Brevity and directness were imposed upon it by the measures of melody. You cannot wind through the polished cadences of Ciceronian periods in a song; you cannot sing a metaphysical argument. But lyrical poetry and musical melody had, in the thirteenth century, all but parted company; only on occasion was poetry set to music. *Canzoni* and sonnets (little songs) were such in name only. The change opened the way to vices which were in time to betray the rich promise and possibilities of Italian poetry. The seeds of corruption were already present in the poetry of the *stil nuovo*. Lacking the curb of music, it ran into an elegance which surpassed in many respects that of Provençal lyric art, but which was of different order and drift, and one that was beset with many pitfalls.

It was, as is the invariable rule, the form in which its matter was draped that won for the new poetry an easy prevalence over the balder Sicilian manner, and grounded Dante's high estimate of Guinicelli and Cavalcanti. These imparted to Italian poetry a smooth-flowing and pliant polish which the lilting measures of Provençal poetry had not. They disclosed to what advantage might be put a closer access to the Latin treasuries than was available to the Provençals. To the poet's quest for freedom of richer expression, new far-reaching paths appeared to open. Dante regarded the ethical doctrinal contents of the new style with considerable indifference. But the metaphysical turn which the Tuscan Muse assumed appealed to some of the most absorbing preoccupations of his mind.

The *stil nuovo* was a learned poetry. Cavalcanti passed for one of the most erudite men of his day. His father, consigned by Dante among the Epicureans in his *Inferno*,[22] had been so deeply addicted to the study of books of philosophy that he was reputed an atheist. Guido Cavalcanti has left no methodical exposition of his philosophical ideas, but his young friend, Dante Alighieri, had in mind the composition of a series of treatises covering the entire field of human knowledge. The plan was evidently abandoned for another, but not before it had been partially put into execution.

Dante was so strongly drawn toward science that he at one time spoke of renouncing poetry in order to devote himself entirely to philosophy. Like most of the great minds of the Middle Ages, he was consumed by the Faustian fever, the frantic desire to master every branch of learning and to penetrate every mystery. Such being his disposition, it was inevitable that he should become deeply absorbed in the study of the Arabian works. If he does not express himself in the same terms as his contemporary, Roger Bacon, who asserted that all thought and science in his day could base themselves only upon familiarity with the Arabian authors,[23] the whole of Dante's works illustrates that opinion. His chief tutor in his youth, Brunetto Latini, a man of encyclopaedic mind, five years before the birth of his illustrious pupil, had spent several years in Spain as ambassador of the Guelfs at the court of Alfonso the Sage. He had met there the Arab and Israelite scholars who were employed, at the instigation of the philosopher-king, in the translation of the Arabian authors.[24]

Dante conceived an enthusiasm for the astronomy and cosmology of the Muslim scholars. He quotes, on the subject of the measurement of the orbit of Mercury, "the proofs given by Al-

Farghani, who declares it to correspond with the twenty-eighth part of the diameter of the earth."[25] And he records the movements of the planets as laid down by the same author, "who, in the *Book of the Aggregation of the Stars,* gives an account of the best observations made on this subject by astronomers."[26] He corrects Aristotle's estimate of the number of the spheres and quotes in full the arguments advanced by Ibn Roschd;[27] he adopts the theory of Ibn Haithan, who originated the idea of "crystalline" spheres; and he cites the conception of epicycles on the lines initiated by Al-Bitroji of Seville, who refuted the Ptolemaic system three centuries before Copernicus.[28]

The interest of Alighieri in astronomy was indeed wholly astrological; he cites with equal deference the most eminent astronomers and also charlatans of a somewhat dubious reputation. "Abú-Ma'shar," he says, "is of the opinion that the conflagration of meteors, which is brought about through the influence of the planet Mars, forebodes the death of a ruling prince and the revolution of kingdoms."[29] The importance attached by Dante to the investigation of the grouping of the heavenly bodies derived from his desire to trace the path of the influences they emit, which are responsible, he believed, for the dispositions of human character and the course of human life. "The rays which emanate from each of the spheres," he says "are the means by which the qualities of each sphere are transmitted to the sublunary world."[30] And, "while the rays of the supreme light of the universe penetrate human intelligences, they are thrown back and reflected by other terrestrial creatures. In order to elucidate this conception of 'light' and its 'emanation' I give here the various conclusions laid down by Ibn Sina on the subject."[31]

This conception of "light" occupies, in fact, an important place in the theories of the Sufi writers of Spain, who in consequence are called *Ischrakiyyin* or "Illuminists." The notion is no less conspicuous in the thought of Dante and the poets of the *stil nuovo.* "Every effect," says Dante in the course of his exposition of those ideas, "participates in the nature of its cause, as is affirmed by Al-Farabi, who declares that every creature is bound by reason of its origin to include some parcel of the divine nature, even as the sun and the other stars participate in the light deriving from the Divine Cause," the light divine being, in the view of Ibn Sina, the analogue of love.[32] This statement, in the same terms as those used by the philosopher of Baghdad, was to serve as the conclusion to the *Divine Comedy.*"

Dante, as the above examples suffice to show, is far from being the pure Aristotelian and orthodox Thomist he was long supposed to be. He is much nearer in his conceptions to so-called "Platonic" and Sufi modes of thought, as indeed he himself makes clear: "The source of this induction (of light or Love) is unanimously stated by all philosophers, including Plato, Ibn Sina, Al-Ghazali and also Denys the Areopagite, however differently they may express themselves, to be ultimately located in the celestial spheres."[33] Consequently, one is not surprised to learn that the great Florentine holds, like the Sufi poets, that "Love is a part of philosophy."[34]

Following the example of his models, he composed his treatise, "On Love," which he called "The Banquet"—*Il Convito* or *L'Amoroso convivio*—in the form of a philosophical exposition dealing with both love and poetry. He presents this work, which he regarded at the time as his *magnum opus*, as a commentary on the *canzoni* with which his arguments are sprinkled. Both in its form and manner, in fact, the *Convito* is written on the model of the works of Ibn Dawūd, Ibn Hazm and Al-Ghazali. Dante's style in these dissertations is far from foreshadowing the verbal splendors of the *Commedia*. The prose of the *Convito*, it must be admitted, is an example of what Voltaire would have called *le style ennuyeux*—the tedious style. "The substance of the entertainment which I have to offer the reader, that is, the poems," he says in his preamble, "might produce an impression of obscurity were they not accompanied by the more substantial nourishment

I have provided, and some might only perceive the material beauty of the verses without apprehending their true worth. But my exposition will furnish the light that reveals the colours entering into the composition of the poems."[35] And he insists at length and repeatedly on the double meaning of his love-poetry, its literal and its allegorical sense.

Like his predecessors, he explains Plato's doctrine of "ideas" or prototypes of "universal forms."[36] Profane love is but a semblance of divine love, the Prime Mover, the First Cause, of all existence. The well-beloved, the *Donna*, the *domina*—and he names Beatrice—"is no other than divine wisdom and philosophy."[37] Love is born through the medium of sight, in other words, through intelligent perception, which is assimilated, in virtue of such apprehension, to First Love. And just as the latter illuminates and animates the world, so does the sight of Beatrice spread the emanations of her light throughout the lover's soul. Just as Love, the creative source of all things, is by nature immortal, so also Love for Beatrice cannot be other than eternal.[38] "Philosophy, that is, the love of wisdom," he says, "is in reality the loving use of knowledge."[39]

The supreme poet of the Italian *trecento* pursues those conceptions of the Sufi mystics of the eleventh century considerably farther than they did. Since the time when Arabian mystical thought had set its mark on the songs of Andalusia and Provence, it had, in fact, undergone notable changes. The last days of Hispano-Moorish culture had seen the emergence of a great thinker, Ibn Roschd (Averroes), who, with measured philosophic balance, had attempted to combine the rationalism of Aristotle with the idealism of Plato, and whose works were to exercise an incalculable influence on the whole thought of Christian Europe. But, side by side with this final manifestation of Arabian philosophy, speculative tendencies were rife that were marked by the excesses of degeneration. Mysticism overflowed the mold of age-long formulae and poured forth a flood of visionary notions.

At the time when Brunetto Latini visited the Arabian academy at Toledo, the world of Islam had been thrown into a ferment by the doctrines of a mystic, Ibn Ali Ibn Arabi of Murcia, who had died twenty years earlier and had been raised to the rank of saint and prophet. Ibn Arabi had begun his career as a Sufi poet. Ibn Roschd himself, struck by the merit of his philosophical writings, had sought him out and consulted him. But Ibn Arabi had shortly after thrown all philosophical sobriety to the winds, and the expression of his mystical exaltation assumed the form of visions and allegories. He was a prolific writer. His chief work, *Al-Futuhat,* "Light" (or "Emanation"), dealing with the "Knowledge of God," explains the effect produced on "intelligences" by the radiations or emanations of the supreme sphere. Taking up an ancient traditional theme, developed by Muhammed Ibn 'Abd Allah Ibn Masarra of Cordova,[40] Ibn Arabi describes the evolutions of "intelligence" under the similitude of the journey of a philosopher. Taking Jerusalem, the center of the earth, as his point of departure, he visited, under the direction of various guides, the circles of hell and Limbo and ascended to the height of the spheres of the Moon, Mercury, Venus, the Sun, Mars, Jupiter and Saturn, eventually reaching the throne of the *Primum mobile.*[41]

A similar allegory appears to have inspired Dante when he speaks, in the *Convito,* of the progressive purification of Love and "of the evolution of life, which rises by degrees from Evil to Good, from Good to Better and from Better to the Supreme Good."[42] It was therefore important to determine with precision the conditions most favorable to the operation and perception of the celestial emanations, sources of all moral progress. This irradiation was thought of in the Middle Ages as an almost physical process. The old formula of the troubadours as to the penetration of love through the eyes was no longer a mere literary conceit, but a "scientific" theory taken quite seriously, and the process was held to be similar in its action to that by which radiations were transmitted to human souls by the spheres. Dante calculates that "if a stone fell from the pole of our celestial hemisphere, it would strike the head of a man placed at a distance of two thousand seven hundred miles west of Rome."[43] But he later changed his mind and accepted the Islamic tradition followed by Al-Arabi, according to which "Paradise is situated within the seventh sphere above Jerusalem, so that if a stone fell from Paradise it would drop exactly on the Rock (of the Temple)."[44]

The "lights" or emanations which affect intelligent minds do not proceed from the spheres themselves, but from the "intelligences" which direct them. "The celestial spheres are in fact set in motion," says Dante, "by intelligences having no corporeal substance, that is to say, by angels."[45] Those intelligences form three hierarchies, each of which comprises three orders of powers, corresponding to the nine spheres: the first hierarchy includes the angels, the archangels and the thrones; the second the commanding lordships, the virtues and the powers; the third the heavenly princes, the Cherubim and the Seraphim.[46]

It was the age when attention was being drawn to the doctrines of the Kabbala. These had been introduced into Spain by Abraham Abúlafa (1210-1291), and long before that date they had been brought to notice by the Jew, Salomon Ibn Gebirol of Malaga (1021-1070), first known for his imitations of Arabian poets[47] and inspired, like Ibn Arabi, by the works of Ibn Massara. The celestial hierarchies of Dante, the order of which had been collated by the talmudists and the pseudo-Denys, correspond to those of the Kabbala: the Ofani, Arelim, Hashmalim, Malakim, Elohim, Bene-elohim, Ishim, Cherubim and Seraphim. The assimilation of man, the microcosm, to the macrocosm, and man as a paradigm, Adam Kadmon, animated by the emanations (*acila*) of the intelligences, or *sephiroth*, are the conceptions that form the kernel of Kabbalistic mysticism as it was disseminated in Italy during the thirteenth century by Menahem ben Benjamin of Recanati. A little later the Italian humanists of the so-called classical Renaissance, Pico della Mirandola, Poggio Bracciolini and Filelfo, were to fall under the spell of those mystic visions. These had already begun to exercise their influence on the poets of the *stil nuovo,* and that influence is clearly to be traced in the modified interpretations imposed on the traditional formulae of the troubadours.

The Italians believed that the ideas which so strangely infused themselves into their love-poetry derived from Plato. Hence the expression "Platonic love" which has passed into our languages. But, having had no opportunity of reading Plato, they in reality drew their conceptions from Alexandrian, Sufi and Jewish sources. What they took for Platonism—much to the amusement of the Greek, Gernistus, who had to explain to the members of the Florentine Platonic Academy that there existed differences between Plato and Aristotle—was in reality far more closely allied to the Neoplatonism of Proclus, Philo and the pseudo-Denys, and not markedly discriminated from the mysteries of the Kabbala.

Meanwhile, the old conventions of Provençal poetry, which bore the mark of their origin from the same sources at an earlier period, were respected by the Tuscan poets. Even the traditional distinction between "noble" or "courteous" love and the coarse feelings of the plebeian and middle classes, incongruous as it was in a society essentially middle class and republican, is given an important position in the works of Guinicelli, Cavalcanti and Dante:*

Guinicelli: *Al cor gentil sempre Amor s'apprende.*

Cavalcanti: . . . *del suo cor gentil.*

Dante: *Amor che a cor gentil ratto s'apprende.*

The whole of the best known *canzone* of Guinicelli has reference to this theme. It is developed by Guido Cavalcanti:

> *Ed a presente conoscente chero*
> *per ch'io ro spero ch'om di basso core*
> *a tal ragione porti conoscenza* . . .[48]

---

* Cf.: "love, that is in the gentle heart begone"—Spenser.

Dante endeavors, not without embarrassment, to explain this fundamental conception of Provençal courtly poetry in terms agreeable to the ideas which inspired the "new style."[49] "Ibn Sīna and Al-Ghazāli considered," he says, "that each soul is of its own nature either noble or base."[50]

Continuing the traditions represented by Sordello and the other Italian troubadours, the poets of the *stil nuovo* devoted themselves to composing variations on invariable burthens and formulae. "Love," after becoming merged with the motor "intelligences" of the third sphere, that of Venus, and with the Prime Mover, retained little of its former connotation of a state of mind or personal sentiment. The symbol of passion is, strictly speaking, no more than an element in their art, an essential element, no doubt, lending itself as no other to the varied modulation of delicate sentiments, but subordinate, from the artistic standpoint, to the contrivance of curiously chiselled poetical gems.

Even as the painters of the Italian Renaissance were to exercise their technique and their talents on prescribed subjects, on madonnas or groups of saints, without necessarily being influenced by theology or piety, so the poets who continued the troubadour tradition showed themselves much more careful of the form than of the literal content of their art. In the commentaries which Dante attaches to his poems in the *Vita nuova*, as well as in his essay on the *Vernacular Tongue*, he applies himself to the discussion of technique, meter and vocabulary. And if those professional dissertations are blended with considerations on the subject of "Love," the latter are, no less than his reflections on prosody and style, essentially literary arguments.

Had Dante been known to us only by his early lyrical poetry, he would in all probability have been scarcely distinguished above the other poets, Cavalcanti, Dino Frescobaldi, Cino da Pistoia, Gianni Alfani, and the few others of Guinicelli's disciples. Sensitive as he was to the influences of his environment, he identified with their style, its merits and its faults. It tokens highly for the power and strength of his personality that he was eventually able, on his own independent impulse, to work himself free of that somewhat nerveless elegance. While retaining the contributions of the *stil nuovo* to wider means of expression, while using in even greater measure its faculties of suggestion and allusiveness, he forged for himself a different and more sinewy language.

In the third *canzone* of the *Convivio* he declares his purpose in explicit terms: "It behoves me," he says, "to abandon the elegant love-rimes which my thoughts were wont to seek. . . . I shall lay aside the sweet style I used in treating of love, and shall speak of the true worth that enobles man in rimes both subtle and rugged":

> *Le dolci rime d'amor ch'i' solla*
> *cercar ne' miei pensieri,*
> *conven ch'io lasci; . . . .*
> *disporrò giù lo mio soave stile,*
> *ch'i' ho tenuto nel trattar d'amore;*
> *e dirò del valore,*
> *per lo qual veramente omo è gentile,*
> *con rima aspr' e sottile.*[51]

And in the series of *canzoni* known as *petrose*, the composition of which is placed by general consent in the last years of the thirteenth century, that is, when the *Commedia* was brooding in Dante's mind, he again declares in plain words: *nel mio parlar voglio esser, aspro*, "my speech shall, I intend, be rugged" (ciii).

Rugged! That is the very antithesis of *stil nuovo* elegance. The Italian commentators are startled, perplexed, and not seldom grieved at the sudden change. It amounts to little less than an apostasy and a revolt. Signor Ortiz deplores that Dante "has *relapsed* into the Provençal style." And in fact Dante went back for the sinewy and concrete vigor which was lacking in the elegant

Latinity of contemporary Italian poetry, and which was demanded by the rising passion of his mood, to the head-fount, to the troubadours, and in particular to Arnaud Daniel, whom he declares to be his master and the "better craftsman"—*il miglior fabbro*.[52] That frequently cited expression is often somewhat misleadingly quoted. Dante places it in the mouth of Guido Guinicelli, and it reads in that context, not "Arnaud Daniel is the best artificer," but "Arnaud Daniel is a better artificer than I am." For all the admiration he bestowed upon "the father of Italian poetry" and of the *stil nuovo*, Dante sets Arnaud Daniel above him.

For Dante, Provençal poetry was represented by the poets of the golden age; the very names of the poetasters subsequent to the crusade and the Inquisition were probably unknown to him. That poetry had, on the other hand, come to Dante and the other poets of the *stil nuovo* by way of the Italian troubadours, all of whom were friends and disciples of the collaborators of the Church. A curious paradox thus came about. While the technique inherited from the troubadours was that of the best phases of their art, the ideas understood to lie behind that art were those of its complete decadence. Like his successors and the majority of educated persons to the present day, Dante was deceived, in all innocence, by the pious fraud practiced by Montanhagol in regard to the old troubadours' conception of "love."

It is no accident that Sordello plays the conspicuous part assigned to him by Dante in the *Purgatorio;* throughout three cantos of the poem, from the sixth to the ninth, he acts as Dante's guide. Even as Virgil was Dante's instructor in Latin poetry, so another Mantuan poet, Sordello, directed his studies of the "modern classics" of his age, to wit, the troubadours. Sordello, who was something of a charlatan, does not owe his reputation to any conspicuous excellence in his poetry, but rather to the authoritarian manner with which he imposed his views, and thus won for himself in Italy the position of recognized authority on Provençal poetry. It was, therefore, inevitable that the Italians should accept Montanhagol's theories and his habit of representing his predecessors as having conformed with them.

Sordello spent most of his life at the Court of Raimon VII of Toulouse. Dante, accordingly, in the sixth canto of the *Paradiso*, sides with Raimon Bérenger and Romieu de Villeneuve against the people of Provence, who were stirred to revolt by the measures which were to lead to the annexation of their country to the kingdom of France. Like most of the Provençal troubadours, Sordello was long a resident at the Spanish Courts, those of Alfonso IX of Leon, Sancho VII of Navarre and Ferdinand III of Castile. He only returned to Italy, at an advanced age, in the retinue of Charles of Anjou.[53] Dante was too young to have met him, but he knew Sordello's famous mistress, Cunizza. However, it was scarcely necessary to have any personal acquaintance with Sordello in order to fall under the influence of his literary and moral theories. They were current coin in the circles of fourteenth century Italian men of letters.

As we have seen, Sordello excelled all the other troubadours in the extravagant affectations of spiritual sublimation which were introduced into Provence on the establishment of the Inquisition. It was in this counterfeit form that the courtly poetry of the troubadours was interpreted to the Italians of the north of the peninsula.

Although Dante was not in a position to perceive their historical causes, he was well aware of the deeper differences between the conception of the *stil nuovo* and those of the troubadours, or the more faithful imitations of the "Sicilian" school. In the *Purgatorio*, he contrives to meet Bonagiunta, an old "Sicilian" poet of Lucca. Dante takes occasion to touch on the widened conception of love of the new Tuscan poetry. "Brother," replies Bonagiunta, "I now perceive what tether held us, the lawyer (Iacopo da Lentino), Guittone and myself, on the hither side of your *stil nuovo*. I know how your quills followed the dictates of your ideal. With us such soaring flight certainly never took place."

> *"O frate, issa vegg'io," diss' elli, "il nodo*
> *che'l Notaro e Guittone e me ritenne*
> *di qua dal dolce stil novo ch'l odo.*
> *Io veggio ben come le vostre penne*
> *di retro al dittator sen vanno strette;*
> *che delle nostre certo non avenne."*[54]

Still less than the love-poetry of the troubadours, even those of the decadence, did the lyrical manner of the *stil nuovo* correspond to the conduct of the authors. We have seen to what point that inconsequence between theory and practice could be carried by a poet like Sordello, who was at the same time the extravagant apostle of spiritualized love in his poetry, and in his private life a notorious and cynical rake. The ecstasy of metaphysical and extra-terrestrial love bears no more relation to reality in the works of Guido Cavalcanti than in those of Sordello. When Cavalcanti chose to exercise his skill in the composition of a particular variety of Provençal lyric, the *pastourelle*, he thus had no difficulties in laying aside theories which would be out of place and in that sense adopting a different style.

> *In un boschetto trova' pasturella*
> *piu che stella bella al mi' parere.*
>
> . . . .
>
> *fra me stesso diss'i: "Or è stagione*
> *di questa pasturella gio' pigliare".*
>
> . . . .
>
> *menommi sott'una freschetta foglia*
> *la dov'i'vidi fior d'ogni colore:*
> *e tanto vi sentio gioa e dolzore*
> *che dio d'amore parvemi vedere.*[55]

I met a shepherdess in a grove and she seemed to me more beautiful than a star. . . . And I said to myself: This is cer-

tainly a good opportunity to enjoy myself with this little
shepherdess . . . she led me to a cool thicket in which I saw
flowers of all colors: and such joy and pleasure I had of
her that I deemed I had a vision of the god of love.

It is a far cry from their vein to the refined key in which most
of the poems of Guido Cavalcanti are modulated. To take the
latter for descriptions of personal experiences and feelings would
be as unreasonable as to suppose that the *pastourelle*, copied almost word for word from a Provençal model, narrates an actual
adventure. Both styles are in equal measure literary conventions.

The chief series of erotic poems by Guido Cavalcanti is addressed to a lady whose name is given as "Mandetta," seen at
Toulouse in the Church of the Daurade during Mass. Petrarch,
it will be recalled, also betakes himself to Provence for his sight,
during divine service, of a lady who was to serve as the pretext
for his effusions during nearly half a century. The Provençal lady
of whom a glimpse is caught at Mass becomes almost a formula.
May we see, in the circumstance that the ideal lady is found in
Provence, a delicate expression of the obligation the Italian poets
acknowledged towards their Provençal masters? However that
may be, the little that is known concerning Cavalcanti's private
life is enough to show that there is no connection between the
metaphysics of love in his poems and the principles which governed his behavior. The latter disclose no sign of sublimation.

Nor does the love experience of Dante Alighieri. Like the
majority of poets, by temperament he was highly sensual. "Side
by side with so much talent and learning," writes Boccaccio, "his
temperament displayed much lewdness of disposition. And this
was the case not only during his youth but even after he had
reached a mature age."[56] Even if the testimony (which was never
disputed and which was in accord with tradition down to the
time of Filalfo and Missirimi) were in need of corroboration, this
is amply forthcoming from the poet's own mouth—*dalla propria*

gota[57]—much to the distress of modern Italian commentators, who twist and squirm to defend Dante's virtue. With great vitality goes, as a rule, a many-sided diversity of moods and tempers. "I am changeable in every guise"—*transmutabile son per tutte guise*—Dante himself says.[58]

It would be a great mistake to think of Dante as always wearing the stern mask of the thinker in which we are accustomed to see him pictured. He had in a high degree the sense of humor, so often lacking in writers straining to the highest themes, as in Milton, for instance. Dante knew full well how to unbend to boisterous and even riotous moods. "With the saints in church, in the taverns with the gluttons"—*nella chiesa co'santi, ed in taverna co' ghiottoni.*[59] It is a very different Dante from the one we commonly picture, a laughing Dante, that we meet in the humoristic *tenson*, in a taste that puts one in mind of Boccaccio, with Forese Donati,[60] who, in Purgatory, recalls the gay life they led together, and what they were then.[61] Another of Dante's associates was the drunken and whoring Sienese poet, Cecco Angiolieri, who, having apparently had a quarrel with his companion, retorts with jocular invectives, telling him in effect: "I know you too well, Dante; you are not a whit better than I am."[62]

Sensuality is the besetting sin which Dante is called upon to confess before he can be admitted to the precincts of Paradise. "My steps have followed after the world's false pleasures"—*col falso lor piacer volser miei passi.*[63] And Beatrice, in her stern indictment, charges that he has been too weak to resist the songs of the sirens.[64] He has fallen so low, she says, that only the sight of the punishments of hell could bring him to better his disposition.[65] And it thus happens that his sins of sensuality and her intervention to save him are the immediate occasion of his otherworld journey.

Throughout Dante's life passes a succession of women. His catalogue almost matches Leporello's. In the very midst of the *Vita nuova*—the classic, as it were, of idealized lyric love—Dante dwells upon other amours. He refers to them under the traditional troubadour convention of the "screen lady," serving to preserve the secret of his real love, although it is hard to see how the device applies in this instance. But he admits that the pretense went so far as to create considerable scandal, and that he addressed "trifles in verse" to those ladies—for there are at least two "screen-ladies," who have been identified as the Fioretta and the Violetta of some of his most charming *canzoni*.[66] Beatrice refers to a third, the *pargoletta*, to whom a series of three of his sonnets is addressed.[67]

No sooner is Beatrice dead than he consoles himself with a *gentile donna, giovane e bella molto;* the confession is also incorporated in his homage to Beatrice and ideal love.[68] And while he is engaged in the composition of the serene harmonies of the *Purgatorio*, his mind is burdened with a new intrigue: Bonagiunta "foretells" the pleasure Dante will have of a certain Gentucca, said to be the wife of Bonacorso, a rich merchant of Lucca.[69] Famed above others by reason of the superb *canzoni petrose*, inspired by a passion which is anything but ethereal, is the lady Petra, identified with Madonna Pietra de' Scrovigni, of Padua.[70] Dante's loves—the list of hints could be extended—range over a considerable variety. For a time he appears to have been much under the influence of a wild and willful little mountain peasant, "la Montanina,"[17] and Boccaccio speaks of an Alpine lass, whether the same or another, "with an enlarged throat"—*alpigina gozzuta*.

The identification of those various ladies is purely conjectural. Not only is Dante so scrupulous in the observance of the rule of troubadour courtly love that he never refers to any except by a *senhal*, but he takes pleasure in enveloping their personality in a cloud of riddles and conundrums which has successfully baffled commentators, each of whom, almost, has some different interpretation to offer on the subject, and as to which is which. So far it is clear only that they were numerous. It is even open to doubt whether Beatrice was Beatrice Portinari. Dante first introduces the name in the *Vita nuova*, with the cryptic sentence: "The glorious Lady of my thoughts, who was by many called Beatrice, as they did not know her real name." It would indeed be somewhat odd if Dante, so punctiliously scrupulous in the observance of the rule of using only a *senhal*, should have broken it only in the case of Beatrice. He says nothing of her marriage nor furnishes any particular as to her identity.

When the character of Italian amatory poetry in the fourteenth century is borne in mind, composed as it is, like troubadour poetry, almost wholly of literary conventions, the discussions as to the reality of Dante's love for Beatrice, which fill the pages of critics, lose much of their interest. Dante's poetic passion could not in any particular have unfolded, from the exquisite filigree of the *Vita nuova* to the apotheosis of the *Paradiso*, otherwise than it did. Whatever might be the deviations and tribulations of his life, his marriage, his numerous love affairs and his periods of wild dissipation, love, or rather Love with a capital, the central theme of his work, could be no other than a consuming passion filling the whole of his existence and occupying all his thoughts. The fact that this love dates from Dante's tenderest infancy is in the best traditions; Bernard de Ventadorn had also known his lady almost from the cradle, Aucassin and Nicolette grew up together. Dante links this circumstance, by the aid of an exhaustive study of the Arabian calendar, with certain considerations connected with the number nine, which symbolizes mystical perfection.

In the works of all the poets writing in the tradition of the *stil nuovo*, right down to Petrarch's day, the occasions of their first beholding their ladies are described in minute detail, while scarcely another incident of their love affairs is circumstantially reported. This treatment is connected with the theory that "Love" penetrates the heart by way of the eyes, and therefore it is only the first encounter of Dante and Beatrice, of Guido Cavalcanti and Mandetta, of Petrarch and Laura, which counts and is worth detailed rehearsal. For the same reason we know nothing of these ladies except their personal appearance and the color of the dress they wore at the time. Whether they were intelligent or stupid, sweet-tempered or irritable, are irrelevant circumstances in the metaphysical theory of love.

The maneuver by means of which Dante pretends to conceal his love and mislead slander by paying court to other young women, who play the part of "screen-ladies," is among the most honorable traditions of courtly love. Again, she is like Laura, under the obligation of dying, in order that she may be elevated to the highest sphere of the empyrean and become one with Divine Wisdom or the Queen of Heaven.

There is no need to be cynical in judging the poet's perfect love. That a momentary meeting should suffice to inspire a tender passion which will last a lifetime without any encouragement, and should outlive its object; that this attachment should not be based on any personal relationship, even the most irreproachable; that it should date from the lover's tenderest years; that it should inspire and sustain a literary activity prolonged into old age—all these things are possible. Human nature is capable of anything when favored by circumstances. But that more than fifty poets should exhibit the same psychological peculiarities of amorous passion at the same period transcends the bounds of plausibility. We may be prepared to believe in the existence of one white blackbird: it is another thing to ask one to believe in a whole flock of them.

Biographical details concerning a certain Monna Bice, daughter of Messer Folco Portinari, encountered by Dante on the 1st May 1274 at one o'clock in the afternoon, married to a certain Messer Simone de Bardi and dying on the 8th June 1290; or concerning a certain Lady de Noves, wife of Sir Hugues de Sade, to whom she bore about a dozen children, or about one a year, seen by Messer Petrarch on the 6th April 1327, Good Friday, in the

Church of Sainte-Claire, situated in the city of Avignon, in the county of Venaissin[72]—all such particulars and a thousand more can add nothing to the likelihood of the story. When one proposes to dedicate a sonnet or a whole sequence of sonnets to a lady who must fulfill certain conditions prescribed by the rules of art, there is no need to be a great poet or a great lover to find, by delving into one's memories, some incident or other which more or less conforms to the conditions required. The lady herself may do her best to fall in with the demands of the poetic passion, but she nevertheless plays quite a minor part in the affair. She is not the occasion of the lyrical work nor does she inspire it; on the contrary, it is the creation of the poet which assigns her a part which she is under the obligation of assuming.

Dante concludes his breviary of love, *La Vita nuova*, with the statement that he hopes to build a literary monument to his lady, the like of which never was dedicated to any woman.[73] By taking over the language fashioned by the lyric art of the troubadours and the poets of the *stil nuovo* in view of conventional themes and stylized emotions, and applying it to the expression of real passions, of bitter suffering, fierce hatred, deep tenderness, profound sadness, and great hopes, by combining the skilled technique of Provençal and Tuscan art with the whole thought and science of his day, Dante created the poetic masterpiece of the new Europe, first in point of time, and never surpassed or equalled since. This monument, which towers at the crossroads of the centuries, and from the pinnacle of whose greatness the eye is carried past the petty futilities and imbecilities of the times toward eternal horizons, is nevertheless constructed from the materials of the stylized art upon which rest, in time, its majestic tiers.

The art of the courtly jongleur, whose affectations raise a smile, forged the speech of Dante. Nor was it their manner and conventions alone which the troubadours of Provence bequeathed to him; they passed on to the supreme poet both the rich harmonies and the prodigious concision which give his language its miraculous quality. Dante avows his fondness for the *trobar clus—le parole oscuro*, which makes sensible the mystery that eludes expression. We find again in him the boldness characteristic of Arnaut Daniel or Peire Vidal, which promotes a common word, transmuted in the magic crucible of style, to the highest uses of language and inspired imagination. Dante is truly an Italian troubadour. The *Divine Comedy*, which, in conformity with the consecrated formulae, raises the ideal lady to the highest spheres, sets the crown upon the amatory conceits of the *Vita nuova* and the *canzoni*. The artificial love which the troubadours sang, the subtilized love of the *stil nuovo*, breaks the envelope of its chrysalis and spreads its wings. It becomes the Love which moves the sun and the other stars—*l'amor che muove il sol e l'altre stelle*.

It is often said that Dante created the Italian language. Would he had. He was, however, too close in time to the outbreak in Italy of a cult that was to have a profound effect upon all European literatures. Already foreshadowed in the trends of the *stil nuovo*, against which Dante had raised his cry of revolt, the Renaissance instituted the doctrinal domination of classicism, that is of Latinity. Latin was the measure of all things. Dante, after excelling in the smooth Latin elegance which the *stil nuovo* induced upon Provençal lyricism, had deliberately curbed the somewhat insipid graces of that mellifluous polish. He had brought back from Arnaut Daniel a more ancient "rugged" directness. To the pundits of the new cult, that rebellion was heresy; Dante was insufficiently Latin, he was "Gothic." Even though the classic zeal did not, in Italy, attain to the vehemence it displayed in France, its effects were very similar. The Italian Renaissance sought to repudiate Dante. He was, as one of the Florentine humanists put it, "banished from the conclaves of the learned, and abandoned to the entertainment of wool-carders and bakers." For centuries, Italy sought to forget her greatest poet. As late as the middle of the eighteenth century, the Jesuit writer S. Bettinelli charged Dante with being devoid of good taste, obscure, ponderous, and that of all the *Commedia*, scarcely a thousand lines are worth preserving.[74]

But by a curious irony, the so-called Renaissance—for the real one, which brought barbaric Europe to life, and made the efflorescence of the fifteenth and sixteenth centuries possible, took place in the twelfth under the influence of Islamic civilization—this so-called Renaissance continued to follow even more closely in some respects than did Dante the tradition inaugurated by the troubadours of Provence. Its founder in Italy was Petrarch. He, the most pampered of poets, crowned with laurel at the Capitol, honored by the European courts and chosen as the ambassador of kings and emperors, was universally recognized as the most eminent representative of the new era.

The work by which the father of the humanist Renaissance has always been best known, however, was even more faithfully modelled, in its subject-matter, inspiration and form, on the troubadour tradition than was Dante's. "Petrarch was the final blossom and perfection of the troubadours," says S. T. Coleridge.[75] The favored poet helped himself so freely at that source that Tassoni, Bembo and others have charged him with plagiarism.[76] Petrarch nowise repels the imputation. To follow the model of amatory lyricism was, in his eyes, no more transgression calling for apology than Virgil's paraphrasing of Homer. In the third canto of his "Triumphs," Petrarch enumerates his literary ancestors. After paying homage to his Italian predecessors, he proceeds:

> In their wake came a company of foreigners, writers in the vernacular. Their leader is Arnaud Daniel, the great master of love, whose elegant and polished style honours the country that gave him birth. Beside him walk the two Peires (Peire Rogier and Peire Vidal), who felt so keenly the strokes of love, the lesser Arnaud (Arnaud de Mareuil) and

all those whom love could not subdue but after a long con-
test. I mean the two Ranbauds (Ranbaud d'Orange and
Ranbaud de Vaqueiras), both of whom sang of Beatrice of
Montferrat. Also the aged Peire d'Auvergne, Giraud (de
Bornelh) and Folquet whose name is the pride of Marseilles,
and who deprived Genoa of that honour when he exchanged
his lyre and songs for a kinder and more devout vocation;
Jaufré Rudel, who took sail to meet death; Aimery (de
Peguilain), Bernard (de Ventadorn), Hugues (de Saint-
Cyr) and many more, whose voice served them as lance and
sword, helm and shield.[77]

Thus by one of the paradoxes which pervade history, the acknowledged representative of the "classical" cult, which came to
wield the tyranny of a dictatorial literary absolutism, was at the
same time the model and immediate source of the directly opposite trend, which classicism fiercely combated. What is true of
Petrarch holds with equal force of the whole influence exercised
by Italy during the formative centuries that followed. Italy was
regarded as the natural heir of classical antiquity, but she was
at the same time the repository of the Provençal tradition. Many
who turned to Italy for closer touch with the "antique," received
instead the "courtly" and romantic inspiration that hales from
Provence. Englishmen who undertook the Italian journey to
breathe in its native fields the perfume of the "antique," returned loaded with the fruits of troubadour tradition. The Italian
influence gave rise, on the one hand, to Racine and French classicism, and on the other to the Elizabethan efflorescence and Shakespeare.

Petrarch's prestige gave birth, throughout Europe, to a lyrical
activity fashioned on the model which he had set. His version of
the troubadour love-song remains probably the best in any language. He is restrained and dignified, and exempt from the added
coloratura in which his imitators indulged. But that perfection
is not the perfection of the troubadours. As with all humanists

and classicists after him, he was debarred by the psychosis of Latinity from piercing to the very qualities that charmed him. He could conceive of no other manner of painting the lily than to overlay it with a coat of Ciceronian and Virgilian varnish.

Latin is the noblest, with one exception, of known languages. Western civilization cannot be pictured without the perfusion in its blood and substance of the speech and thought which first differentiated it from the barbarian world. But the fact remains that attempts to impose more Latinity on speech and expression that have grown independently of the Latin model have been uniformly disastrous. For one thing the insensate incongruity of applying the syntax of a highly inflected language to idioms which have entirely shed desinential inflections imparts an un-couthness even to the most musical of languages. Boccaccio's prose, the admired model that trails its influence even in modern literary Italian, with its gerunds, participles absolute and trans-positions, in its gawkiness occasionally approaches German at its worst.

Petrarch, sincerely and enthusiastically admiring his models, no more understood them than Pope, sincerely and enthusiastically admiring Homer, understood him, when he attired him in the garb of his rhyming couplets, and made him express himself in smart antitheses like a coffee-house wit. It is owing to that tone-deafness, begot of the blind cult of Latinity, that Petrarch was in-capable of understanding Dante. Dante was, to Petrarch's think-ing, insufficiently Latin. His art was not the smooth-flowing elegance of his declared guide Virgil, but of a quality immea-surably superior. And it is owing to the same incapacity that the far-spread and momentous renewal of the troubadour tradition, translated into the "perfected" form in which Petrarch garbed it, begot the failures of taste which blurred, in England, the luster of Elizabethan brilliancy.

Before long, that misconception killed poetry in Italy itself. The swarms of disciples and imitators of Petrarch further "im-

proved" on his improvements of the troubadour genre and manner, and turned out a Petrarchese poetry larded with conceits
and trinketed with gauds and ornaments like an old whore. And
when the classicizing Puritan, Milton, went to Italy for inspiration, he found there nothing but "flattery and fustian."

In sixteenth-century France the center of the cult of Petrarchist
poetry was at Lyons, in the circle of Louise Labé and Maurice
Scève. Clement Marot, on his release from the Conciergerie and
the Châtelet, where he had been confined for "eating bacon in
Lent," joined the Court at Lyons, and there made the acquaintance of the followers of Petrarch and composed the first sonnet
in French. The new type of composition was soon rendered
illustrious by Ronsard. This interesting technical development
articulated the whole theory of love as it had arisen out of the
orthodox passion of such as Montanhagol, Guiraut Riquier,
Sordello, Guinicelli, Cavalcanti and Dante. Antoine Heroet gave
a lengthy exposition of its principles in his *Parfaite Amye*, and
Maurice Scève repeated, in his *Delie,* the spiritualized passion of
Dante and Petrarch. Joachim du Bellay, in spite of the passages
of invective in his *Deffense* and his poem *Against the Petrar-
chans*, was, like all the rest of the Pleiad poets, a Petrarchan. He
celebrated, in fifty sonnets, his immortal and etherealized love
for *Olive,* as Ronsard did his for *Cassandre.* The brief flowering
of the Italianate blossoms in France, however, was smothered
almost at its birth by the "Pleïade" itself and the classical movement.

Strange though it may appear at first blush, the Provençal
tradition was much more continuous and lasting in England than
in France. Before the French pseudo-classical reaction had crossed
the channel, England had produced its palmary literary glory
in the Elizabethan age, and the classical reaction could not assume the destructive violence that it had in France. Before it had
reached these Islands, England had Elizabethan literature, derived directly from Italy without its having passed through

France. The manner, style, metrical models, and the very themes and conceits of the troubadour tradition, which had moulded Italian lyrical poetry, became transported, bodily one might say, into England. There it was the more readily endenizened owing to the poetical art having, from the first, grown there as an off-shoot of the Provençal stock.

The English poets, Raleigh, Spenser, Sidney, Marlowe, Shake-speare, while probably unaware of those Provençal origins, were fully conscious of their Italian ties and of that migration. Fore-most in bringing about the latter was a poet whom Sir Arthur Quiller-Couch regards as "one of the glories" of English poetry and "one of the heroes of our literature," Sir Thomas Wyat. He had made a sojourn in Italy, and it was he, chiefly, who brought "the flame of lyrical poetry to England, the flame of the Petrar-chists, caught from the Troubadours."[78]

It is of interest to note that Wyat, "who led our poets to Italy" and introduced the sonnet and much else that became characteris-tic of a new phase of English poetry, showed a particular fond-ness for an archaic stanzaic form, which had passed out of usage among the Italian poets themselves. That form is no other than the Hispano-Mauresque *murabba'*, the technological seed of the whole lyrical evolution. Thus he sings:

> And wylt thow leve me thus?
>> Say nay, say nay, for shame,
>> to save thee from the blame
>> of all my greffe and grame;
> And wylt thow leve me thus!
>> Say nay, say nay!
>
> And wylt thow leve me thus
>> that hath lovyd thee so long
>> in welth and woo among?
> And is thy heart so strong
> as for to leve me thus?
>> Say nay, say nay!

Or again:

> Fforget not yet the tryde entent
> of suche a truthe as I have ment,
> my great travay so gladly spent,
>   Fforget not yet.

and:

> That deth or mercy be ende of my smert,
> take with the payne whereof I have my part;
> and ekes the flame from which I cannot stert:
> And leve me then in rest I you require.[79]

That popular form of Provençal poetry, as we have seen, became established in English lyrical poetry during the latter part
of the thirteenth century. It retained its dominant position down
to the verge of the Elizabethan age, within hailing distance, one
might say, of Shakespeare. The lyrical effusions on which King
Henry VIII plumed himself bear very much the same cast and
manner as those of the Count de Poitiers:

> Pastime with good company
> I love and shall, until I die.
> Grudge who lust, but none deny.
> So God be pleased, thus live will I.
>   For my pastance,
>   Hunt, sing and dance,
>   My heart is set.
>   All goodly sport
>   For my comfort
> Who shall me let?

Wyat is the more emblematic of the great transition which he
was paramountly instrumental in bringing about, in that he uses
the ancient *murabba'* form side by side with its Italian derivative,
which he introduced into England—the sonnet.

Shakespeare* went to school with the Italianate sonneteers. It has been deplored that he was an Elizabethan. But his faculty, no less than his failings, is a product of his age, and had he written in another, the Augustan, say, or the Romantic, we should not have known the quality that enthralls us. The Tudor English, excited by the rout of the Armada, had had revealed to them potentialities and a plasticity in words which they had not before suspected. And Shakespeare found his powers in revelry. There is nothing intrinsically reprehensible, so far as I can perceive, in giving rein to a glamorous mastery of diction. A burst of verbal coruscation is often amusing; it sometimes strikes us with breathtaking excitement, as:

> Not poppy, nor mandragora,
> Nor all the drowsy syrups of the world,
> Shall ever medicine thee to that sweet sleep
> Which thou ow'd'st yesterday[80]

and that is the mark to which great poets aim. What conflicts with that aim is *habitual* indulgence of that verbal profligacy.

In a sober, judicious, but appreciative appraisal of Shakespeare, Walpole says: "He cannot be simple." That is a grievous disability. Besides producing artificiality, uniform verbal glamour cannot but be at times forced, as is only too apparent when Shakespeare's inspiration—as not so seldom happens—sags to the level of contemporary turgidity. Yet but for that vice, the conquest of language wherein consists Shakespearean magic would not have been achieved.

Shakespeare towers like a mountain peak above the surrounding foothills, but is of one substance and structure with them. That cast and texture was imported, wittingly and avowedly, from Italy; and the Italians had it, wittingly and avowedly, from

* An alternate version of this section on Shakespeare is given in the Appendix.

an older poetic fabric. The blossom of Elizabethan splendor was a new burgeoning from the Provençal stock. In his *Biographia literaria*, Coleridge, who knew nothing of Provençal poetry, characterizes the Elizabethans—not very acutely, it is true—in words that might apply with equal, indeed greater aptness to the troubadours:

> The imagery is always general: sun, moon, flowers, breezes, murmuring streams, warbling songsters, delicious shades, lovely damsels, cruel as fair . . . are the materials which are common to all, and which each shaped according to his judgment or fancy, little solicitous to add or particularize. . . . (They) derive their chief attraction from the manner of treating them; from impassioned flow or picturesque arrangement. . . . They placed the essence of poetry in the *art*. The excellence at which they aimed consisted in the exquisite polish of diction combined with perfect simplicity. This their prime object they attained by avoidance of every word and phrase which none but a learned man would use; by the studied position of words and phrases, so that not only each part should be melodious in itself, but contribute to the harmony of the whole . . . and lastly with equal labour, the greater because unbetrayed, by the variation and various harmonies of their metrical movement. . . . Superior excellence in the manner of treating the same subject was the trial and test of the artist's merit.

The wealth of Shakespeare's poetic resources enables him to substitute gold for pinchbeck, and diamonds for glass in the confection of his jewels. But their mode and manner conform to the time's tastes and fashions. Form and resonance take precedence over matter, and the profundity of the latter, often, like the *trobar clus*, more apparent than real (his philosophy does not extend much farther than that of the man in the street), is above all one more instrument in the production of the magic of his art. His thought, his invention, nay, his very insight into character and his dramatic sense, are subservient to the primary aim of verbal music and verbal splendor. These are not mere vehicles for the expression of their contents, but the very essence of his, as of all poetry.

Product though he was of his age, Shakespeare bears the token of true artistic intelligence, in that he grew, learned, mellowed. In his more youthful production, tipsy with the wealth at his disposal, he riots in its prodigal spending. He thumps his target with the scattering discharges of a blunderbuss of words and images. As, to cite at haphazard:

> The gaudy, babbling and remorseful day
> Is crept into the bosom of the sea,
> And now loud-howling wolves arouse the jades
> That drag the tragic, melancholy night.[81]

That is bombast. It is wholly bad. Nothing is added to the main image by the volley of irrelevant epithets and subsidiary images —"babbling," "remorseful," "loud-howling wolves," "jades," "tragic melancholy." On the contrary, the main image is wholly obliterated under the dump of irrelevancies. The old jongleur, Cercamon, is immeasurably nearer to true poetry when he says simply:

> *Quan totz le segles breuneziz.*

The intended image is there, clear, picturesque, and vivid, as it is not in Shakespeare.

But at the turn of the century and of his life's maturity, Shakespeare, ripened and sobered, returns unto himself. Abandoning comedy and the pomp of patriotic chronicle-plays, where he had found free scope for his verbal abundance to play revel without overmuch concern for the emotional quality of poetry, he entered the period of the great tragedies. His advice to the players in Hamlet, not to tear passion to tatters, sounds very much like

self-rebuke, and a recantation of his too fond attachment to
Elizabethan exuberance. Othello says: "She was false as water,"
and the words are telling! But in *The Winter's Tale*, Shakespeare
had said:

> . . . false
> As o'er-dy'd blacks, as wind, as waters; false
> As dice are to be wish'd by one that fixes
> No bourn 'twixt his and mine.

The Shakespeare of the great tragic period, of Hamlet,
Othello, Lear, Macbeth, has banked and stilled the torrent of his
eloquence and thereby lifted it to a higher level. He has for the
most part, though not entirely, discarded his blunderbuss, and
hits the mark with a single level shot. He has accordingly grown
to an artistic stature which he had not previously attained. And
in that strange, almost inexplicable, farewell to art, *The Tempest*,
in which he breaks and buries his staff, and abjures his rough
magic, Shakespeare takes his place in the highest seats of poetry.

> We are such stuff
> As dreams are made on, and our little life
> Is rounded with a sleep.

And in the measure that he hardens to the spell of the Pe-
trarchizing version of troubadour tradition, Shakespeare dis-
closes an affinity to a purer form of that same tradition. He draws
very close to Dante:

> *La vostra nominanza è color d'erba*
> *Che viene e va.*[82]

> What is man,
> If his chief good and market of his time
> be but to sleep and feed? A beast, no more.[83]

That is poetry of the high order. The incisive edge of the brief exhortation of Ulysses to his aged companions, however, has an emotional and a dramatic poignancy which Hamlet's philosophical soliloquy has not:

> *Considerate la vostra semenza;*
> *Fatti non foste per vivere come bruti,*
> *Ma per sequir virtute e conoscenza.*[84]

> I have lived long enough: my way of life
> Is fallen into the sere, the yellow leaf.[85]

That is also great poetry. How its quality stands by the side of Dante's each must pronounce for himself.

> *Al poco giorno, ed al gran cerchio d'ombra*
> *Son giunto, lasso ! ed al bianchir de colli,*
> *Quando si perde lo color nell'erba.*[86]

> To the failing light and the great encircling shade
> I am now come, alas! and the greying of the hills,
> when in the verdure the colours fade.

The evolution whose main outlines have been sketched above constitutes a chapter of literary history. But literature is the blood of the mental life of humankind, which is transmitted from generation to generation. The conventions and idealizations of the poets, however removed they may appear from the real life of the time and from that of their authors, have had a profound effect on European civilization. The "courtesy" of twelfth-century Provence reappears in seventeenth and eighteenth century "gallantry"; it comes up again in the novel of the nineteenth century. Whatever the distance may be between literature and life, the written word sets a deep impress on the mind and the emotions of the human heart. Romantic feeling would never have existed had it not been sustained by novels and poetry. National psychology and social tradition are in a large measure the products of literature.

The emotions that spring from sex constitute a biological fact. They are independent, as regards their source, of all the conventions and principles laid down by the human spirit. The forms that these impulses assume, however, are sensitive in the highest degree to the influences expressed by literature. Literature and religion have often changed the aspect and character of such forms. The East and the West, the North and the South, display differences which appear to affect the very nature of the human heart and which have been set down to race, blood, or climate, but which are in a far greater degree the result of social traditions, conventions and habits of mind, transmitted by environment and diffused and perpetuated by the words of writers and poets.

Europe, at the dawn of its revival after the centuries of darkness which followed the collapse of the ancient world, underwent one of the most remarkable of such transformations. It would be necessary, in order to measure the extent of the change, to recall what were the ideas and feelings in Greek and Roman antiquity on the subject of women and love, what their character was in the barbaric world and finally how these topics are regarded by uncivilized and primitive people. Such a survey, which we have undertaken elsewhere and of which the present work only represents a fragment, would enable a just estimate to be reached of the ground covered by this "immensely far-ranging revolution" and this "new conception of love" for which the troubadours of Provence have long been praised.

The part they had in that revolution was, in reality, very indirect. It was not through the dialectical subtleties of courtly love nor through the so-called neo-platonism of the Italian poets and the Petrarchists that the change of feeling in question was brought about. It was imposed on European literature, on fiction and on poetry, by a power of quite another order of vehemence, persistence and authority: the power of the Church.

The Fathers of the Church regarded sexual love as the essence of sin and woman as "the gate of hell."[87] They accounted chastity more important than the doctrines of the Christian faith.[88] "The lightest stain upon our chastity," declared Tertullian, "is harder for us to bear than death."[89] "The kingdom of heaven," he said again, "is the home of eunuchs."[90] Origen castrated himself.[91] Saint Ambrose believed that the extinction of the human race was preferable to its propagation through sin.[92] "Married persons," he wrote elsewhere, "should blush for the state in which they live."[93] "Every woman," said Clement of Alexandria, "should be overwhelmed with shame at the thought that she is a woman."[94]

Extravagant and morbid as they may appear to us, those doctrines lie at the foundation of the attitudes, accounted moderate and reasonable, which are held by the average European and American in this respect. It is a subject which, as the philosopher Ibn Hazm of Cordova once said, "is often treated frivolously in jest, but may become a very serious and solemn matter." It is to the pressure which the doctrines of the Church Fathers exerted for centuries on European thought and literature, that the feelings and ethical canons of civilized nations owe the traits of character by which they are distinguished. They have effected a compromise between the brutal impulses of the savage and the ascetic frenzy of the imperious passion which disturbs the human mind; they have clothed love in a web woven of the light and graceful arabesque of poetry.

But has this expedient solved the problem? It would be rash to say so. The blind impulses of the great biological forces have not developed in view of conditions which are peculiar to the human race, the conditions, namely, of social life. Between those two factors, biological and social, irreducible contradictions exist which it is beyond the power of any compromise to reconcile. Yet, artificial as may be the idealizations which the lyrical and romantic spirit tried to impose upon passion, it cannot be contended that they are more so than any other adjustment of the dilemma which has hitherto been attempted by humanity. And they have at least made a leading contribution to the creation of the sublime fiction which the human spirit has cast, like a veil, over life, over its hideousness and misery, and which we call art. The troubadours called it joy and youth.

Appendix

Two fragments which were with Briffault's translation of *Les Troubadours* may be of some interest. Editors should have some qualms about the submission to public view and criticism of the rough drafts of a deceased author who might well have altered them considerably had he lived to put them in a form he deemed fit for print. This is especially so in the case of a fastidious author such as Briffault. His extensive revisions of *The Mothers*, even after it was in proof, came near to driving the publisher to distraction. The detailed revisions, and revisions upon revisions penned in the manuscript of *The Troubadours* indicate that after a quarter of a century he had changed little in this respect.

The first item appears to be an alternate, probably deleted, version of the passage on Shakespeare. The second, more interesting, item, which deals with the derivation of Dante's *"terza rima,"* exists in two versions. The one version appears to have been written as a result of inferences Briffault based on extrapolation, before he had been able to locate any examples of this form which predated Dante. Then later he must have located the cited examples, which confirmed his conjecture nicely, rewritten the passages to include them, and at the same time deleted the original suppositions on which the conjectures were based. Only the second passage is included here.

SHAKESPEARE

Shakespeare went to school with the Italianate sonneteers. It has sometimes been deplored that he was an Elizabethan. But his faculty, no less than his failings, is a product of his age, and had he written in any other we should not have known the quality that enthralls us. He appears to have been inspired with a genuine poetic ambition and to have had a sense of vocation. From the start he attained, with "the first heir of his invention," to universal favor. On the strength of *Venus and Adonis, Lucrece* and his first sonnets alone, Richard Barnsfield (1598) places his name among the immortals. He betters himself by court connections; he was well on the way to becoming the leading lyric and narrative poet of the age. Then a strange thing happened. We know nothing of the circumstances which led to his association with the stage. The rare signposts which help us to plot out the trend of his career fail us entirely at its critical turning-point. "Became stage-struck" is a phrase that recurs in comments; but there is no indication of such an outburst of enthusiasm; much rather the reverse. The successful poet, the "immortal," accepted hack-work, re-writes, odd, almost menial tasks, and even small parts on the boards. One conclusion only accords with the known traits of Shakespeare's character. To put it bluntly, he abandoned lyric poetry and took to the theater because it paid better. He commercialized his gift, quite in the same manner as the novelist of today who grinds out three books a year and buys a villa at Monte Carlo. The thought of Edmund Spenser dying of penury may not have been absent from his mind.

In the sixteenth century the theater sprang into sudden prominence in every country of Europe, in Italy, in Spain, in France, in England. Printing had revolutionized the conditions of literary diffusion; but books were still a privilege of the relatively well-to-do classes; they were out of reach of the great masses of the people. The medieval popular jongleur, once the universal provider of entertainment, had practically died out. More exactly, he had modified the form of his activities; he enacted, on the boards of fairs, thrilling scenes of miracle or murder, scraps of patriotic history, clowneries and buffooneries. The play was the thing which filled the gap in popular entertainment. The theater which thus sprang up had little connection, save in name, with Greek drama or even Roman comedy. It was a form of entertainment which supplied a popular need.

THE TERZA RIMA

The derivation of Dante's *terza rima* has been much discussed, and to little purpose. Some have thought that he invented it. But the *terza rima* was current in popular Italian poetry. The following example is from the early twelfth century, and in Cremonese dialect:

> *Noioso sun et canto di noio*
> *che mi fa la ria gente noiosa.*
> *Io vedo l'uomo, come l'è più croio*
> *tanto elege vita più grecosa*
> *in vestire, in parlare de rigoio*
> *et in fare ogni consa disdignosa.*

> > Gherardo Petecchio, "Frotula noie moralis," cited by G. Lipparini, i, p. 48. Cf.p. 34. Cf. iv, p. 26. Ctrambolli per Tisbe.

The close affinity of early Italian popular poetry with the *zajal* form has already been noted. It is manifest in the following anonymous piece:

> *E la mia donna zogliosa*
> *vidi con altre danzare.*

> *Vidili con allegranza*
> *la sovrana de la belle,*

che di gioi' menava danza
di maritate e pulcelle.
La'nde presi gran baldanza
tuttor danzando con elle:
ben rassembla piú che stella
lo so viso a reguardare.

> (*Ibid.*, p. 125) Cf. iv, p. 28. Giovanni Dominici
> (1356-1419) "Di', Maria dolce."

But Provençal poetry, and that of all Romance languages, introduced from an early date a variation in the *zajal* model. Each line
of the latter, save the concluding one of the strophe, employed
the same rhyme. The Arabic language being almost destitute of
tonic accent, each syllable being uttered with equal emphasis, no
opportunity was lost in Arabic poetry of stressing the beat of the
rhyme by repetition of the same rhyme. Romance languages, on
the contrary, are rich in tonic variations. The hammer-like beat-
ing of time on one rhyme is needless, and was rightly regarded as
not altogether pleasant. Hence Romance poets preferred an al-
ternation of rhymes, either in couplets or interwoven. In popular
Italian poetry, that interwoven poetry in sets of three lines appears, by no means uncommonly, if allowance is made for the
dearth of documents. Dante did not invent the *terza rima*, nor
did he evolve it by variation on the virtuosity of the more sophis-
ticated troubadours. He found it ready to his hand in popular
Italian poetry.

Bibliography

'Abd Al-Wahid Ibn 'Ali, al Marrakushi. *Histoire des Almohades,* trans. and annot. E. Fagnan. Algiers, 1893.

Alfonsi, Petrus. *Disciplina Clericalis.* 1854. See Migne, J. P. *Patrologiae Cursus Completus, etc.* Vol. 157, 1844.

Alpetragius. *Planetarum theoria,* trans. Calo Calonymos. Venice, 1531.

Alphonse de Liguori. *The Glories of Mary,* trans. R. A. Coffin, London, 1868.

Altamira y Crevea, R. *Historia de España y de la civilización española.* 4 vols. Barcelona, 1900-11.

Amari, M. *Storia dei Musulmani di Sicilia.* 2nd ed. Catania, 1933.

Amir, Ali, Rt. Hon. Maulawi Saiyid. *A Short History of the Saracens.* London, 1899, 1921.

Ancona A. di, and Comparetti, D. *Le Antiche rime volgari.* 5 vols. Bologna, 1875-88.

Andraud, P. *La Vie et l'oeuvre du troubadour Raimon de Miravel, étude sur la littérature et la société méridionale à la veille de la guerre des Albigeois.* Paris, 1902.

Andrés, Juan. *Dell' origine, progressi e stato attuale d'ogni letteratura.* 8 vols. Parma, 1782-1822.

Anglade, J. *Histoire sommaire de la littérature méridionale au moyen âge, des origines à la fin du XVᵉ siècle.* Paris, 1921.

————. *Le Troubadour Guiraut Riquier, étude sur la décandence de l'ancienne poésie provençale.* Paris, 1905.

————, ed. *Les Poésies de Peire Vidal,* Paris, 1913.

————. *Les Troubadours, leurs vies-leurs oeuvres-leur influence.* Paris, 1908.

Appel, C. *Bernart von Ventadorn, seine Lieder mit Einleitung und Glossar.* Halle, 1915.

————. *Provenzalische Chrestomathie. Mit Abriss der Formenslehre und Glossar.* Leipzig, 1895.

Aubri de Trois-Fontaines. *Alberici Monachi Trium Fontium Chronicon.* Hanover, 1698.

Audiau, J. *Les Troubadours et l'Angleterre. Contribution à l'étude des poètes anglais de l'amour de 1250 à 1400.* 2nd. ed. Paris, 1921.

Barbieri, Giammaria. *Dell' origine della poesia rimata.* Modena, 1571.

Baret, Eugène. *Les Troubadours et leur influence sur la littérature du Midi de l'Europe: Avec des extraits et des pièces rares ou inédites.* 3rd ed. (of *Espagne et Provence*). Paris, 1867.

Bartsch, K. *Chrestomathie provençale.* Elberfeld, 1868.

Bédier, J. *Les Légendes épiques: Recherches sur la formation des chansons de geste.* 4 vols. Paris, 1908-13.

Bédier, J. and P. Hazard. *Histoire illustrée de la littérature française.* 2 vols. Paris, 1923-24.

Bembo, P. *Prose scelte; Degli asolani; Della volgar lingua; Lettere scelte di Pietro Bembo, con profazione del Francesco Costero,* ed. E. Sozogno. Milan, 1880.

Besly, J. (the Elder). *Histoire des comtes de Poictou et ducs de Guyenne; contenant ce qui s'est passé de plus memorable en France, depuis l'an 811, jusques au roi Louis le Jeune,* ed. J. Besly, the Younger. 2 vols. Paris, 1647, 1840.

Birch-Hirschfield, A. *Ueber die den provenzalischen Troubadours des XII und XIII Jahrhunderts bekannten epische Stoffe.* Halle a. S., 1878.

Blunt, Anne and Wilfrid. *The Seven Golden Odes of Pagan Arabia.* London, 1903.

Boccaccio, G. *Vita di Dante Alighieri.* Rome, 1544.

Boeddeker, K. *Altenglische Dichtungen des MS. Harl(eian) 2253.* 1878.

Braga, Th. *Cancioneiro portuguez da Vaticana. Ediçao critica restituida sobre o texto diplomatico de Halle, acompanhada de um glossario e de uma introducçao sobre os trovadores e cancioneiros portugueses.* Lisbon, 1878.

Brechillet Jourdain, A. L. M. M. *Recherches critiques sur l'âge et l'origine des traductions d'Aristote et sur des commentaires grecs ou arabes employées par les docteurs scolastiques.* Paris, 1819.

Brockelman, C. *Geschichte der arabischen Literatur.* 2 vols. Weimar, Berlin, 1898 [1897]-1902.

Canello, U. A. *La Vita e le opere del trovatore Arnaldo Daniello.* Halle, 1883.

Carducci, G. *Cantilene, ballate e strambotti.* Pisa, 1871.

Cartier, J. *Bref Récit et succinct narration de la navigation faict en MDXXXV et MDXXXVI.* Paris, 1654. Facsimile reprint, 1863.

Casiri, M. *Bibliotheco arabico-hispana escurialenses, sive librorum omnium mss. quas Arabice ab auctoribus magnam partem Arabo-Hispanis compositos biblioteca. Coenobi Escurialensis complectitur, recensio and explanatio.* 2 vols. 1760, 1770.

Caussin de Perceval. *Essai sur l'histoire des Arabes avant l'islamisme et jusqu'à la réduction de toutes les tribus sous la loi musulmane.* 3 vols. Paris, 1847-48.

Cedrenus, Georgius. *Georgii Cedreni Annales, siue Historial ab exordio mundi ad Isacium comnenum usque compendium.* Basel, 1566.

Cercamon. See Jeanroy, A.

"Cesarius of Heisterbach," in D. C. Munro, ed., *Medieval Sermon Stories.* Philadelphia, 1901.

Chabaneau, C. "Biographies des troubadours," in Claude de Vic, *Histoire générale de Languedoc.* Vol. 10 (1880). Paris, 1872-1893.

Chabaneau, C., and Anglade, A. See Jean de Notredame.

Chambers, E. D. and Sidgewick, F. *Early English Lyrics, Amorous, Divine, Moral and Trivial.* London, 1907.

Champollion-Figeac, J. J. *Hilarius, a writer of Latin Verse in France. Hilarii versus et ludi.* Paris, 1838.

Chavarri, E. L. See López Chavarri, E.

Chaytor, H. J. *The Troubadours and England.* Cambridge, 1923.

de Coincy, Gautier. *Miracles de la Sainte Vierge.* Paris, 1857.

Coleridge, S. T. *Notes and Lectures upon Shakespeare and Some of the Old Poets and Dramatists with Other Literary Remains,* ed. Mrs. H. Coleridge. 2 vols. London, 1849.

Coulet, J. *Le Troubadour Guilhem Montanhagol.* Toulouse, 1898.

Crescini, Guilhem Figuiero. *Manualetto provenzale.* Verona, Padova, 1892. *Manuale per avviamento agli studi provenzali . . .* 3rd ed. Milan, 1926.

Crescimbeni, G. *L'Istoria della volgare poesia.* Rome, 1698.

Dadin de Hautesserre (Dadinus Altserra). *Rerum aquitanarum libri quinque, in quibus Vetus Aquitania illustratur.* Toulouse, 1648.

Dante. *La Divina Commedia.* Florence, 1840-42.

Dejeanne, J. M. L. See Marcabru.

Diez, F. *Die Poesie der Troubadours.* 2nd ed. Leipzig, 1883.

———. *Leben und Werken der Troubadours.* 2nd ed. Leipzig, 1882.

Döllinger, J. J. *Beiträge zur Sektengeschichte des Mittelalters.* Munich, 1890.

Dozy, R. P. A. *Historia Abbadidarum, praemissus scriptorum Arabum de la dynastica locis nunc primum editis.* (*Scriptorum Arabum loci de Abbadido.*) 2 vols. Lugduni Batavorum, 1846-52.

———. *Histoire de Musulmans d'Espagne, jusqu'à la conquête de l'Andalousie par les Almoravides,* 711-1110. 4 vols. Leiden, 1861.

———. *Recherches sur l'histoire politique et littéraire de l'Espagne pendant le moyen âge.* 3rd ed. 2 vols. Paris, Leiden, 1881.

Dryden, J. *Dramatic Essays.* 1912. Reissued London, New York, 1954. (Everyman's Library no. 568.)

Dumont, J. *De la versification latine en Anjou pendant les XIe et XIIe siècles.* Angers, 1865.

Ermengaud, Matfré. *Lo Breviari d'amor,* ed. G. Azais. 2 vols. Béziers, Paris, 1862-81.

Eusebius. See Seyssel, C. de.

Faral, E. *Les Jongleurs en France au moyen âge.* Paris, 1910.

Farmer, H. G. *Studies in Oriental Musical Instruments.* London, 1931.

Ferrai, Maria. *La Poesia amorosa nei migliori poeti del dolce stil nuovo. Guido Guinicelli, Guido Cavalcanti, Dante Alighieri, Cino La Pistoia.* Siena, 1900.

Ferri, G. *Laude di frate Jacopone da Todi secondo la stampa florentina del 1490.* [Documenti di storia letteraria]. 1910.

Fetis, F. J. *Histoire générale de la musique depuis les temps les plus anciens.* 5 vols. Paris, 1869-76.

Ford, Ford Madox. (pseud. H. M. Hueffer). *Provence. From Minstrels to the Machine.* Philadelphia, London, 1935.

Foxwell, A. K., ed. *The Poems of Sir Thomas Wiat.* London, 1913.

Gaspary, A. *Die sicilianische Dichterschule des dreizehnsten Jahrhunderts.* Berlin, Leipzig, 1878.

———. *La Scuola poetica siciliana del secolo XIII,* trans. Leghorn, 1882.

Gaufridi, Jean de. See Jean de Gaufridi.

Gérard de Crémone et Jean de Séville (Johannes Hispalensis), *Liber aggregationibus scientiae stellarum.*

Gérold, Théodore. *La Musique au moyen âge (Les Classiques français du moyen âge).* Paris, 1932.

Gibb, E. J. W. *History of Ottoman Poetry.* London, 1900.

Gidel, C. A. *Les Troubadours et Pétrarque.* Angers, 1857.

González Palencia, Cándido Angel. *Historia de la literatura arábigo-española.* Barcelona, Buenos Aires, 1928.

Grangeret de Lagrange, Jean Baptiste André. *Anthologie arabe, ou choix de poésies arabes inédites, traduites pour la première fois en français, et accompagnées d'observations critiques et littéraires.* Paris, 1828.

Gröber, Gustav. *Grundriss der romanische Philologie.* 2 vols. Strassburg, 1888.

Guillaume de Saint Pathus. *Vie de Saint Louis, par le confesseur de la reine Marguerite.* 1761.

Guillaume de Tudèle. *La Chanson de la croisade contre les Albigeois,* ed. P. Meyer, 2 vols. Paris, 1875-79.

Guittone d'Arezzo. *Rime.* 2 vols. Florence, 1828.

Guizot, F. P. G. *Collection des mémoires rélatifs à l'histoire de France depuis la fondation de la monarchie française jusqu'au 13ᵉ siècle; avec une introduction, des suppléments et des notes.* Paris, 1823-35.

Hartmann, M. *Das arabische Strophengedicht.* Leipzig, 1896, etc.

Hawkins, John. *"A General History of the Science and Practice of Music."* 5 vols. London, 1776.

Hoffmann, K. *Joufray's altfranzösisches Rittergedicht.* Halle, 1880.

Ibn Khaldūn. *Prolégomènes historiques d'Ibn Khaldoun,* trans. Baron W. M. de Slane. 2 parts. Paris, 1862.

Jean de Gaufridi. *Histoire de Provence.* 2 vols. Aix, 1694.

Jean de Notredame. *Vies des plus célèbres et anciens poètes provençaux,* ed. C. Chabaneau and J. Anglade. Paris, 1913.

Jeanroy, A. *Les Chansons de Jaufré Rudel.* Paris, 1915.

———. ed. *Les Chansons de Guillaume IX., duc d'Aquitaine (1011-1127). (Les Classiques français du moyen âge).* 1913.

———. *Les Origines de la poésie lyrique en France au moyen-âge: Etude de littérature française et comparée, suivre de textes inédits.* Paris, 1889.

———. *Les poésies de Cercamon.* Paris, 1922.

Jebb, S. *Fratres Roger Bacon - - - Opus Majus ad Clementum quartum pontificen Romanum.* London, 1733.

Joinville, J. *Histoire de Saint Louis. Credo et lettre à Louis X. Texte original, accompagné d'une traduction par N. Wailly.* Paris, 1874.

Jubinal, Achille. *Nouveau recueil de contes, dits, fabliaux et autres pièces inédites du XIIIᵉ, XIVᵉ, et XVᵉ siècles pour faire suite aux collections de Legrand d'Aussy, Barbazan et Meon.* 2 vols. Paris, 1839-42.

Klein, O. ed. *Die Dichtungen des Mönchs von Montaudon.* 1885.
Koken, C. J. G. W. *Guittones von Arezzo, Dichtung und sein Verhaltniss zu Guinicelli von Bologna.* Leipzig, 1886.
Kolsen, A. *Beiträge zur alt provenzalischen Lyrik (42 erstmalig bearbeitete Dichtungen).* Florence, 1939.
Lafiteau, Jean-Baptiste. *Moeurs des sauvages amériquains comparées aux moeurs des premiers temps.* 2 vols. Paris, 1724.
Langfors, Arthur. *Les Chansons de Guilhem de Cabestanh.* Paris, 1924.
Langland, William. *The Vision of Piers Plowman,* ed. W. W. Skeat. Oxford, 1886.
Lea, H. C. *A History of the Inquisition in the Middle Ages.* 3 vols. London, 1888.
LeJeune, Paul. *Relation de ce que s'est passé en la nouvelle France en . . . 1633. Envoyée au . . . Provincial de la Compagnie de Jésus.* 1634.
Levi, Ezio. *Poesia di popolo e poesia di corte nel trecento.* Leghorn, 1915.
López Chavarri, *Música popular española.* Barcelona, Buenos Aires, 1927.
Lowinski, V. *Zum geistlichen Kunstlied.* Berlin, 1898.
Lucka, E. *Die drei Stufen der Erotik.* Berlin and Leipzig, 1924.
─────. *The Evolution of Love,* trans., London, 1922.
Luederitz, A. *Du Liebestheorien der Provenzalen bei den Minnesaenger der Staufzeit. Eine literarhistorische Untersuchung.* Weimar, 1897.
Mahn, C. A. F. *Die Werke der Troubadours, in provenzalischer Sprache, mit einer Grammatik und einem Worterbuch.* 5 vols. Berlin, 1846-86.
─────. *Gedichte der Troubadours in provenzalischer Sprache.* 4 vols. Berlin, 1856-73.
al-Makkari. *The History of the Mohammedan Dynasties in Spain, Extracted from the Nafku-t-tib min ghosni-l-andalusi-r-rattib wa tarikh Lisana-d-Din Ibni-l-Khattib, by Mohammed al-Makkari, a native of Telemsan,* trans. P. de Gayangos y Arce. 2 vols. London, 1840-43.
Marcabru. *Poésies complètes,* ed. J. M. L. Dejeanne. Bibliothèque Méridionale, Vol. XII. Toulouse, 1909.
Mariana, Juan de. *Historia general de España.* 20 vols. Madrid, 1817-22.

Massignon, L. F. J. *Al-Hallaj, Martyr mystique de l'Islam* . . . *Etude d'histoire religieuse, etc.* 2 vols. Paris, 1922.

Mayans y Siscar, Gregorio. *Orígenes de la lengua española.* 2 vols. Madrid, 1737.

Menéndez y Pelayo, M. *Antologia de poetas líricos castellanos desde la formación del idioma hasta nuestros días.* 13 vols. (Biblioteca Clásica) Madrid, 1890-1908.

Menéndez y Pidal, R. *Poesía juglaresca y juglares.* Madrid, 1924.

du Méril, E. *Theatri liturgici quae Latina superstant monumenta edita recensuit, inedita vulgavit, annotationibus illustravit E. du Méril. Origines latines du théâtre moderne.* Cadomi, 1849.

Meyer, P. See Guillaume de Tudèle.

——. *Recueil d'anciens textes bas-latins, provençaux et français accompagnés de deux glossaires.* Paris, 1874-77.

Migne. *Patrologia Cursus Completus bibliotheca universalis . . . omnium S. S. Patrum, Doctorum, Scriptorumque ecclesiasticorum qui ab aevo apostolica ad usque Innocenti iii tempora floruerent . . .* Series (Latina) prima. Accurante, 221 vols., Paris, 1857-1912. Series Graeca, 162 vols., Paris, 1857-1912.

Mila y Fontenals. *De los trobadores en España.* Barcelona, 1861.

Monaci, E. *Crestomazia dei primi secoli, con prospetto delle flessione grammatticale e glossario.* Citta di Castello, 1912.

Morandi, L. *Antologia della nostra critica letteraria moderna.* Citta di Castello, 1893.

Munk, S. *Mélanges de philosophie juive et arabe.* Paris, 1857.

Nicholson, R. A. *A Literary History of the Arabs.* London, 1914.

——. *The Mystics of Islam.* London, 1914.

——. *Studies in Islamic Mysticism.* Cambridge, 1921.

Nostradamus. See Jean de Notredame.

Nykl, A. R. *El cancionero del seih, nobilisimo Visir, Maravilla del tiempo, Abu Bakr, ibn 'abd-al-Malik Aben Guzmán-Ibn Quzman,* ed. with Spanish trans. of selected extracts. Madrid, 1933.

——. *A Book Containing the Risala Known as The Dove's Neck-Ring, About Love and Lovers, Composed by Abu Muhammed 'Ali ibn Hazm al-Andalusi.* Paris, 1931.

Nyrop, C. *Storia dell'epopea francese. nel medio evo,* trans. Egidio Gorra. Turin, 1888.

Ordericus Vitalis. "Historia ecclesiastica" in A. Du Chesne, *Historiae Normannorum Scriptores antiqui.* Lutetiae, Paris, 1619.

Ozanam. *Les poètes franciscains en Italie au XIIIe siècle*, trans. from Italian. Paris, 1852.

Palacios, Asín. *Abenhazam de Córdoba y su historia crítica de las ideas religiosas.* Madrid, 1927.

———. *Aben massara y su escuela.* Madrid, 1914.

———. *La escatología musulmana en la Divina Comedia.* Madrid, 1919.

Paris, Gaston. *Histoire poétique de Charlemagne.* Paris, 1865.

———. *La Poésie du moyen âge. Leçons et lectures.* 6th ed. Paris, 1906.

———. *Mélanges de littérature française du moyen âge.* Paris, 1912.

———. *Poèmes et légendes du moyen âge.* Paris, 1900.

Pätzold. *Die individuellen Eigenthumlichkeiten einiger herrvoragender Troubadours in Minneliede.* Marburg, 1882.

Petrarch. *Epistolae.* Basel, 1554.

Pierre de Vaux-de-Cernay. "Historia Albigensium et sacri belli in eos suscepti," in M. Bouquet, *Recueil des historiens des Gaules et de la France*, Vol. XIX. Paris, 1722.

Pulci, Luigi. *Morgante maggiori.* Florence, 1482.

Puy-Laurens, Guillaume de. *Chronique de Guillaume de Puy-Laurens, contenant l'histoire de l'expédition des Français contre les Albigeois*, trans. from Latin to French by F. R. B. Guizot, 1823 (orig. 1636).

Quadrio, F. S. *Della storia e della ragione d'ogni poesia volumi quattro.* 5 vols. Bologna, Milan, 1739-52.

Quatremère, E. H. *Mélanges d'histoire et de philologie orientale.* Paris, 1861.

Quiller-Couch, Sir Arthur. *On the Art of Writing.* Cambridge, 1916.

Rajna, P. *I reali di Francia.* Bologna, 1863.

Raynouard, F. J. M. *Choix de poésies originales des troubadours.* 6 vols. Paris, 1816-21.

Renan, J. E. *Averroès et l'averroïsme, essai historique.* Paris, 1852.

———. *Histoire générale et système comparé des langues sémitiques* - - - *Première partie. Histoire générale des langues sémitiques.* Paris, 1855. 5th ed., Paris, 1878.

Renart, J. *Galeran de Bretagne: Roman de XIIIe siècle.* Paris, 1925.

Ribera Tarrago, Julian. *Disertaciones y opúsculos. Edición colectiva que en su jubilación del profesorado le ofrecen sus discípulos y amigos, 1887-1927. Con una introducción de M. Asín Palacios.* 2 vols. Madrid, 1928.

————. *La enseñanza entre los musulmanes españoles.* Zaragoza, 1893.

————. *Música de las cántigas (of Alphonso X, King of Castile and Leon).* 2 parts. Madrid, 1922.

Ribot, T. *La Psychologie des sentiments.* Paris, 1896.

Richard, A. *Histoire des comtes de Poitou 778-1204.* 2 vols. Paris, 1903.

Ruckert, F. *Die Verwandlungen des Abu Seid Von Serug, oder Die Makamen des Hariri.* 3rd. ed. 2 vols. Stuttgart and Tubingen, 1844.

Ruffhead, O. *The Life of Alexander Pope . . . With a critical essay on his writings and genius.* London, 1769.

Ruiz, Juan. *El libro de buen amor.* Edición prologo y notas de Alfonso Reyes. Madrid, 1917.

de Sade, l'abbé. *Mémoires de la vie de Pétrarque.* Amsterdam, 1764-67.

Saige, M. J. J. G. *Les Juifs du Languedoc antérieurement au XIV siècle.* Paris, 1881.

Salvador-Daniel. *La Musique arabe.* Algiers, 1863.

Salverda de Grave, J. J. *Le Troubadour Bertran d'Alamanon.* Toulouse, 1902.

de Sandoval, P. *Crónica del ínclito emperador de España, Alonso VII . . . sacada de un libro muy antigo escrito de mano . . . par relación de los mismos que lo vieron, etc.* Madrid, 1600.

Schack, A. F. Von. *Poesie und Kunst der Araber in Spanien und Sizilien.* 2 vols. Stuttgart, 1877.

Scherer, W. *Geschichte der deutschen Literatur.* Berlin, 1883.

Schmidt, C. G. A. *Histoire et doctrine de la secte des Cathares ou Albigeois.* 2 vols. Paris, 1849.

Schofield, W. H. *English Literature from the Norman Conquest to Chaucer.* London, 1906.

Seyssel, C. de, trans. *L'Histoire ecclésiastique d'Eusèbe.* Paris, 1532.

Silvestre de Sacy, Baron A. J. *Traité élémentaire de la prosodie et de l'art métrique des Arabes.* Paris, 1831.

Simonde de Sismondi, J. C. L. *Histoire de la littérature du Midi de l'Europe.* 4 vols. Paris, 1813.

de Slane, W. M. See Ibn Khaldun.

Stimmung, A. *Bertram de Born; sein Leben und seine Werke.* Halle, 1879.

————. *Seconde Biographie de Bertram de Born.* Halle, 1892.

Stronski, S. *Le Troubadour Folquet de Marseille.* Cracow, 1910.

Tassoni, A. *Considerazione sopra le rime del Petrarca . . . col confronto di luoghi de' poeti antichi di vari tempi.* Modena, 1609.

Tharaud, Jérôme and Jean. *Marrakech; ou Les seigneurs de l'Atlas.* Paris, 1920.

Thomas. *Le Roman de Tristan,* ed. J. Bédier. (Soc. des anciens textes français). Paris, 1902-05.

Tiraboschi, G. *Storia della letteratura italiana.* 11 vols. Modena, 1772. 95.

Viardot. *Histoire des Arabes et des Mores d'Espagne, traitant de la constitution du peuple arabe-espagnol, de sa civilisation, de ses moeurs et de son influence sur la civilisation moderne.* 2 vols. Paris, 1851.

Vincent de Beauvais. *Speculum historiale.* Douai, 1624.

Weinhold, K. *Die deutschen Frauen in dem Mittelalter.* 2 vols. Vienna, 1882.

Zenker, R. *Die Gedichte des Folquet von Romans.* Halle, 1896.

Zuccolo, Lodovico. *Discorso delle ragione del numero del verso italiano.* Venice, 1623.

Notes

I. INTRODUCTION

1. "The lack of originality among the poets of northern France has frequently been noted, at least insofar as the *chanson d'amour* is concerned. The sentiments they express, the manner of presenting them, the style, the stanzaic structures of their poems, are all copied from the troubadours."—Théodore Gérold, *La Musique au moyen âge*, p. 169.

"The art of the singers of the south burst forth in the chateaus of Flanders, of Burgundy, of Champagne . . . These love songs were copied and translated by our northern minstrels, and from these translations they frequently went on to more-or-less free imitations."—Paulin Paris, in *Histoire littéraire de la France*, Vol. XXIII, p. 519.

"This ancient French lyrical poetry, such as it was developed in this period, is the complete complement of that of Provence, to which it is related in form and content. The similarity can be found in the most casual elements of the composition."—J. Bédier and P. Hazard, *Histoire illustrée de la littérature française*, Vol. I, p. 28.

"The courtly poetry of the lands of the *langue d'oui,* and particularly their lyrical poetry, are largely in debt to the poetry of the troubadours. The amorous poetry of the north is considerably inferior to its southern sister . . . with respect to their degree of finesse and variety of ideas, as well as their elegance of expression."—Paul Meyer, in *Romania*, XIX, 1890, pp. 42, 7.

2. J. Anglade, ed., *Les poésies de Peire Vidal*, pp. 118 and iv.

3. C. Appel, ed., *Bernart von Ventadorn*, No. xxvi. Appel put

Bernard's visit in the year 1155 and thought that he went to England for the coronation of Henry II. *Ibid.*, lvi ff.

4. The author of *Roman de Joufroy* writes:

Uns dancheus qui l'alait querant
est venus a Londres errant.
Marchabruns ot non li messages
qui molt par fu corteis e sages.
Trovere fu molt de gran pris.
Bien le conuit li rois Henris
qu'assez l'ot en sa cort veu . . .
"Bien vegnanz, fait li rois Henris,
Marchabruns, soiez el pais."

A squire who went to seek him came to London without delay; he was remarkably courteous and well-mannered, and he was a *trouvère* of considerable merit. Indeed King Henry recognized him, for he had seen him frequently at his court. "Be welcome in our country, Marcabru," King Henry told him.

(K. Hoffmann, *Joufray's altfranzösisches Rittergedicht,* Halle, 1880, verses 3599 ff.). Queen Matilda, wife of Henry I, was renowned as a patroness of poets.

In the thirteenth century, Savaric de Mauleon, another troubadour, lived in England. Jean de Nostredame called him "The Englishman." Jean de Nostredame, *Les Vies des plus célèbres et anciens poètes provençaux*, ed. C. Chabaneau and J. Anglade, p. 66.

5. Jean de Gaufridi, *Histoire de Provence* (1684), Vol. I, p. 101. Jean, Duke of Brabant, who was present, indulged in the composition of some poems in Provençal. *Histoire litteraire de la France,* Vol. IX, p. 177.

6. A. Luderitz, *Die Liebestheorien der Provenzalen bei den Minnesaenger der Staufzeit,* 1904; K. Bartsch, *Deutsche Liederdichter;* K. Bartsch in *Zeitschrift für deutsches Alterthum,* Vol. XI, pp. 145-162. The minnesinger Rodolphe de Neuchâtel translated one of Peire Vidal's poems (J. Anglade, ed., *Les Poésies de Peire Vidal,* No. XXVIII). "The direct imitation of the Provençal and the French Muses only lasted a short while," said Bartsch, "but the indirect imprint of Romance lyric art on that of Germany remained profound. This imprint penetrates German thought and its epic form in structure

and spirit. The sentiments related to sexual relations were to show this influence for a long time to come." (*Liederdichte*, pp. ix ff.) The German poets of a later epoch came to ridicule the courtly conventions, and Walther von der Vogelweide, the greatest and the last of the minnesingers, expressly rejected the influence of the troubadours, but his works nevertheless show their influence very clearly.

7. H. J. Chaytor, *The Troubadours and England;* W. H. Schofield, *English Literature from the Norman Conquest to Chaucer;* Jean Audiau, *Les Troubadours et l'Angleterre.*

"It is evident that English lyric poetry is greatly indebted to the troubadours . . . Every study of English stanza forms must take the Provençal lyric art as its point of departure."—Chaytor, p. 135.

"The influence of the troubadours on the English poets has been as real as their influence on any other European literature."—Audiau, p. 129.

"The second half of the twelfth century . . . already acknowledges the establishment under Provençal influence of that official *chanson d'amour* or *chanson courtois*, which ultimately succeeded in impressing itself upon the imagination of the Renaissance no less than upon that of the Middle Ages, and may be said to have fixed the type of literary romantic sentiment, from the *Canzionere* of Petrarch to *The Angel in the House* . . . The moment is fundamental for the understanding of all subsequent literature in England as well as in France."—F. K. Chambers, p. 281.

8. Owen Ruffhead, "Life of Pope," p. 425.

9. John Dryden, "Dramatic Essays" (ed. *Everyman*, p. 274).

10. "Pro se vero argumentatur alia, scilicet *oc*, quod vulgares eloquentes in ea primitus poetati sunt tamquam in perfectiori dulciorique loquela."—Dante, *De vulgari eloquentia*, I, x.

"At the time that it flourished the Provençal language was held in esteem throughout the western countries, and held by far the highest place among all languages. So that every man, be he French, Flemish, Gasconian, Burgundian, or of any other nationality, who desired to write well, especially in verse, would write in the Provençal language, whether or no he was a Provençal."—P. Bembo, *Della volgare lingua*, ed. Sonzogno, pp. 150 f.

"All of the pre-sixteenth century schools of courtly lyric derive, directly or indirectly, from that brief flowering of that art which appeared in Languedoc."—M. Menéndez y Pelayo, *Antologia des poetas liricos castellanos,* Vol. I, p. lxxviii.

11. The language of the troubadours is not the dialect of any given district, but was formed by the adoption of words and phrases from all dialectical varieties found from Aragon to Limousin. It was thus a composite literary language, what the older critics called a "no-language," and the Greeks, who frequently employed such super-dialectical blends, called "common" language. In much the same manner Chaucer eked out the insufficiencies of London English by drawing upon northern, Kentish, and western dialects. Troubadour speech is closely related to the Galician and Catalan of the period.

12. J. Anglade, *Les Poésies de Peire Vidal*, p. 60.

13. Bertram de Born, *Poésies,* ed. A. Stimmung, *Romainsche Bibliothek*, Vol. VIII (Halle, 1892), p. 140.

14. U. A. Canello, *La Vita e le opere del trovatore Arnaldo Daniello* (Halle, 1883), p. 105 f.

15. Gaston Paris, *Histoire poétique de Charlemagne*, p. 150.

16. *The Art of Writing.* Lecture IX.

17. C. Appel, ed., *Bernart von Ventadorn*, p. 220.

18. Dante, *Vita nuova*, xxv. In the *Convito* (I, ix) Dante adds that likewise, "many noble princes, barons and knights" did not know Latin. Count Guilhem de Poitiers, the originator of courtly poetry, knew only very little Latin (A. Richard, *Histoire des comtes de Poitou*, Vol. I, p. 444), "only enough to say his prayers" (A. R. Nykl, *The Dove's Neck-Ring*, p. cix, n. 16).

19. K. Weinhold, *Die deutschen Frauen in dem Mittelalter*, p. 188.

20. G. Schoepperle, *Tristan and Isolt*, Vol. II, p. 439.

21. Raymond d'Agyles, *Histoire des Francs qui ont pris Jérusalem,* in Guizot, *Collection des mémoires relatifs à l'histoire de France*, Vol. XXI, p. 144. The use of the term "Provençal" to indicate the literature of the lands of the *langue d'oc* became widespread only in the thirteenth century. Probably this usage was due to the Italians, who found it natural to designate all of that literature by reference to the region which was nearest Italy and with which it had the most intimate relations.

22. A. Jeanroy, in *Revue des Deux-Mondes*, Jan. 1899, p. 351. "In spite of some similarities between the two forms of poetry it does not appear that there was any contact either direct or indirect, between the two."—J. Anglade, *Sommaire de la littérature méridionale au moyen âge*, p. 20.

In this respect, Renan shared the ideas current in his academic milieu: "As for the literary and moral influences, they have been greatly exaggerated; neither Provençal poetry nor chivalry owed any-thing to the Moslems. There was an abyss which separated the form and the spirit of Romance poetry from the form and the spirit of Arabic poetry; there is no proof that the Christian poets were aware of the existence of Arabic poetry, and one can assert that if they were, they were incapable of understanding its language and spirit."— *Histoire des langues sémitiques,* p. 397.

Although carrying all of the assurance on which the authority of a great scholar rests, this affirmation is grossly in error. Had Renan forgotten the oft-cited declaration of Bishop Alvarez of Cordova? "A large number of people compose poems in Arabic, which by their elegance, surpass those of the Arabs themselves" (*Indiculus luminosus,* in Migne, *Patrologia latina,* Vol. CXXI, col. 566), an assertion confirmed by Al-Maqqari, who reproduced a copy of these poems which Christian poets had composed in Arabic. A manuscript of ecclesiastical decrees at Madrid contains a dedication in Arabic verse by a priest named Vincent (A. González Palencia, *Historia de la literatura arábigo-española,* p. 272 f.). King Alphonse, the Wise, who had one of the pleasantest of the Arab fantasies diffused throughout European literature, the tale of the statue and the ring; his brother, Fadriquez, who was the author of the *Libro de los engaños et los asaiamentos de las mujeres;* Duns Scotus, who was a poet as well as a theologian, were all familiar with Arabic poetry.

Juan Ruiz, Archpriest of Hita, the most illustrious of the medieval Spanish poets, knew Arabic poetry well and imitated it (Menéndez y Pelayo, *Estudios de crítica literaria,* 2 da Serie, p. 390; J. Fitzmaurice-Kelly, in *Encyclopaedia Britannica,* 14th ed., 1938, Vol. XXI, p. 155). The *Poema de Yuçuf,* entirely Arabic in inspiration, is the work of an Aragonese poet who used Arabic characters when he wrote in his native language (Fitzmaurice-Kelly, *loc. cit.*). In one of the most widely circulated books of the Middle Ages, the *Disciplina clericalis,* which was translated into all of the European languages, Petrus Alphonsi attests that Arabic poetry was available to everyone after 1106 (ed. Paris, 1824, p. 6). The author of *Averroès et l' averroïsme* could not have been unaware of the fact that Ibn-Roschd, in his commentary on Aristotle's *Poetique,* presented the rules of Arabic prosody.

Petrarch wrote: "As for Arabic poets, I am well acquainted with them" (*Epistolae,* Bâle, 1554, Vol. II, p. 904). Whatever faults may be attributed to the author of this declaration, he was neither an idle boaster nor a liar. Renan, however, wanted to contradict him with a lie: "How could Petrarch have known Arabic poetry?" he wrote, and he returned to his assertion: "The Middle Ages had not the slightest notion of it" (*Averroès et l' averroïsme*, p. 261, note). Petrarch, who was a better authority than Renan with respect to what he knew or did not know, indeed could not have had any knowledge of Arabic poetry if it had not been known in the Middle Ages, for the humanists of his time would have been the last people to seek knowledge of it. We admit freely that neither Petrarch's information on this item, nor that possessed by the medieval clergy and literati, with the exception of those in Spain, amounted to much. Petrarch, violently orthodox and moved by a special hatred towards the Arabs, described their poetry as "flabby, nerveless and obscene" (*loc. cit.*). The question is not of much importance for us, for neither the learned men nor books had any more to do with the diffusion of song in the eleventh century than they do in the twentieth century. Be all this as it may, one should not place much confidence in the precision of Renan's statement, nor of the expressions of many others who hold to the theory of the autochthonous origin of troubadour poetry.

23. Diez wrote: "As models for this style of poetry I have cited liturgical poetry, popular songs and some relics of ancient Latin lyrical composition. But how this poetry (of the troubadours) differs from all others! And with what rapidity it developed! It resembles a fairy garden which appears suddenly at the wave of a magician's wand" (*Leben und Werken der Troubadours*, p. xii).

According to Jeanroy, Provençal literature "appeared to us from the start as having been removed from any foreign influence; it burst forth like a flower, rising from the earth without root or stem" (*Revue des Deux-Mondes*, Jan., 1899, pp. 350 f.).

Indeed, it is in similar conclusions, making appeal to the supernatural, that all of the theories—the Latin hypothesis, the popular song hypothesis, the Limousin hypothesis, the May festival hypothesis— which regard the advent of Provençal poetry as an autochthonous blossoming culminate. Such theories, in spite of their rhetoric, are confessions of failure. This error would have been avoided by an examination of the sources of the foreign influences which the hypotheses in question would deny, but to which their failure would oblige us to give attentive consideration, even if there were no other reason for doing so.

What could be simpler and apparently more reasonable than to envisage an evolution having a local popular poetry as its point of departure? Nevertheless, this hypothesis, which is so simple and so easy to suggest, at once encounters difficulties which cannot be over-come. We are indebted to Alfred Jeanroy, whose industry in the search of data and their precise presentation is worthy of considerable admiration, for having revealed, in the very act of attempting to estab-lish this theory, the difficulties with which such an undertaking is confronted. Indeed, he saw himself in the position of having to make use of one of the most formidable frameworks of doubtful conjectures that had ever been called upon to support a speculation of this type, and to conclude by excusing himself for his inability to offer anything more than "belabored and cold hypotheses."

Although not committing himself, J. Bédier pricked these specula-tions with a point of fine irony by qualifying as "divinatory" the work of Jeanroy and asking himself if the theory of Gaston Paris, who derived all of the works of the troubadours, the Petrarchists and of the trouvères from the May festivals of the late Middle-Ages, was only a myth" (*Revue des Deux-Mondes*, May, 1896, pp. 146 f. and 172). Indeed these hypotheses are derived from the realms of divination and myth rather than that of criticism. We shall see that the traits of the popular poetry on which Jeanroy tried to found the structure of his conjectures ran through the Hispano-Mauresque poetry, just as it was the custom to embellish these latter with an illusion to Spring.

24. Eugène Baret, *Les Troubadours et leur influence sur la littéra-ture du Midi de l'Europe*, p. 44 f. In fact, Baret recognized the im-portance of the Arabic influence and insisted on it; yet the editors of the *Larousse du XXᵉ siècle* found it desirable to cite this passage without any reference to the existence of Moorish Spain.

Dr. J. Dumont obtained some fragments of Latin poetry which orig-inated in Anjou and date back to the time that courtly poetry was de-veloping in this area (*De la versification latine en Anjou pendant les XIᵉ et XIIᵉ siècles,* Angers, 1865). Neither in form, nor in style, nor in content do they exhibit any similarity, even the most remote, to any kind of popular poetry or to that of the troubadours.

"There is no relation between this ancient civilization and trouba-dour poetry."—Paul Meyer, *Revue critique*, 1867, p. 172.

"Latin poetry had long since died out."—A. Jeanroy in the *Revue des Deux-Mondes*, 1899, p. 350 f.

"Those who knew Latin . . . exerted no influence on the popular poetry, which they detested."—Gaston Paris, *La Poésie au moyen âge,* 1913, p. 22.

The poetry of the troubadours "originated outside of the educated circles of the time."—J. Anglade, *Histoire sommaire de la poésie méridionale*, p. 20.

"It is generally admitted that Provençal poetry is not related to Latin poetry."—L. M. Brandin, in the *Encyclopaedia Britannica*, 1932, Vol. XVIII, p. 638.

25. Rudolph Erckmann, "Der Einfluss der spanisch-arabischen Kultur auf die Entwicklung des Minnesangs," *Deutsche Vierteljahrschrift für Literaturwissenschaft und Geistesgeschichte*, 1931, p. 240 f.; C. Appel, in *Zeitschrift für romanische Philologie*, Dec. 1932; R. Schröder, in *Germanisch-romanische Monatschrift*, 1933, pp. 162 ff.

26. Although completely espousing Diez' opinion concerning the autochthonous origin of troubadour poetry, the French writers on Romance literature could not suppress a smile when the same Diez similarly wanted to represent as indigenous the poetry of the German minnesingers. (Anglade, *Les Troubadours*, p. 321, note 22). This latter opinion is as widespread in Germany as the notion of the autochthonous origin of Provençal poetry is in France. W. Scherer wrote: "The courtly song of love arose in Austria and Bavaria from popular songs. We should regard it as an inheritance of the most remote past" (*Geschichte der deutschen Literatur*, p. 202). Even this was surpassed. The Visigoths were credited with having brought popular poetry to Germany (M. Hartmann, *Die arabische Strophengedicht*, p. 237).

The French writers on Romance literature, however, yielded nothing to the Germans in patriotic ardor, and their sentiments led them to equally surprising conclusions. Jeanroy's speculations bear on the imitation of a lyrical style of poetry from the north of France, "today lost," but which was cultivated by the foreigners, "since they considered everything which came from France to be of the highest quality (*Origines de la poésie lyrique en France*, pp. xxiii, 125). Thus, "in our eyes the old German lyric art represents an obscure phase in the progress of the French lyrical poetry"; "it was poetry from northern France, or southern France, which influenced the first Italian works"; and it seemed probable to him that "most of the themes popular in Portugal reached that country from France" (*Ibid.*, pp. 125, 306, 334). Portugal was one of the oldest and most celebrated and most fertile homes of the popular Hispano-Arabic song (R. A. Nicholson, *History of Arabic Literature*, p. 364). But not content with attributing to northern France the origin of the popular poetry of all other countries, Jeanroy and Gaston Paris, reversing the historical evidence, want to trace to northern France the inspiration which led to the flourishing of Provençal poetry in the south. Gaston Paris wrote that the hypothetical popular poetry which preceded that of the troubadours "was cultivated in the north and ended by returning to revive in the south the most ancient styles, which had fallen into disuse" (*Mélanges de littérature française du moyen âge*, p. 571).

On the other hand, the Italians—among whom the thread of tradition had never been broken, and who always admitted the dependence of their poetry on that of Provence when the latter remained completely unknown in France—always regarded the matter of the derivation of Provençal poetry from Spain as being beyond dispute. Perhaps Dante was aware of this circumstance (*De vulgari eloquio*, II, xii). In the sixteenth century Giammaria Barbieri devoted a chapter to "La propagation de la poésie rimée des Arabes parmi les Espagnols et les Provençaux" (*Dell'origine della poesia rimata*, Modona, 1571, pp. 44 ff.). The same sentiments are expressed by Lodovico Zuccolo (*Discorso delle ragioni del numero del verso italiano*, Venice, 1623, p. 10); G. Crescimbeni (*L'Istoria della volgare poesia*, p. 6); G. Tirasboschi (Preface to his edition of Barbieri, pp. 11 ff.); F. S. Quadrio (*Della ragione d'ogni poesia*, Vol. II, p. 299); P. G. Andrés (*Dell'origine, progressi e stato attuale d'ogni letteratura*, Vol. II, pp. 66 ff. and the whole volume); J. Sismondi (*Histoire de la littérature du Midi de l'Europe*, 1813, pp. 38 ff.). These testimonials have little authoritative value; what they show is that in Italy, in the absence of traditional and no doubt unconscious prepossessions, there was no need for a condescending attitude toward the suggestion that Provençal poetry was of Hispano-Arabic origin. One would be inclined to believe that the Italians were aware of a tradition bearing on this matter, or a "legend" from a more authentic source than the conjectures of some philologists. A trivial, but significant, detail is the fact that Verdi's Opera, *Il Trovatore*, has for its locale not Provence, but Spain.

27. "It is necessary to seek a unique point of departure in some intermediate region, Poitou, Le Marche, Limousin . . . There are serious reasons for believing that all of the lyrical poetry of old France had its origin in that district . . . and spread thence to the north and south."— Gaston Paris, *Mélanges de littérature française du moyen âge*, p. 571.

"The question of its origins is in any case resolved. Songs existed in Poitou. Apparently numerous popular songs were composed in this part of France, where the dialects of *oc* and those of *oïl* were in contact . . . It is indeed in Limousin and partly in Poitou, most likely on the common boundary of these two provinces, that the origins of troubadour poetry may be located. Was not the first troubadour Guillaume VII, Count of Poitiers?"—J. Anglade, *Les Troubadours*, p. 8.

"The circumstances which led to the development of courtly poetry at the court of Poitiers and in the neighboring castles did not result from a nexus between such poetry and popular local poetry. As Jeanroy himself said, "I will admit that I do not see the basis for the generally accepted opinion that Guillaume composed in the Limousin tongue, or at least that the language he employed was based on Limousin."— *Les Chansons de Guillaume IX*, p. xiii, note 3.

28. Dimitri Scheludko, who enumerates in detail the various theories put forth to account for the origin of the art of the troubadours, and who is particularly prone to attack suggestions of a Hispano-Mauresque derivation, is nevertheless only able to oppose such suggestions with a declaration of faith. He sees in Provençal poetry a manifestation of the "spirit of the whole of the Middle Ages" (*Beiträge zur Entstehungsgeschichte der altprovenzalischen Lyrik*, in *Zeitschrift für französische Sprache und Literatur*, 1929, pp. 1-38, 201-266, and *Archivum romaïcum*, 1927, pp. 201 ff., 1928, pp. 30-127). This formula is certainly comprehensive enough to accommodate all tastes. However, this "very spirit of the Middle Ages," at the time of the twelfth century renaissance, had itself arisen, in all its aspects and elements, from the contact made by Europe at this date with the civilization of Islam.

II. MOORISH ORIGIN

1. R. A. Nicholson, *A Literary History of the Arabs*, p. 416.

2. H. A. R. Gibb, art. "Arabic Literature," *Encyclopaedia Britannica*, 14th ed., 1938. Vol. II, p. 195.

3. R. A. Nicholson, *loc. cit.* The Hispano-Moorish poets "broke with tradition and their works much more resemble those of the Europeans than those of the Arabic poets" (A. S. Tritton, art. "Shi'r," in *Encyclopédie de l'Islam*).

4. C. P. Caussin de Perceval, *Essai sur l'histoire des Arabes avant l'islamisme*, Vol. II, pp. 314 ff.; E. H. Quatremère, *Mélanges d'histoire et de philologie orientale*, p. 225; Anne and Wilfrid Blunt, *The Seven Golden Odes of Pagan Arabia*, p. 14; Syed Ameer Ali, *A Short History of the Saracens*, p. 455.

5. In his account of *Tauk al-Hamama* (*Zeitschrift der deutschen morgenländischen Gesellschaft*, LXIX, pp. 192 ff.), I. Goldziher gives a list of the predecessors of Ibn Hazm. R. A. Nicholson's *The Mystics of Islam* is the best general survey of Sufi literature. On this subject, see also: *Selected Poems from the Divani Shamsi Tabriz*, by the same author; I. Goldziher, *Vorlesungen über den Islam*; E. J. W. Gibb, *History of Ottoman Poetry*, Vol. I, pp. 32 ff.; Grangeret de Lagrange, *Anthologie arabe*, pp. 41 ff., 132 ff.

The writings attributed to Denys, the Areopagite, were one of the favorite reference books of the Sufi mystics; they were at the same time the source of European medieval mysticism. The pseudo-Denys inspired both Al-Ghazāli and Abelard.

The Sufi assimilation of profane love with divine love was not entirely abstract and symbolic; the amorous experience was regarded as necessary for the comprehension of God. Love (*'isk*) is the union of the created with the creator. "There is no more sublime Master in the universe," they said; and again, "Love is not its own goal, but a bridge leading to the truth" (Gibb, *op. cit.*, Vol. I, pp. 20 f.). The anguish of the lover was compared to the separation of the soul from the object of its happiness, that is to say, divine love. The "cruelty" of the beloved represented the difficulties which confront intelligence in its efforts to understand God. Thus the experience of earthly love—"the science of hearts," *'ilm al-qulub* (Massignon, in Hastings, *Encyclopedia of Religion and Ethics*, Vol. XII, p. 16)—was itself indispensable to the comprehension of the amative relation between man and God (*Ibid.*, p. 22). Cf. Grangeret de Lagrange, *Anthologie arabe*, p. 41: hymns of Ibn al-Farīd (1) to love and (2) to wine.

6. A. R. Nykl, "The Dove's Neck-Ring," p. cv. "Certain adepts of philosophy," said Ibn Dawūd, "have claimed that God—may His name be exalted—created every soul in a round form, like a sphere; then he cut each soul in half and placed each half in a separate body. And each body which encounters the body containing the other half of its soul is loved by it as a result of the original affinity. And it is thus that human beings associate with one another in obedience to the necessities of their nature. And thus did Jamil speak." (L. Massignon, *La Passion d'Al-Hallaj*, Vol. I, p. 177.) Ibn Dawūd praised "those who love, but remain chaste and do not manifest their love . . . If the very chastity of lovers, their isolation from filth and their heed of their purity were not protected by religious laws and by mores, it would still be the duty of each of them to remain chaste in order to render their

desire eternal" (*ibid.,* p. 174 f.). "This refined conception of human love, this poetic theme of 'very pure profane love,' " said Massignon, encountered in Ibn Dawūd a singularly fervent and sincere interpreter. He is the genuine precursor of Ibn Quzmān of Cordova; anticipating the latter, he sang of courtly love, the themes of which, popularized by the new metres of the *mowashshahat,* would come to influence the lyrical impulse of the poets who composed in the *langue d'oc,* Provençals, Catalans, Galicians, and Italians. Thus the first systematization of idealism appeared in Arabic as a result of the inversion of the cult of divine love. It is the only ideal acceptable to the Zaharite theologian" (*ibid.,* p. 176).

7. R. Dozy, *Scriptorum arabum loci de Abbadidis,* Vol. II, p. 75, n. 57. "Of all of the Spanish authors, Ibn Hazm was the most eminent by virtue of the extent and depth of his knowledge of the sciences cultivated by the Arabs, his profound mastery of the Arabic language, and his talents as an elegant writer, as a poet and as a historian" (Ibn Bachuwal, cited by Ibn Khallikan, ed. De Slane, Vol. II p. 268). Al-Maqqari claimed that the Almohade Al-Mansūr once said, "All men of learning must need have recourse to Ibn Hazm" (*Analectes,* II, p. 160).

8. The text of *Tauk al-Hamama fi ul-Ulfa wa'l Ullaf* (The Dove's Necklace, Of Love and Lovers) by Mūhammad 'Ali Ahmad Ibn Hazm al-Andalousi, was published by D. K. Petrof, Leiden, 1914. A translation in English by A. R. Nykl appeared in Paris in 1931, under the title: *The Dove's Neck Ring, About Love and Lovers.* On Ibn Hazm, see: C. Brockelman, *Geschichte der arabischen Literatur,* Vol. I, p. 400; R. Dozy, *Histoire des Musulmans en Espagne,* Vol. III, pp. 341 ff.; Goldziher's account of Nykl's edition in *Zeitschrift der morgenländischen Gesellschaft,* Vol. LXXIX, pp. 192 ff.; and Asín Palacios, *Abenhazam de Córdoba y su historia crítica de las ideas religiosas,* Madrid, 1927.

9. *Tauk al-Hamama,* trans. Nykl, p. 6.

10. *Ibid.,* p. 112.

11. *Ibid.,* p. 137.

12. *Ibid.,* p. 141.

13. *Ibid.,* pp. 31 f.

14. *Ibid.,* pp. 28 f.

15. *Ibid.,* p. 13.

16. E. Garcia Gomez, *Poemas arábigo-andaluces,* p. 97.

17. Grangeret de Lagrange, *Anthologie arabe,* pp. 33, 36, 41.

18. The terms traditionally used in the courtly poetry of the troubadours, such as *Joi, joven, gilos, enoyos* (generally used as a synonym
for "spouse,") *leial, mezura, lauzengier* (slanderer), were identified
with their equivalents used in the same manner in the Hispano-Moorish
poetry (A. R. Nykl, *El cancionero de Aben Guzmán*, p. xlvii; Lichten-
staater, in *Islámica*, 1931, p. 17). It is interesting to note that these
terms were employed in the oldest Sufi poetry in an allegorical sense.
Thus, *washi*, the term equivalent to *lauzengier*, stood for the logical
faculty. (R. A. Nicholson, *Studies in Islamic Mysticism*, p. 178). Cf.
note 5, above.

19. See: Jérôme and Jean Tharaud, *Marrakech, ou Les Seigneurs
de l'Atlas*, pp. 173 ff.

20. R. Altamira, *Historia de España*, Vol. I, pp. 287 ff.; J. Ferrandis
Torres, *La vida en el Islam español*, p. 14; J. Ribera, *Disertaciones y
opúsculos*, Vol. I, pp. 345 ff.

21. Al-Maqqari, tr. Gayangos, *History of the Mohammedan Dynasties in Spain*, Vol. I, pp. 161-167; Clément Huart, in *Journal asiatique*, 1881, pp. 5 ff.; A. Cour, *Ibn Zaidoun, un poète arabe d'Andalousie*.

22. Ibn Khaldūn, *Prolégomènes*, trans. De Slade, Vol. II, pp .415 ff.

23. With the exception of the zither and the harp, which originated
in the Orient at an earlier date, all of the musical instruments in use
in the Middle Ages were of Moorish origin. The *rabab*, ancestor of
the violin as well as of the rota, the gigha and the rebeck, was also
the original form of the viol (usually six-stringed and without frets),
the instrument which was most often used to accompany lyrical singing. The Arabs imported it from Persia, but they perfected it by the
invention of the bow (*aws*). Seven different forms of the Moorish
rabab are known to us: the rectangular viol (*murabba'*), the round
viol, shaped like a boat, a pear or a hemisphere (*kamandja*), the pan-
dora and the open-framed *rabab*. The archpriest Ruiz mentioned the
"loud rabab" and the "Moorish rabab." Ordinarily it had two strings.
The lute "was apparently introduced into Europe in the tenth century
by the Moors." The oldest known representation of a lute is found
on an ivory carving from Cordova. The carving, which bears the date
968, is preserved in the Louvre. A large variety of instruments was
developed in Andalusia and passed on to Christian Europe, See T.
Gérold, *La Musique au moyen âge*, pp. 368 ff.; M. Brenet, "Notes sur
l'histoire du luth en France," *Rivista musicale*, 1898; E. López Chavarri, *Música popular española*, pp. 74 ff.; H. G. Farmer, art. "Rabab",

Encyclopedie de l'Islam; H. G. Farmer, *Studies in Oriental Musical Instruments;* Salvador-Daniel, *La Musique arabe* (Algiers, 1879); Ibn Khaldūn, *Prolégomènes,* trans. De Slane, Vol. II, pp. 417 ff. Menéndez Pidal, *Poesía juglaresca,* pp. 55 ff.

"The origins of the music of the Middle Ages are oriental in the sense that the songs of the troubadours are inspired by those of the Arabs" (L. J. Fétis, *Histoire générale de la musique,* Vol. V, pp. 7 f.).

24. Martial, VI, lxi.

Edere lascivos ad Baetica crusmata gestus
Et Gaditanis ludere docta modis.

"Crusmata," from χρονω, Latin *pulso,* were a type of castanets. The Betis was the Guadalquivir which gave its name to the province of Baetica. Cf. on the dances of Cadiz: Martial, I, 42, 12; XIV, 203; Juvénal, *Sat.,* XI, 162.

25. S. De Sacy, *Traité élémentaire de la prosodie et de la métrique des Arabes,* pp. 2 ff.; A. S. Tritton, art. "Shi'r," in Th. Houtsma, *Encyclopédie de l'Islam;* Weil, art. "Arud," *ibid.*

26. Martin P. W. Hartmann, *Das arabische Strophengedicht: I. Das Muwassah,* pp. 112 ff.; Weil, *loc. cit.;* Mohammed Bencheneb, art. "Muwashshah," *Encyclopédie de l'Islam.*

27. M. Hartmann, *op. cit.,* p. 218: "Most authors do not make any distinction between *muwashshah* and *zajal*"; Georges S. Colin, in Hesperis, XVI, 1933, p. 166: "The *zajal* is purely and simply a *muwashshah* written in the Spanish dialect, rather than in the classical language."

28. Hammer-Purgstall, "Sur les formes artificielles de la poésie arabe," *Journal asiatique,* 4th series, Vol. XIV, 1849, p. 249.

29. Ibn Khaldūn (III, p. 361), cited by M. Hartmann, *op. cit.,* p. 216: "The Bedouins also have another type of poetry, arranged in stanzas of four lines, the last of which has a rhyme differing from that of the first three, so that the fourth rhyme is repeated in each *bait* to the end of the poem." Cf. René Basset, "Un épisode d'une chanson de geste arabe," *Bulletin de correspondance africaine,* 1885, pp. 136 ff., 142, n. 1, 144, n. 3.

"Tradition says that at the time of Harūm a young female slave inaugurated the fashion of writing verse in the vernacular tongue, although the pedantically minded did not consider it poetry." A. S. Tritton, art. "Shi'r," *Encyclopédie de l'Islam.*

According to Casiri, the encyclopedic writer Ibn 'Abd Rabbihi (860-

939), who flourished at the court of the Umayyad Caliphs, was the inventor of the *muwashshaha* (Michael Casiri, *Bibliotheca arabico-hispana escurialensis*, Vol. I, p. 127). According to Ibn Khaldūn, Muqaddan Ibn Mū'afa al-Qabri al-Darir (c. 880) was its inventor, (Ibn-Khaldūn, *Mugaddima*, ed. Quatremère, Vol. III, p. 404, trans De Slane, Vol. III, 436). Ibn Bassam (*Al-Dhakhira*, p. 200) also attributes the "invention" of this genre to Al-Qabri. A great deal of weight may not be attached to the assertion that Al-Qabri was actually the "inventor." In the Middle Ages, in both Muslim and Christian countries, the "invention" of all sorts of things was attributed to anyone who distinguished himself in their use. Ibn Khaldūn, after having named the "inventor" of the *muwashshaha*, adds: "It is true that some ballads were circulating in Spain before his time." The dates are really the noteworthy items. Strophic poetry, *muwashshahat* and the *azajal*, was widespread in Spain in the tenth century, and apparently even in the ninth.

"We have certain knowledge of five *muwashshahat* dating from 1027 to 1030" (Hartmann, *op. cit.*, p. 210).

We present the transliteration of the first strophes of a *zajal* dating from the beginning of the eleventh century:

> *Ma ladda li charbû rahi 'ala riyadi l-aqahi;*
> *lu la hadim al-washahi, ida ata fi's-shabahi;*
>
> > *Au fi'l-asûl*
> > *adha yaqûl*
> > *ma li-shemûl*
> > *latamat khaddi,*
> >
> > *Wa li's-shemal*
> > *habbat fa mal*
> > *gûsn i'tidal*
> > *dammahu bûrdi.*

—Abû Bakr al-Abjad (d. 1031), Ibn Khaldūn, III, p. 394; tr. De Slane, p. 428.

The *murabba'* form, *aa, bbba, ccca*, is regular; the *marqaz* is repeated. The theme of the song is love. "I have never been pleased when she fulfilled her promise in the evening and told me in the morning: 'It was wine which brought color to my cheeks; it was the North Wind which smote my face.' She is among those who slay hearts; just seeing her walk fills me with concern. May her eyes cast me back into iniquity!

Sweet lips, lined with pearls, assuage the fire which consumes me. I am ill with love; I shall never break my promises, and I shall not cease to hope, however unconcerned you may appear."

30. M. Hartmann, *op. cit.*, p. 215; R. Dozy, *Supplément aux dictionnaires arabes.*

31. Friederich Ruckert, *Die Verwandlungen des Abu Seid von Serug, oder Die Makamen des Hariri*, Vol. I, p. 88.

R. A. Nicholson has also translated many pieces drawn from Hariri's *Maqama.*

> I ride and I ride
> through the waste far and wide,
> and I fling away pride
> to be gay as the swallow;
>
> Stem the torrents fierce speed,
> tame the mettlesome steed,
> that wherever I lead
> youth and pleasure may follow.

—Literary History of the Arabs, p. 335.

The following strophes are by Muhammed Ibn Hasan al-Nawaji (d. 1455). The text is given by Grangeret de Lagrange, *Anthologie arabe*, p. 202.

> Come hand the precious cup to me
> and brim it high with a golden sea!
>
> Let the old wine circle from guest to guest
> while the bubbles gleam like pearls on its breast,
> so that night is of darkness dispossessed.
> How it foams and twinkles in fiery glee!
> 'Tis drawn from the Pleiads' cluster, perdie!
> . . . .
> Alone with me in the garden green
> a singing-girl enchants the scene.
> Her smile diffuses a radiant sheen.
> I cast off shame for no spy to see,
> and Hola! I cry, let's merry be.

—R. A. Nicholson, op. cit., p. 417.

32. J. Valera, according to A. F. Von Schack, *Poesie und Kunst der Araber in Spanien und Sizilien*, Vol. II, p. 272.

33. The Arabic text of the *zajal* is given on p. 176, note 58, in the original French version of this book. I add a transliteration of this passage from A. R. Nykl, *El cancionero de Aben Guzmán*, p. 266 f, and a translation.

Kefa les yakun mai f'al-gurbah ham,
Wa halaitu galbi li-Umm al-Hakam?

Baga mahha galbi w'ana f'as-safar,
Wa shatt an-naharu wa sar men shahar
Wa gabat li munyah wa gaba'l-qamar:
Wa ba' da faraqaha gani 'n-nadam!

Min al-wahshah f'al-gurbah galbi yafur
Li Sultanata 'd-dunya namdi nazur
Wa qad tammat a'wan tammat shahur
Wa'ishqi li-Umm al Hakam les yatam!

Li Umm al Hakam nahwa beina 'l-gawar;
Li-Umm al-Hakam haddu ka'l-gullanar;
Li-Umm al-Hakam 'aineine 'n-sud, kibar;
Muharraqah bi-sh-shaqfi tashar umam!

Fa ya sukkaran muntahab f'al-madaq!
Bi-haqqi dika 'sh'shiffatein 'r-riqaq
La tausa dimam al-qubal w'al-inaq
Wa afkir 'ala sahhati w'at-tubam!

Wa ufi li anna muhibbak wafi;
Wa da'al-hurugh w ahtagab w'ahtafi
Wa saddiq li-man qallah al-haira fi
Wa iyyak tuti man yaghi lak yanam!

Wa kun li-rasuli qariga 'l-highab!
Wa in kan wa tada wa tursil kitab
Bi-dammi nusattar ileik al-gawab
Wa nabri 'izami makana 'l-qalam!

How could I not be sad, I who, upon leaving,
leave my heart by my lady, Al-Hakam?

I left her my heart and took my leave
and the days are so long they appear to be months;
clouded is my joy, overcast is my moon,
and sadness overwhelms me since I left.

My heart throbs alone and abandoned.
Go! Go! find the sovereign lady of this world!
The months pass, the years pass,
but my love for my lady, Al-Hakam, abides.

Al-Hakam moves forward, proudly among ladies,
Al-Hakam has cheeks like the flowers of the pomegranate,
Al-Hakam has eyes large and black,
which ravish the soul and confound men.

Oh! exquisite and savory sweetness!
Ah, God! those delicate lips!
Do not forget their vows, our kisses, our embraces,
and dream of my love and my pain.

Be faithful, for I am your faithful lover;
do not go out, keep silence and be prudent;
believe those who speak well of me,
and pay no attention to those who speak ill of me.

Hide this message that no one may see it;
and if you deign to write me
I shall write my answer with my blood
and shall fashion a pen from my broken bones.

34. Bartsch, *Chrestomathie*, col. 245. In Bartsch's transcription the refrain is repeated after each verse, whereas in the manuscript only the first two words are. Concerning this, see Jeanroy, *Origines*, p. 413.

35. *Zeitschrift für romanische Philologie*, IV, p. 503.

36. C. Appel, *Provenzalische Chrestomathie*, p. 90.

37. C. Raynouard, *Choix de poésies originales*, Vol. II, p. 236. Another of Gaucelm Faidit's "albas" begins:

> *Us cavaliers si jazia*
> *ad la re que plus volia*
> *soven baizan li dizia:*
> *Doussa res, ieu que farai?*

> —C. Appel, *Provenzalische Chrestomathie*, p. 90.

An "alba" of Cadenet has the following form:

> *s'anc fui beha prezada*
> *ar sui d'ant en bas tornada*
> *qu'a un vilas sui donada*
> *tot e per sa granmanentia.*

> —C. Raynouard, *Choix de poésies*, Vol. III, p. 251.

38. P. Bembo, *Della volgare lingua*, p. 184 f., ed. Sonzogno.
— According to Leone Allacci, a strophe of the model *aaabb*, attributed
to Vincenzo d'Aleano, would be the oldest example of Sicilian poetry:

> Rosa fresca aulentissima ca pari in ver l'estate
> le donne te desiano, pulcelle maritate
> trahame deste focora se teste a bontate
> per te non aio abento nocte e dia
> penzado pur di voi madonna mia.

The piece dates only from the last years of the twelfth century.—
(G. Tiraboschi, *Storia della letteratura italiana*, Vol. IV, Part II, pp.
384 f.)

A popular thirteenth-century Italian song had the following form:

> Babbo meo dolce cosi tu mal fai
> che'd io sum grande e marito no me dai.

> Mal fa'tu, babo, che non me mariti
> ched io son grande e son mostrata a diti;
> Ben m'ai tenuta cum tego assai,
> fal pur di ora, s'tu'l di'far ca mai.

> "Figliola mia, non te far meravegla
> s'io t'o tenuta cotante in famegla
> c'on dal te fatto ancor trovai
> ch'l sper de deo travarelo agi mai."

> —Ezio Levi, *Poesia di popolo e poesia di corte nel
> trecento*, p. 40. Cf. G. Carducci, *Cantilene,
> ballate e strambotti* (Pisa, 1871), pp. 42, 54,
> 62, 65.

39. A. Jeanroy, ed., *Les Chansons de Guillaume IX*, p. 28 f.

40. *For hire loue y carke ant care,*
    for hire loue y droupne ant dare,
    for hire loue my blisse is bare,
       ant al ich waxe won;
    for hire loue in slep y slake,
    for hire loue al nyht ich wake,
    for hire loue mournyng y make
       more then eny mon.

Or again:

   Heo is coral of godnesse,
   heo is rubie of ryhtfulnesse,
   heo is cristal of clannesse,
      ant banner of bealte.

    —K. Boeddeker, *Altenglische Dichtungen des Ms. Harl.*
    2253, pp. 169. 171, f.

One of Walther von der Vogelweide's pieces contains perhaps a relic of the popular Provençal form:

   Von Rôme voget, von Pülle künec, lât iuch erbarmen,
   das man mich bî rîcher kunst alsus siht armen.
   Gerne wolte ich, möhte ez sîn, bî eigem fiure erwarmen.
   zahi wie'ch danne sunge von vogellînen . . .

    —Walther von der Vogelweide, ed. O. Güntter, p. 68.

The rare examples in France are even more obviously in the "Provencializing" style:

   A ma dame, barade, présenter
   te voel; di te par moi sous celer
   ke de sa cose empirier et grever
      n'est pas courtoisie.

    —*Chansonnier de Noailles*, B. N. Mss. fr. 12615, Paul
    Meyer, *Romania*, XIX, p. 30. Cf. A. Jeanroy, *Origines*
    de la poésie lyrique, pp. 506-9.

The rhyme-pattern *aaab* became extremely common in England. Indeed, from the beginning of the thirteenth century until the verse of the Elizabethan age, and within not many years from Shakespeare, the *murabba'* model dominates English lyrical stlyle, at least so far as its surviving relics enable us to judge. In E. K. Chambers and F. Sidgewick's anthology of *Early English Relics,* out of 102 examples, 44 are pure *murabbas*. That surprising circumstance appears to arise from the fact that, in direct opposition to what happened in France, the authors of those verses are all, or nearly all, clerics. Their subjects are mostly religious. Being under no obligation of decking themselves with elegant variations to curry favor with courtly clients, the writers of church-lyrics continued in the use of their original form. A large proportion are Christmas carols, as, for example, the one cited in note 45.

There are, however, not a few amatory lyrics, e.g.

> As I lay sleeping,
> in dreames fleeting,
> ever my sweeting
> is in my mind.

> —Sir John Hawkins, *A General History of the Science and Practice of Music,* Vol. III, p. 25; Chambers and Sidgewick, **XXXIX**, 15th c.

It is notable that Chaucer, drawing his poetical models immediately from France, uses the *aaab* pattern but once (*Anelida and Arcite,* verses 220 ff.), while that ordonnance held the field among his ecclesiastical contemporaries. His sources were "courtly"; those of Church ditties were "popular." The prevalence of the form among the latter again bears witness to its having been more widespread in France and Provence than direct evidence would indicate.

41. F. Sabatier, "Saint François d'Assise," p. 419; see: Fr. Ozanam, *Les Poètes franciscains en Italie au XII siècle;* Della Giovanna, *S. Francesco giullare.*

42. *Laude di frate Jacopone da Todi,* ed. G. Ferri, p. 90. For example:

O amor de povertate
regno de tranquillitade

Povertate, via secura,
non ha lite ne rancura,
de latron non a paura,
ne de nulla tempestata.

43. *Sucurra, donna, aiuta*
   Ch'al tuo figlio se sputa
   E la gente lo muta:
   Onlo dato a Pilato.
      . . . .

44. *O signor, per cortesia*
   mandami la malsania!

   A me la freve quartana,
   La continua e la terzana,
   La doppia cotidiana,
   colla grande idropesia.

45. E. K. Chambers and F. Sidgewick, *Early English Lyrics*, p. 117; Bodleian Library, English Poetry, *e I.*
46. Chambers and Sidgewick, *Early English Lyrics*, p. 146; Bodleian Library, English Poetry, *e I.*
47. Chambers and Sidgewick, *Early English Lyrics*, p. 80; Bodleian Library, Rawlinson, c. 813.
48. Here is such an example; it is a popular noel:

   In hoc anni circulo
   vita datur saeculo
   nato nobis parvelo
   de Virginie Maria.

   —E. du Méril, *op. cit.*, p. 6.

The monk Hilaire, who was of English origin, according to Mabillon, and a disciple of Abelard, favored in his verse a form which has a Provençal cast.

Ad honorem tui, Dari,
quia decet letari,
omnes ergo pari,
    Gaudeamus,
Laudes tibi debitas referamus.

> —*Hilarii versus et ludi*, ed. J. J. Champollion-Figeac,
> p. 51 f. Cf. pp. 14, 25, 27, 41.

The jongleurs who composed *Mystères* for the churches very often used similar forms which were frequently bilingual. See E. du Méril, *Origines latines du théâtre moderne*, pp. 225, 241. All of these examples belong to an epoch in which Provençal poetry was supreme. Sometimes they would be entirely in Provençal:

E resors es, l'escriptura o dii;
Gabriels soi en trames aici;
Atendet lo, que ja venra praici.
    Gaire no y dormet
aisel espos que vos hor' atendet.

> —*Mystère des vierges sages et des vierges folles*, in
> C. Raynouard, *Choix de poésies des troubadours*,
> Vol. II, p. 141.

The English monks and song-makers, who travelled constantly back and forth between England and France, were remarkably polyglot. Pieces in three languages are far from uncommon. For example:

A celuy que pluys eyme en monde,
of alle tho that that I have found,
    Carissima,
saluz od treye amour,
with grace and joye and alle honour,
    Dulcissima.

Sachez bien, pleysant et beele,
that I am right in good heele,
    Laus Christo!

et moun amour doné vous ay,
and also thine owene night and day
   in cisto.

> —Camb. Gg. iv, 27; Chambers and Sidgewick, *Early
> English Lyrics,* VIII, early XVth century.

I add the following for its quality:

Scripsi haec carmina in tabulis,
Mon hostel est en mi la vile de Paris,
may I sugge namore, so wel me is;
yet I deye for love of hire, duel hit ys.

> —Harleyan, 2253.

   The jongleurs who wrote miracle-plays frequently used similar bilingual forms. See E. du Méril, *Origines latines du théâtre moderne,* pp. 225, 241.

   49. E. du Méril, *Poésies populaires latines du moyen âge,* p. 26.

   50. A. Jeanroy, *Origines de la poésie lyrique en France,* pp. 76, 338. Paul Meyer dates these productions still later, placing them toward the end of the thirteenth century (*Romania,* XIX, 1890, p. 25).

   51. A. Jeanroy, *Origines,* pp. xiii, 125.

   52. A. Jeanroy, *Les Chansons de Guillaume IX,* p. xiv.

   53. A. Jeanroy, *Origines,* pp. 105, 106, 108.

   54. M. Hartmann, *Das arabische Strophengedicht,* pp. 100 f.

   55. A. Jeanroy, *Origines,* p. 412.

   56. A. Jeanroy, *Les Chansons de Guillaume IX,* p. xiv.

   57. A. Jeanroy, *Origines,* p. 398, note. There was another rule of the Hispano-Moorish songs which was also imposed on the lyrical poetry of the troubadours: In both cases the songs were constrained to consist of seven or eight stanzas. This rule is observed with great regularity in both cases. "The commonest number of *baīt* is "seven," said Ibn Khaldūn (*Histoire des Berbères et des dynasties musulmanes de l'Afrique septentrionale,* trans. by De Slane, Vol. III, p. 541).

   58. Marcabru, who had a liking for the *murabba'* form, adheres closely to the Andalusian rhythm. A. R. Nykl compares a strophe from the "l'Etourneau" series with a *zajal* of Al-Abjad (note 29):

Ma ladda li charbû rahi
'Ala riyadi l-aqahi
Lû la hadim al-washahi
Ida ata fis chabahi
    Au fil-asûl
    Adah yaqûl
    Ma li-sh-shemûl
    Latamat khaddi?
    W a li's-shemal.
    Habbat fa mal
    Gusn i'tidal
    Dammahu bûrdi.

      —Al-Abjad

Ai! com' es encabalada
La fals'a razo daurada
Denan totas vai triada;
Va! ben es fols qui s'i fia.
    De sos datz
    C' a plombatz
    Vos gardatz
    Qu' enganatz
    N'a assatz,
    So sapchatz,
    E mes en la via.

      —Marcabru

59. J. Anglade, *Les Poésies de Peire Vidal*, p. 23.

60. C. Appel, ed., *Bernart von Ventadorn*, p. 260.

61. Alphonse d'Aragon, in Raynouard, *Choix de poésies*, Vol. II, p. 118.

62. Gaucelm Faidit, in A. Kolsen, *Dichtungen der Troubadors*, p. 30; C. Appel, *Provenzalische Chrestomathie*, p. 90; Gauceran, in A. Kolsen, *op. cit.*, p. 17 f.; Bertram de Born, *Poésies*, ed. Stimmung, p. 145; Folquet de Romans, in Crescini, *Manualetto provenzale*, p. 225; le Moine de Montaudon, ed. O. Klein, pp. 44, 84; Peire Cardenal, in C. Raynouard, *Lexique roman*, Vol. I, p. 459; Guilhem Rainols et Magret, *Histoire littéraire de la France*, Vol. XVII, pp. 538 ff.; Guilhem Figuiera, in Crescini, *Manualetto provenzale*, p. 327; Arnaud Plaguès, *Hist. litt. de la France*, Vol. XVII, p. 636; Nicolet de Turin, *ibid.*, p. 626.

63. Ibn Sanā' al-Mūlk intoned the praises of the Hispano-Moorish songs with oriental prolixity and extravagance. "Those who do not recognize the natural beauty in them, once they have heard them," he wrote, among other things, "exhibit a dull, parochial nature, a lack of sensitivity and intelligence, a stupified spirit, possessing no element of good education, and foreign to any refinement. Such, in my opinion, is the character of any man who is able to remain indifferent upon hearing them" (Hartmann, *op. cit.*, p. 52).

64. Ibn Bassam, *Al-Dhakira*, in Raynouard, *Choix de poésies*, Vol. II, p. 118.

65. 'Abd al-Walid al-Marrakishi, *Histoire des Almohades*, tr. E. Fragnan, p. 77 f.

The Arab authors, such as Ibn Khaldūn, say that the popular poetry (*zajal*) was derived by imitation of the literary strophic poem (*muwashshaha*). This is nothing but a scholastical preconception. To the contrary, Hartmann and most of the orientalists believe that the strophic literary poem is an imitation of the popular poem (Hartmann, *op cit.*, pp. 209, 218; Z. Veil, art. " 'Arud," *Encyclopédie de l'Islam*).

66. In Dozy's opinion, the name of Ibn Quzmān is not related to the Visigoth name, Guzman, as one might suspect and as Gunzburg seems to have believed. It is thoroughly an Arab name. He is very often mentioned by Arabic authors, notably in Ibn Khaldūn, in Maqqari, in Al-Muhibbi and in Ibn Bassam. Rosen disputed his right to the title "vizir," and was followed by Brockelmann (*Geschichte der arabischen Literatur*, Vol. I, p. 272); but Dozy proved, in a letter to Gunzburg, that Ibn Quzmān was fully entitled to it. It is necessary to recognize, however, that the title was frequently attributed to someone without that person's actually exercising the implied functions. After the fall of Al-Mu'tamid, Ibn Quzmān returned to Cordova, but also travelled considerably in many parts of Spain. The interesting question is: What sort of person was he? Rosen and Brockelmann represent him as a "poor wretch," almost a beggar, living on the charity of his benefactors. His Diwān contains many pieces dedicated to his patrons, and he often complains of his poverty; The *Diwān* itself is dedicated to Al-Washki Ibn Hamdin. It is necessary, however, to take into account the fact that he imitated the style of the popular singers, although he was a cultivated man. All things considered, it is probable that, relying on the largesse of his benefactors, he led a life very similar to that of the majority of the troubadours.

67. The *Diwān* of Ibn Quzmān, of which the only manuscript is found in Leningrad, having come there by way of Syria, was published in phototype by Baron David von Gunzburg in Berlin, in 1896. It was number 136 of the Arab Mss. in the Asiatic Museum. Twenty-four pages of the manuscript are missing. Victor Rumanovitch von Rosen published a short account of the Ms. with extracts (*Notice sommaire des manuscrits arabes du Musée asiatique*, St. Petersburg, 1881, pp. 242-254). The distinguished Arabic scholar, Dr. Julian Ribera y Tarrago, deserves the credit for having first drawn attention to the importance of the Diwān (*Discurso leído en la Real Academia Española: "El cancionero de Aben Guzmán,"* Madrid, 1912; reprinted in *Disertaciones y opúsculos*, 1928, Vol. I, pp. 3 ff.) A. R. Nykl, of

the Chicago School of Oriental Languages, published a partial trans-scription, with a transliteration in Latin letters and translations of a member of the *azajal* of the *Diwān* (*El cancionero de Aben Guzmán*, Madrid, 1933). See in addition: F. J. Simonet, "Las anacreonticas de Ibn Guzmān," in *La ilustración española y americana*, Madrid, 1885, no. 45, pp. 331 ff.; A González Palencia, *Historia de la literatura arábigo-española*, pp. 107-112, 329-332; G. S. Colin, in *Hespéris*, XVI, 1933, pp. 161-170; Jean de Goeje, art. "Ibn Kozman," *Encyclopédie de l'Islam;* Fehim Bajraktarevic, *ibid., Supplément.*

68. Arabic scholars, accustomed to literary Arabic, and unfamiliar with the Arabic spoken in the twelfth century, refer to the songs of Ibn Quzmān in terms which recall those used by Ibn Bassam. Dozy claims that the poems of Ibn Quzmān are composed "in an unin-flected vernacular." "The language of these songs," says M. Ribera, "is not the poetic language taught in the schools, but certainly the vulgar tongue which was current in Cordova; it contains jests, coarse speech and the vulgar jokes of the street. It is the language of students and gamins and represents the commonplaces of domestic expression." (Julian Ribera y Tarrago, *Disertaciones y opúsculos:* "El cancionero de Aben-Guzmán," I, p. 41). These descriptions are likely to produce an erroneous impression. One must not imagine that Ibn Quzmān committed grammatical blunders or that his language was uncultivated and hardly literate. This is no more true of Ibn Quzmān than it was of Dante when he wrote in the "vulgar tongue" instead of Latin and when he used the coarsest of words in "The Divine Comedy."

69. *Al-Mostathref fi kulli fennin mostazref,* cited by Hammer-Purgstall, "Sur les formes artificielles de la poésie arabe," *Journal asiatique,* 4th series, XIV, p. 249.

Another type which would have delighted Marcabru and which was represented in Ibn Quzmān is cited and discussed in the Hamasa of Abū Tammam Habib ibn-Aws (d. 850). It has for its theme *Madhammati 'l Nisa,* "The abuse of women" (R. A. Nicholson, *The Literary History of the Arabs,* p. 130).

70. Admittedly it is necessary to take account of Arabic usage, which, not allowing the naming of a woman directly, very often led to the substitution of the masculine gender for the feminine in speak-ing of the object of amatory passion. "Why does one so often find among the Muslim poets so many pieces in which the object of their love is depicted by attributes which are not those of the female sex?" asks De Slane. And he answers: "It was considered improper to make references to sex, either in conversation or in writing. Therefore, it

became necessary to depict the beloved object by using adjectives and verbs of the masculine gender . . . this change of gender is even permitted in some cases by the spirit of the Arab language . . . Even today, in Cairo, the musicians who run about the streets must use the masculine gender when the matter of love comes into their songs; otherwise, public morality would be offended and the singer would be exposed to severe punishment for having lacked decency and broken a police regulation. "The Moslem poet has thus been forced to abide by this rule posed by public opinion" (De Slane, "Sur le sens figuré de certains mots qui se rencontrent dans la poésie arabe," *Journal Asiatic,* 3rd series, VII, p. 175.) And August Cour noted: "The beloved object was depicted by epithets and with traits proper to the male sex. Whatever the motive may have been, an ancient fear of magic, or sexual jealousy, or the influence of Islam, this dissimulation is a fact; and this fact is recognized by public approval, the supreme authority in literary matters" (A. Cour, *Ibn Zaidoûn: un poète arabe d'Andalousie,* p. 135.)

The meticulous protocol of Arabic etiquette which requires that on each encounter with a friend or an acquaintance one enquires individually about the health of all the male relatives, does not allow one to mention wife, daughter or mother, and to do so would be an inexcusable affront. An analogous situation is found in Provençal poetry, in which the *senhal,* by which the lady is designated, is sometimes masculine. Thus Bernard de Ventadorn extols Marguerite de Turenne under the name of "Tristan" (ed. C. Appel, p. 254), and Bertram de Born addresses Maheut, viscountess of Talleyrand, by the term "fair lord" (A. Stimmung, *Bertran von Born,* p. 13). The term *midons,* "my lord," was in general use.

71. C. Raynouard, *Choix de poésies originales des troubadours,* Vol. II, p. 249. Also Bernard de Ventadorn:

No es meravelha s'eu chan
melhs de nul autre chantador.

—Ed. C. Appel, p. 188.

72. For example, the second strophe of the tenth *zajal* is thus conceived:

Ya mutarnani *Silibato*
tun hazin, *tun benato*
tara l-yaum *wastato*
lam taduq fih ger loquaima.

O my poor Salviato (*Silibato*), you (*tun*) are sad and vexed (*penado*), this day will be a ruined (*gastado*) for you (*tun*); you haven't tasted a single morsel.

One encounters such words as "nabbali" (*navaja,* dagger) and *Fulano* (so and so). In item number lxxxiv, an old Spanish woman speaks a mixture of Spanish and Arabic. Cf. *azajal* xix, xx, lxxxii, xlix, cii. See J. Ribera, *Disertaciones y opúsculos,* Vol. I, p. 36.

In a thirteenth century Portuguese song book, in the Vatican library, there is found a song of the *murabba'* model in Portuguese, mixed with phrases in a corrupt Arabic.

> *Eu, velida, non dormia,* lelia d'outra
> *e meu amigo venia; e doy* lelia d'outra
>   *non dormia e cuidaba*
>   *e meu amigo chegava*
>   *E meu amigo venia*
> *e d'amor tan ben dizia;*
>   *e meu amigo chegava*
> *e d'amor tan ben cantava: e doy* lelia d'outra

—Th. Braga, *Cancionero portugez da Vaticana,* no. 415

One frequently finds a large number of bilingual pieces in Christian Europe dating from the same time. Generally the main part is in Latin, the refrain in Provençal. For instance a manuscript in the Vatican contains a bilingual "aube" (reproduced in facsimile in E. Monaci, *Facsimili di antichi manoscritti,* fol. 78; Cf. J. Schmidt, in *Zeitschrift für deutsche Philologie,* XII, pp. 333, 41). The monk Hilarius has many pieces with Provençal codas (*Hilarii versus et Ludi,* pp. 14, 25, 27, 41). Latin is sometimes mixed with English:

> Esto memor mortis
> Jam porta fit omnibus ortes
>   saepe sibi juvenes
>   accipit ante senes.
> *Syth alle that in thys worlde hath been*
>   in rerum natura
> *or in this worlde was seen*
>   in humana cura.

—(E. du Méril, *Poésie populaire latine du moyen-âge,* p. 7, cf. p. 123, note.)

73. "Aragonais was very similar to Valencian, or, more properly, to Limousinian." Mayans y Siscar, *Orígenes de la lengua española,* Vol. I, p. 54. Cf. C. Michaelis de Vasconcellos and Th. Braga, *Geschichte der portugiesischen Literatur,* in Groeber, *Grundriss der romanische Philologie,* Bd. II, Abt. 2, p. 134, n.

74. A. González Palencia, *Historia de la literatura arábigo-española,* p. 111.

75. J. Ribera y Tarragó, *Disertaciones y opúsculos,* Vol. I, p. 71.

76. Dante, *Vita nuova,* XXV: "E non molto numero d'anni passati, che apparino prima questi poeti volgari ... Se volemo cercare in lingua d'oc e in quella di si, noi non troviamo cosedette anzi lo presente tempo per cento e cinquanta anni."

77. This is also the view of A. R. Nykl. "I am of the opinion," he wrote, "that Guilhem de Poitiers was responsible for the beginning of the formative period of this poetry." (*The Dove's Neck-Ring,*" p. cviii.) The case, however, is not singular. Everything seems to indicate that the diffusion of Provençal poetry and of "courtly" ideas into northern France was largely due to the personal action of the granddaughter of the troubadour prince, Aliénor d'Aquitaine, and that of her daughters, Marie de Champagne and Aélis de Blois. This is the opinion of Gaston Paris (*Romania,* XII, 1883, pp. 523 ff.).

78. Ibn Khaldūn, III, p. 426, cited by Ribera, *Música de las cántigas,* p. 60 f. The share of the expedition commander, Guillaume de Montreuil, consisted of not less than 1,500 young girls. Some were sent to the Emperor of Byzantium (Menéndez Pidal, *La España del Cid,* Vol. I, p. 165 f.).

79. This may be concluded with certainty, in the opinion of A. Richard, although it is not expressly stated (*Histoire des comtes de Poitou,* Vol. I, pp. 404 ff.). Count Guilhem was not at Poitou nor was he in Provence. The daughter of Count Guillaume IV of Toulouse, the young queen of Aragon—she was between 20 and 22 years of age—was the legitimate heiress of the count. She would not have been able to consider returning to the shire of Toulouse, where her uncle (Raimon de St. Gilles) would certainly not have tolerated her presence. In view of the privileges due her, one may suspect that suitors for her hand were not lacking, but the Duke of Aquitaine was able to supplant all of them. Young, charming, handsome, he had all of the personal qualifications which would enable him to conquer the heart of a young woman ... The date of the marriage is not known, but there is every reason to believe that Guillaume did not long delay,

for he was the husband of Phillippa before the end of the year 1094.

Guillaume spent the summer and the autumn of 1094 on the preparation for and the consummation of this union, for to eliminate the competitors that were necessarily in his way, he certainly did not hesitate to make use of his personal charm. Thus for a long time he was away from Poitou, leaving the field free for rivalries and ambitions to break out unchecked . . . The celebrations and the entertainments of all sorts which necessarily accompanied Guillaume's marriage were too much to his liking for him to allow them to be interrupted. . . . History does not record any trace of the Duke of Aquitaine during the year 1095.

As A. R. Nykl observes (*op. cit.,* p. lxvii), it would have been the reverse of everything we know about the customs of the time if there had not been in the retinue of the young queen of Aragon some jongleurs or some female singers similar to those who were present at the capture of Barbastro. Thus Guilhem of Poitou would have had the occasion then to familiarize himself with the Moorish song.

80. Ordericus Vitalis, *Historia ecclesiastica,* ed. A. le Prévost, Vol. IV, p. 132. The chronicler is poorly informed with respect to the doings and the trial of the Count of Poitiers in the Holy Land. He was never in captivity. After the annihilation of his army in Anatolia, Guilhem de Poitou spent about a year midst the luxuries and pleasures of Antioch as the guest of Tancrède. This was another excellent opportunity for him to get to know the Moorish songs, which were then current in Syria. (See above, note 30).

81. Gaston Paris, *Histoire poétique de Charlemagne,* p. 48. Cf. R. Briffault, *The Mothers,* Vol. III, p. 425 ff.

Ribera put forth the thesis that the form of the Provençal heroic song (*chanson de geste*) was itself derived from a Hispano-Moorish form. ("*Discurso leído ante la real academia de historia,* "La épica entre los musulmanes españoles.") The *Chanson de Roland* owes its origin and its inspiration to the crusades in Spain from 1018 to 1120, in which a large number of French knights took part. Certainly the heroic tales were widely diffused among the barbaric nations; but the rhymed forms were not. The latter were of the form of the Arabic *qasīda.*

The opinion of J. Bédier, according to which the *chansons de geste* would have been composed in connection with pilgrimages, such as that of Santiago de Compostela (Bédier, *Les Légendes épiques*) is in accord with Ribera's theory. Groeber compares the *chansons de geste* with a sort of a Baedeker, which would have recalled to the pilgrims, the myths associated with the places which they had visited.

82. Juan Ruiz, *El libro de buen amor,* coplas 115-117.

83. Calderón de la Barca, *"Amar después de la muerte,"* Jorn. I, esc. i, *Biblioteca de autores españoles,* Vol. XII, p. 681.

For comments on the *zajal* in Spanish literature, see J. Ribera, *Disertaciones y opúsculos,* Vol. I, pp. 68 ff. The *murabba'* form of versification is found yet today in popular songs in Morocco (Rafael Arévalo, *Método práctico para hablar el árabe marroquí,* Tangier, 1909, p. 146).

84. P. de Sandoval, *Crónica del ínclito emperador Alonso VII,* p. 68. The authors of *L'Histoire générale de Languedoc* (Vol. III, p. 694) raise some doubts concerning this enfeoffment, but their objections do not seem capable of dismissing the detailed account of the chronicler. This account is repeated by Zurita, an Aragonese historian, who certainly would have had reason to raise doubts, if such existed, concerning the claims of the King of Castile. The Aragonese Kings' affirmation of their rights to the shire of Toulouse dates back to 1093 (A. Richard, *Histoire des comtes de Poitou,* Vol. II, p. 403).

85. C. Raynouard, *Lexique roman,* Vol. I, p. 512.

86. *Le Troubadour Folquet de Marseille,* ed. S. Stronski, p. 85. Cf. Bernard d'Auriac:

> *Nostre reys qu'es donor ses par*
> *vol desplegar*
> *son gomfano.*

> —C. Raynouard, *Chiox de poésies,* Vol. IV, p. 241.

Mathieu Paris (1213) spoke of heretics *in partibus Tolosanis et Aragonum regno.*

87. *Poésies de Marcabru,* ed. Dejeanne, p. 109. "Reial" was very common in France as a battle-cry. It was also used in Portugal (Manuel Mila y Fontanals, *Trovadores en España,* p. 79, n.). The oldest Provençal money, coined by the counts of Toulouse, bore the crown of Aragon and was known by the names, "royal sous" or "crown sous" (Jean de Gaufridi, *Histoire de Provence,* Vol. I, p. 78).

88. E. Baret, *Les Troubadours et leur influence sur la littérature du Midi de l'Europe,* p. 24.

89. R. Dozy, *Recherches sur l'histoire et la littérature de l'Espagne pendant le moyen âge,* Vol. I, p. 99.

90. J. Anglade, ed., *Les Poésies de Peire Vidal*, p. 2.

91. Juan de Mariana, *Historia de España*, Book IX, ch. 1.

92. R. Dozy, *Histoire des Musulmans en Espagne*, Vol. III, pp. 83 ff.; R. Altamira, *Historia de España*, Vol. I, pp. 215 f.

93. R. Dozy, *Recherches sur l'histoire et la littérature de l'Espagne*, Vol. I, pp. 215 f.

94. R. Altamira, *op. cit.*, Vol. I, p. 262; R. Dozy, *Recherches*, Vol. I, p. 201.

95. Dadin de Hauteserre, *Rerum aquitanarum libri v*, p. 513, citing the *Chronicon malleacense*. There seems to have been some confusion concerning Guilhem's two principal expeditions into Spain. Nevertheless, the chronicle explicitly gives June 17, 1115 as the date of the victory gained by the count and his Limousin knights at Cordova. Fauriel says that he was on all of these expeditions. (*Histoire de la poésie provençale*, Vol. I, p. 464). Cf. Besly, *Histoire des comtes de Poitou* (1647), pp. 434, 437; *Recueil des historiens des Gaules et de la France*, Vol. XII, pp. 119, 413.

96. Jaufré de Vigeois, in *Recueil des historiens des Gaules et de la France*, Vol. XII, p. 425.

97. J. Anglade, *Peire Vidal*, p. 58 f.

98. Dejeanne, *Poésies de Marcabru*, p. 108.

99. *Ibid.*, p. 109.

100. J. Ribera, *La epica entre los musulmanes españoles*, p. 12.

101. Al-Maqqari, *Analectes*, Vol. I, p. 247.

102. A. González Palencia, *Historia de la literatura arábigo-española*, p. 56.

103. Milá y Fontanals, *Los trobadores en España*, p. 102.

104. *Ibid.*, pp. 261 ff.

105. 'Abd al-Wahid, *Histoire du Maghreb*, trans. by Dozy, p. 72 f.

106. R. Dozy, *Histoire des Musulmans d'Espagne*, Vol. III, p. 31.

107. *Les Poésies de Cercamon*, ed. A. Jeanroy, p. 21.

108. J. Anglade, *Peire Vidal*, p. 12.

109. *Annales du Midi*, Vol. XXI, p. 317; Menéndez Pidal, *Poesía juglaresca y juglares*, p. 167.

110. R. Menéndez Pidal, *Poesía juglaresca y juglares*, p. 140 f. Cf. "Chronicon Adelfonsi imperatoris," in *España sagrada*, Vol. XXI, p. 354.

111. Al-Maqqari, *Analectes*, Vol. II, p. 424.

112. P. Sandaval, *Crónica del ínclito emperador Alonso VII*, p. 70 f.

113. *Chronicon Adelfonsi imperatoris, España sagrada,* Vol. XXI, p. 379.

114. *Roderici toletani archepiscopi de rebus Hispaniae,* 1155, Book VII, Chapter IX, in *Recueil des historiens des Gaules et de la France,* Vol. XII, p. 383.

115. R. Menéndez Pidal, *Poesía juglaresca,* p. 152.

116. P. Mariana, *Historia de España,* Book XI, Chapter III. Cf. *Recueil des historiens des Gaules et de la France,* Vol. XII, p. 413, note.

117. *Histoire littéraire de la France,* Vol. XVIII, p. 571.

118. R. Altamira, *Historia de España,* Vol. I, p. 425.

119. V. A. Canello, *Arnaldo Daniello,* p. 105. Of the eighteen of his songs which we possess—a very small fraction of his total works— at least three deal with a lady of Aragon who, judging by the numerous puns on *l'aura,* must have been named Laura. Arnaud would not have lost his love "for all the riches of Lucerna," or "for the throne of the kingdom of Ebro" (xvi and x). Lucerna, today Lucena, which he mentions in two songs, is a town in the province of Valencia. In Arnaud Daniel's time Lucerna was a Moorish village, the *taïfa* of Valence not having been annexed by the Christians until 1238. Lucerna was the scene of the novel, *Enfance Vivien,* to which Arnaud Daniel frequently refers.

120. A. Jeanroy, "Les Troubadours en Espagne," *Annales du Midi,* XXVII, p. 147.

121. *Seconde Biographie de Bertram de Born,* ed. Stimmung, p. 54.

122. C. Chabaneau, in *Histoire générale de Languedoc,* Vol. X, p. 223, n. 5.

123. *Ibid.*

124. *Ibid.*

125. A. Jeanroy, "Les Troubadours en Espagne," *Annales du Midi,* Vol. XXVII, p. 146.

126. C. de Lollis, "Il Canzoniere provenzale, Codex Vat. 523w", *Studi di filologia romanza,* Vol. III, p. 610.

127. Menéndez Pidal, *Poesía juglaresca,* p. 149.

128. The only historical trace of the passage of Guilhem de Cabestanh into Spain is the appearance of his name in the list of knights who took part in the battle of las Navas de Tolosa. It is given by Pero Anton Beuther and regarded by Chabaneau as being authentic. The Provençal biography of Cabestanh consists merely of a romantic legend, but it is significant that in this tale the prince who avenges the

murder of the lovers is none other than the king of Aragon, Alphonse
II.

129. Milá y Fontanals, *Trobadores en España*, p. 324.

130. Menéndez Pidal, *op. cit.*, p. 147.

131. Menéndez Pidal, *op. cit.*, p. 9.

132. *Ibid.*, p. 23 f. C. Michaelis de Vasconcellos (*Cancioneiro de
Ajuda*, Vol. II, p. 650) thought the word to be Provençal. In Italian
the word was *zieglero* (G. Crescimbeni, *Istoria della volgare poesia*,
p. 96), thus apparently confirming Ribera's conjecture. Cf. also
Menéndez Pidal, *Poesía juglaresca*, p. 23.

133. Giraud Riquier, Epître lxxiv, vv, 87f., in Mahn, *Werke der
Troubadours,* Vol. IV, p. 210.

134. P. Meyer, *Recueil d'anciens textes*, i. 82; Crescini, *Manualetto
provenzale.*

The old French term "gouliar" is never applied, as some have
erroneously assumed, to any kind of jongleur. It was a popular
epithet referring to noisy, drunken and disorderly bands of Latin-
quarter students. However, it may be that, like several French pejorative designations, such as "savate" (Sp. *zabatos*) for old shoes, "hab-
ler", boaster, bragger, from Sp. *hablar,* to speak, that "gouliar" was a
pejorative application of the Italian *guillaro.*

135. P. Rajna, *I reali di Francia*, Vol. I, p. 588.

136. G. Crescimbeni, *L'Istoria della volgare poesia*, (1714), p. 96.
Any association with the German Ziegler, a brickmaker, can be safely
excluded.

G. Crescimbeni. *Istoria della volgare poesia*, p. 96. The most common designation in Italian is *gioellero*, which is usually interpreted
"provider of joy" (from *gioia*). It is, however, to be noted that this
is a Tuscan form, while the activity of the early Italian jongleurs and
troubadours was almost entirely confined to the north of the Apennines. Now among the most distinctive characteristics of all northern Italian dialects are (1) that the soft *g's* become sibillants, (2)
that there are no *i* diphthongs, (3) that there are no reduplicated
consonants (*Zorzo* for "Giorgio", *Shosa* for "Chioggia", *losa* for
"loggia"). Thus the Tuscan form gioellero would in its original form,
in northern Italy, be *zozeller*, which is essentially similar to *zoellero*,
and comes very close to the Arabic. C. Michaelis de Vasconcellos
thinks—quite likely rightly so—that the Italian appellation derived
from the Provençal (*Cancioneiro de Ajuda*, Vol. II, p. 658). The
French "Ségrier" is clearly a rendering of the Italian or the Provençal
term.

137. Ibn Khaldūn, *Prolégomènes,* tr. De Slane, Vol. III, p. 425; Hammer-Purgstall, "Note sur les mowaschschahah et les ezajal," *Journal asiatique,* 3rd series, Vol. VIII, 1899, p. 160.

138. Menéndez Pidal, *op. cit.,* p. 135.

139. Menéndez Pidal, *Poesía juglaresca,* p. 31.

140. A. Jeanroy, Dejeanne et Aubry, *Quatre poésies de Marcabru,* 3rd song; J. Ribera, *La jota aragonesa,* pp. 138 f.; *Id. La música arabe en las canciones de trobadores, troveros y minnesinger.*

"The *jota* is the supreme dance of Aragon, whose fanaticisms of love, heroism and religion it symbolizes. When an Aragonese speaks of the *jota* it is with the fervor of an enthusiast, with the sacred passion that one offers to a deity. It represents a veritable pagan cult." (Raoul Laparra, "La Musique populaire en Espagne," *Enc. de la musique.*)

In order to allow readers who are musicians to make a comparison I present (pp. 244-45) Jeanroy-Aubry's transcription of Marcabru's song, followed by an example of the *jota.* The notation of the modal system does not provide any indication of the rhythm. It thus allows the singer to alter it at will and to introduce all sorts of variations. In Marcabru's song the stanza consists of lines of eight syllables and a refrain of four syllables. This is also the structure of the *jota.* It very much resembles that of the fandango, and it is difficult to make an absolute distinction between the two. According to Larrámendi, in his *Coreografía de Guipúzcoa,* the Basque fandango is a variant of the Aragonese *jota.* (E. López Chavarri, *Música popular española,* p. 124.) "The melody of the dance is not always identical with that of the couplets. When the singer begins, the instruments become silent, except for the guitars which mark the rhythm," (E. Lopez Chavarri, *op. cit.,* p. 114, n.) The cadence is 3/4 or 6/8. Sometimes, as at Valence, the *jota* is danced and sung to a very slow measure.

141. T. Gérold, *La Musique au moyen âge,* p. 91.

142. Jean Renart, *Galeran de Bretagne,* ed. Lucien Foulet, vv. 1168 ff.

143. The subject of popular Spanish poetry prior to the poetry of the troubadours is too large a theme and requires research sufficiently impracticable under prevailing circumstances for me to discuss it fully. I shall confine my efforts to outlining its general traits. Hartmann and Ribera, as well as many Arab authors, are in agreement in believing that the *marqaz,* or the *khargaz,* of the Andalusian *azajal,* which were composed in the romance tongue, represent fragments of some popular songs which were wholly composed in that language.

Pax in no . mi . . ne Do . . . mi . .

. ni! Fetz Mar . . ca . brus los motz e.l

so. Au . jatz que di : Cum nos a

fait, per sa dous . . sor Lo Seigno .

. rius ce . le . . . sti . . . aus Pro . . bet de

nos un la . va . . . dor, C'anc, fors ou .

tra . . mar, no'n fon taus, En de lai

en . . ves Jo . . sa . . phas; E d'a . . quest

de sai vos co . . . nort.

This theory is reminiscent of Jeanroy's hypothesis concerning the origin of the refrains, but it is rather more likely in this case, since it is a matter of two distinct languages and not of a mere "tradition" for which there is no proof. However, there is no doubt that the Spanish dances, and in particular the Aragonese *jota*, which harks back to a time prior to that of the Roman occupation and is very likely of oriental origin (Phoenician, Syrian), were accompanied by songs. Gaston Paris and Jeanroy, as well as others (Du Méril, for example) are rightly in agreement in considering the songs which accompanied the dances, the *ballettes*, the *caroles* as the most characteristic and most indisputable forms of popular poetry. As in all other cases, we do not possess any Spanish dancing songs dating back to before the twelfth century. But these forms vary little; thus we are justified in forming an opinion, on the basis of those we have, concerning the nature of those from an earlier era. But those extant, which are very abundant in the song books, have the form of the Andalusian *zajal*. For example:

> Tres morillas me enamoran
>   en Jaén,
> Axa, Fátima y Marién.
>
> Tres morilias tan garridas
> iban a coger olivas
> y hallábanlas cogidas
>
>   en Jaen
> Axa, Fátima y Marién.
>
> Y hallábanlas cogidas
> y tornaban desmaidas
> y las colores perdidas
>
>   en Jaén
> Axa Fátima y Marién.

> —(*Cancionero de palacio*, cited by E. L. Chavarri,
>   *Música popular española*, p. 245.)

The Portuguese song book in the Vatican abounds in such examples.
   These dancing songs—"almost invariably composed in three couplets, each of which is followed by a refrain," a form Jeanroy attributed to the French influence (*Origines de la poésie lyrique en France*, p.

308, f.)—reproduce the oldest type of the Spanish dancing song. The Castillian dialect did not exist in the eleventh century, or else it was a dialect of absolutely no importance. There is little doubt that the language of these Spanish *ballettes* was essentially the same as that of Aragon, the language of the jongleurs and the troubadours, "Provençal." "Not long ago all of the singers and troubadours in our land, although they came from Castille, or Andalusia, or Estremadura, composed their works in the Galician language, that is Portuguese." So said the marquis of Santillana in the fifteenth century (cited by Gottfried Bain, *Geschichte der spanischen Literatur*, in Groeber, *Grundriss der romanischen Philologie*, Bd. II, Abt. 2, p. 389. Cf. above, note 73). There was a Romance language which extended, if we exclude slight local variations, from Seville and Cordova as far as Toulouse and Poitiers.

There is a persistent popular tradition which would place the origin of the Aragonese *jota* in Valence and further would attribute its "invention" to the Arabs. This tradition indicates that the Aragonese people were aware of the influence which Arabic music and poetry exerted on their national dance, although this dance, which has for them the importance of a cult, probably arose even earlier.

144. *Parnasse occitanien*, p. 340; C. Raynouard, *Lexique roman*, Vol. I, p. 382.

It may very well be, and it is even probable, that the count of Poitiers, who was a man with an alert and extremely inquisitive mind, acquired at least a few fragments of Arabic during his sojourns in Spain and at Antioch. M. A. R. Nykl (*The Dove's Neck-Ring*, p. cxiii) noted that the nonsense rhymes the count introduced into his *Farai un vers por mi sonelh* (No. 5 in the Jeanroy edition) had a decidedly Arabic appearance. Here is the strophe according to Bibliothèque Nationale, Ms. fr. 856, which Mahn adopts:

> Aujatz ieu que lur respozi;
> anc fer ni fust no y mentagui,
> mais que lur dis aital lati:
>   "Tarrababart
> marrababelio riben
>   saramahart."

Nykl suggests that this is a mixture of Arabic and Turkish and interprets thus: *Tara wara-l-bab* (look behind the door); *marat* or *marten* (women); *biliorum* (I know), *ben* (myself); *sar nnhar bard* (it is cold today).

Without attempting a reconstruction, which would only be con-jectural, I propose rather:

Tarra bab, arra (or *aya*)	Please close the door!
Marhaba!	May God increase thy bounty!
	(fig.; A very common greeting.)
'eulen (Maghrabine form)	I know (that you are)
ryah bent	a deceitful girl.
Sarra ma hard.	How cold it is!

Taking into account the defective Arabic and the errors of numerous copyists, the galimatias of the man who pretends to be dumb appear to be passably intelligible. It is not a matter, of course, of correctly de-ciphering these galimatias, but to show that they are amenable to transliteration.

The linguistic "abyss" between the Arabic world and the Latin world in the thirteenth century, as imagined by Renan and as is gen-erally assumed, certainly did not exist. The many Arabic words in our languages bear witness against this supposition. Linguistic diffusion always consists of a transference of the language of the most civilized culture to that of the least civilized. Modern Europeans are of the opinion that the now decayed Arabic world is half barbaric; but in the twelfth century just the opposite was true: compared to barbarous Europe, the Arabic world was highly civilized. A large number of the Arabic words which have passed into our language are scientific words which we have obtained by means of books and education. But there are many others which have come by way of the daily commerce between the two peoples and which presuppose a certain, linguistic knowledge, even if only of the "pidgin" type, on the part of the Europeans. Words relating to commerce and government, such as "douane" (customhouse) from *diwan*, "amiral" (admiral) from *émir* or émir *al-bahr*; nautical terms, such as "cable" from *habl*, "goudron" (tar) from *gatran*, "caravel" (*garaf*), etc.; names of com-modities: "café," "sucre" (sugar), "candi" (candy), "chandelle" (candle) from *candil*, "jarre" (jar), "coton" (cotton), "baldaquin" (baldachin) from *bagdadi*, the name of a fabric which came from

Baghdad, "baraque" (hut, barracks); names of flowers: "lilas," "jasmin," etc.; names of articles of clothing: "chemise" from *kamis,* "jupe" (Eng. jupe, shirt) or "jupon" from *jubba,* "savate" (shoe, sabot) from *sebbat.* The jongleurs called their musical instruments by their Arabic names. Words of Arabic origin, which imply a very intimate knowledge of a spoken language, are found in Provençal. For example: *galaubia* = magnificence, generosity; *galib* = chivalrous, literally, "resembling 'Ali," Islam's ideal knight. Cf. "algarade" (Arab. *al-garah* = incursion).

145. *Histoire littéraire de la France,* Vol. IX, p. 174.

146. See miniature from the manuscript of "Cantigas de Santa Maria," Bibl. Escurial (b. I. 2), reproduced as Figure 24 in the original French version of this book (Robert Briffault, *Les Troubadours,* Paris, Editions du Chêne, 1945).

147. C. Chabaneau, in *Histoire générale de Languedoc,* Vol. X, p. 127.

148. It has been said that on the occasion of the battle of Calatanazor (in the province of Soria), in which Al-Mansūr's armies had undergone a reverse in 998 or 1002, a singer depored the disaster in a *planh* which was sung alternately in Arabic and in the vernacular Romance tongue (Mariana, *Historia de España,* Book VIII, Chapter IX). Father Mariana's sources are Lucas de Tuy and Rodriquez Jiminez de Rada, archbishop of Toledo, who both wrote approximately a century after the event. The chronological confusion into which these authors typically fell has raised doubts concerning the authenticity of this Christian victory. However, this has nothing to do with the incident in question. Although the tale was, after the manner of the clerics of that time, embellished with miraculous incidents—the song would have been sung in Cordova the very day of the battle, but the singer suddenly vanished—the circumstance that he uttered in his song in both languages is put forth quite naturally. This indicates, at least, that similar bilingual presentations were not unusual in the eleventh century and that in Cordova itself a similar duplication was necessary in order that the entire population understand such announcements. At the end of the thirteenth century, Guiraut Riquier, "the last of the troubadours," feeling the need of finding a patron, addressed himself to the Muslim emirs, seeking the position of singer at their courts (J. Anglade, *Les Troubadours,* p. 287). In an earlier era, the Hispano-Moorish singers themselves turned in the same way to the Spanish princes.

149. E. Renan, *Averroès et l'averroïsme*, p. 159. The abundant importation of novels, fables, narratives, etc., from the Islamic world to the West is generally recognized. Gaston Paris writes: "Whence came these tales which were so widely spread throughout Europe, many of which are popular even today? Most of them have their origin in the East . . . The Arabic importations took place through two very different locations: Syria and Spain . . . In the East, the crusaders, who lived very intimately with the Moslem population, received many of these tales by word of mouth." (*La Littérature française au moyen âge*, p. 119 f.). The extent of this light type of literature is so great that Paris devoted a whole volume to its study (*Les Contes orientaux dans la littérature française du moyen âge*), and Groeber has a long chapter on it. The *Disciplina Clericalis* was translated into French, German, Italian, English, Catalan, the language of Bearn and Icelandic; it gave rise to a whole line of tales. A vast literature of *fableaux* and *fablieux* extended through the time of Boccaccio and the Italian story-tellers, up through the sixteenth and seventeenth centuries. In France, *Floire et Blanchefleur, Aucassin et Nicolette,* the *Estormi* of Huoun Peucele, Rutebeuf's *Testament de l'âne*, the *Longue nuit,* the *Vilain mire*, from which Molière took the theme of his "The Doctor in Spite of Himself," are derived directly from the repertories of the Arab and Hispano-Moorish story-tellers. The very novels of chivalry are adorned in oriental garb and sometimes, as for example in the case of *Enfance Vivien*, are actually Arabic stories. Even hagiology and the lives of the saints are derived from the same source, as for example, *Barlaam et Josaphat* (G. Paris, *op. cit.*, pp. 233 ff.). Thus tales and narratives freely crossed this abyss which was deemed "uncrossable" to popular song.

Jeanroy aptly said, "If there is a buoyant, winged poetry which flies easily and rapidly from mouth to mouth, it is lyrical poetry." But he added: "From early times our dances have also travelled beyond our frontiers" (*Origines de la poésie lyrique*, p. 125). In what direction? Surely not as a foreign importation into Spain, the cradle of the dance from time immemorial and, for the last two centuries, of lyric poetry also.

Ribera remarks on this subject: "This preference that the troubadours have shown for Spain, their frequent trips, and constant intercourse with that country, have been interpreted by scholars as indications of the influence of the poets from beyond the mountains on the poetry of the peninsula. The possibility has not occurred to their jaded imagination that the effect of these perpetual visits could have operated in the opposite direction, and that the Provençal singers may have learned anything bearing on that 'new form of art' which had seen the light of day long ago in Spain" (*La música de las cántigas*, p. 142 n.).

150. Benjamin of Tudela, cited by Sabatier, *op. cit.*, p. 7.

In 1195 the council of Montpellier forbade Christians to serve as domestics in the houses of Saracens or Jews (Manse: *Sacr. conc. nova et ampliori coll.*, Vol. XXII, col. 669). "Decrevit etiam, ut Judaei sive Sarraceni nullam super Christianos habeant potestatem, nec eos Christianis praeficere quiquam praesumant, neque sub alendorum peurorum obtentu, nec pro servitio, nec alia qualibet causa, in domibus suis servientes Christianos aut Christianas permittantur habere." Very probably the Jews played an important role in the diffusion of the Andalusian song, as well as in the diffusion of all Arabic literature and all the knowledge of the Arabs. The Spanish Jews were very often jongleurs by profession. Indeed the Jews have a predilection for the profession of music and song. Even today in Morocco most of the popular musical and dancing establishments are to be found in the *mellah* (ghettos) and the musicians, singers and dancers are Jews. "Many of the musicians in the service of the Spanish Kings were Jews, as the *livres de raison* of the royal houses attest" (E. López Chavarri, *Música popular española*, p. 27).

Juan Ruiz mentions the festivities with Jewish female singers (*Libro de buen amor*, couplets 1513 f.). During the reign of Alphonse X, "judging from accounts dating from the succeeding reign, the king's palace employed a large number of Moorish and Jewish jongleurs" (R. Menéndez Pidal, *Poesía juglaresca*, p. 138). After the Almorivade conquest these Jewish jongleurs went everywhere; they were to be found even in England. Always great polyglots, the Jewish jongleurs were the interpreters of the songs which they chanted to their Provençal confreres. Moreover, a large number of Spanish Jews, following the example provided by all of the literate persons of Moorish Spain, cultivated poetry, composing it either in Arabic or in the romance tongue. Many of the most celebrated among them settled in Provence. The famous Aben-Ezra, himself the translator of Averroes and the Arabian philosophers, composed songs. Of the multitude of Jewish poets living in Provence, one may cite Abraham Bédersi de Béziers, Joseph Ezobi de Perpignan, Isaac Gorni, Al Mazizzi, Sulami (Renan, in *Histoire littéraire de la France*, Vol. XXVII, pp. 723 ff. Cf. *Histoire générale de Languedoc*, Vol. III, p. 865; G. Saige, *Les Juifs du Languedoc antérieurement au XIVe siècle*).

III. AMOUR COURTOIS

1. Diez and Jeanroy discovered the "germs" of courtly love in the poems of Guilhelm de Poitiers (Jeanroy, *Les Chansons de Guillaume IX*, p. xvii and f.). These "germs" are indeed embryonic. But Jeanroy goes even further. "The courtly formulary is given us complete in all its aspects in the songs of Guillaume IX" ("La poésie provençale au moyen âge," *Revue des Deux-Mondes*, 1903, p. 668 f.). All the examples which Jeanroy cites to support this assertion are found in similar form, and even more distinct and mature, in the Hispano-Moorish poetry in the treatise of Ibn Hazm and in the songs of Ibn Quzmān.

(a) "The type of mystical exaltation which has as its cause and as its goal the faith of the beloved woman, as well as love itself, has already been designated under the word *joi*; the enthusiastic hymn that the poet sings in its honor (IX) . . . naturally assumes the existence both of the phenomenon and of its name."

The hymn to love which Ibn Farid sings is even more fervidly enthusiastic (Grangeret de Lagrange, *Anthologie arabe*, p. 33). Similar hymns abound in Hispano-Arabic poetry (cf. *Ibn-Khaldûn*, ed. De Slane, Vol. III, p. 427.) The definition which Jeanroy gives of "joy" is his own invention. Nothing which approaches it is found in the work of any other troubadour. But Jeanroy's imaginary definition rather closely resembles the *tarab* of Sufi poetry.

(b) "During this period there was the assimilation of the 'service of love' to the feudal service . . . The use of the expressions *escriure en sa carta* and *retenir* is certainly authentic."

Ibn Hazm, 39: "The sword has become the slave of the hilt"; 40: "in love the haughty become humble"; 76: "the duty of the lady is to return love to her lover."

(c) "At this period, finally, the respective attitudes of the woman and of the lover were fixed":

"I give the rules of love in 50 chapters" (Ibn Dawūd, in *The Dove's Neck-Ring*, p. civ.)

(d) "The one disdainful and inexorable" (of a woman) (VII, VIII, IX, X).

"The gazelle becomes a lioness" (Ibn Hazm, 39). "She is haughty and disdainful among women" (Ibn Quzmān, cxii). The "cruelty of the well-loved" is the subject of an entire section of Sufi doctrine (Gibb, *History of Ottoman Poetry,* Vol. I, p. 22).

(e) The lover repelled (VII).

"When you reproach me I shall become the most miserable of mortals. Nevertheless death for the love of you would be sweet" (Ibn Hazm, 39, 40, 60).

(f) So timid he dares not to declare himself (IX, X).

"He who loves but remains chaste and does not reveal his secret" (Massignon, *La passion d' al-Hallai,* Vol. I, p. 174).

(g) Relying on patience (VII).

"He who does not show evidence of patience will weep" (Ibn Dawūd, *The Dove's Neck-Ring*, p. cv).

(h) Already we praise women for their worldly traits of character (IX).

"She is a sultaness among women" (Ibn Quzmān, cxii).

(i) And for the man, love is considered as the source of these very qualities (VII).

"He who is incapable of courage and chivalry is incapable of pious love" (Ibn Hazm, p. 3).

(j) The courtier, finally, is the evident opposite of the villian (VII).

"No one deviates from loyalty unless he is of low birth and lacking refinement" (Ibn Dawūd), *The Dove's Neck-Ring*, p. cv).

On this count Jeanroy certainly bears notable witness to the formulation in all its aspects of courtly love in Moorish Spain. I do not think, however, that we should be justified in pushing too far the attribution of courtly conventions to the Arabs.

2. Jaufré de Vigeois, in *Recueil des historiens*, Vol. XII, p. 424.

3. C. Chabaneau, in *Histoire générale de Languedoc*, Vol. X, p. 217. Chabaneau thinks that Ventadorn's court of Eble was a school of courtly poetry whence sprang many generations of troubadours (*Revue des langues romanes*, XXXV, p. 382).

4. Ed. Stimmung, p. 54.

5. Ed. Dejeanne, p. 149.

6. *Histoire générale de Languedoc*, Vol. III, p. 859.

7. Raoul Glaber, "Historiae sui temporis," in *Recueil des historiens des Gaules et de la France*, Vol. X, p. 42.

8. Jaufré de Vigeois, in *Recueil des historiens*, Vol. XII, p. 144.

9. P. Andraud, *La Vie et l'oeuvre du troubadour Raimon de Miraval*, p. 162.

10. Let a single example suffice to show the contrast, which could be amply illustrated, between the conduct of the Muslims and that of the "Christians." I take it from the history of *Jérusalem*, by Besant and Palmer: "It was agreed that the lives and property of the defenders of Acre would be spared on the conditions that they pay 200,000 dinars, free 500 captives and return the True Cross ... Saladin made a down payment of 100,000 dinars, but refused to pay the rest or to hand over the prisoners until he had some guarantee that the Christians intended to keep their word and to free the inhabitants of Acre. ... The money was weighed out, the prisoners brought to be freed and the True Cross presented. Richard the Lion Hearted, who was encamped at Merj'Ayun, had the prisoners of war placed behind him on a hill. Suddenly at a signal from King Richard, the Christian soldiers threw themselves on the unfortunate prisoners and put them all to the sword. Confronted with the spectacle of this atrocity, Saladin maintained the dignity and the humanity of his chivalrous character. The proud Saladin did not deign to sully his honor by making reprisals. He simply refused to give up the money or the Cross and sent the prisoners back to Damascus. Who, Saladin or Richard the Lion Hearted, was the true knight?"

As for the orders of knighthood, it has been demonstrated that the institution is considerably older in the Islamic world than in the Christian (Hammer-Purgstall, "La Chevalrie des Arabes antérieure à celle de l'Europe," *Journal asiatique,* 1849, 4ᵉ série, Vol. XIII, pp. 5 ff.). The Almohades were an order of chivalry. Cf. C. J. Wehe, *Das Ritterwesen,* Vol. I, pp. 132 ff. Viardot, *Histoire des Arabes,* Vol. II, p. 196; Wacyf Boutras Ghali, *La Tradition chevaleresque chez les Arabes.*

"Chivalry was born of the mingling of the Arabic people and the peoples of the north" (Châteaubriand, *Etudes et discours,* ed. 1841, p. 396).

11. Stendhal, *L'Abbesse de Castro,* Preface.

12. Miguel Cervantes, *El ingenioso hidalgo don Quijote de la Mancha,* Part I, Ch. XXIII.

13. A. Stimmung, in Grober, *Grundriss der romanischen Philologie,* Vol. II, pp. 19 f.; J. Anglade, *Les Troubadours,* pp. 27 f.

14. *Histoire littéraire de la France,* Vol. XXIII, p. 512.

15. C. Raynouard, *Choix des poésies,* Vol. II, p. 160 f.

16. The profession of singer or minstrel was under a church ban from the time of Charlemagne. "He who brings actors, mimes and dancers into his house is forgetting the host of devils that he lets in along with them," said Alcuin. "God forbid that the devil should establish himself in a Christian home" (Alcuin, in Pertz, *Monumenta Germaniae Historica, Epistolae Karolini Aevi,* Vol. II, Epistola, CLXXV, p. 290). Leidrad, Archbishop of Rheims, denounced "the songs of the poets, the ostentations and the verses of actors, which corrupt the soul" (*ibid.* p. 541). These anathemas were repeated by many Councils (E. Faral, *Les Jongleurs en France au moyen âge,* pp. 272 ff.). The Sixth Council of Paris defined the duties of kings to be: "To prevent theft, to punish adultery, and to refuse to maintain jongleurs" (Migne, *Patrologiae cursus,* Vol. CXXXIX, col. 477). Jongleurs were refused the sacraments, "because they are the ministers of Satan" (W. Hetz, *Spielmanns-Buch,* p. 317; E. Gautier, *Epopées françaises,* Vol. II, p. 11). As the disgrace, however, continued to manifest itself, the church began to adapt itself and to compromise. Poems dealing with heroic deeds, particularly those of Christian heroes, were exempt from condemnation (E. Gautier, *op. cit.,* p. 11; Faral, *op. cit.,* p. 67; C. Nyrop, *Storia dell' epopea francese,* pp. 279 ff.). This is probably the reason for the prevalence of the *chanson de geste* in France. Later on, companies of jongleurs were enrolled in the service of the Church; they composed sacred canticles and religious plays.

17. Gui d'Ussel:

Ben feira chanzoz plus soven
mas enoja.m tot jorn a dire
qu'eu plang per amore e sospire,
quar o sabon tuit dir comunalmen:
per q'eu volgra mots nous ab son plasen,
mas re no trob q'autra vez dit uo sia.
De cal gisa.us pregarai doncs, amia?
Aqo meteis dirai d'autre semblan,
qu'aiai farai senblar novel mon chan.

Gladly would I make more songs, but it would be bothersome
to say continually that love makes me weep and sigh, for anyone can say as much. To this agreeable melody I should like
to put some new words, but I can find nothing that has not
already been said. How then, my love, should I address my
entreaties to you? I shall say the same thing in a manner
which appears different, thus apparently giving the form of
novelty to my song.

—*Les poésies des quatre troubadours d'Ussel,*
edited by Jean Audiau, p. 27.

18. F. Diez, *Geschichte der Troubadours,* pp. 117 f.; A Birch-
Hirschfeld, *Ueber den Troubadours des XII, und XIII. Jahrhunderts*
bekannten epische Stoffe, p. 40; L. Sudre, "Les Allusions à la légende
de Tristan dans la littérature du moyen âge," *Romania,* XV, p. 534f.

19. F. Diez, *Die Poesie der Troubadours,* pp. 128 ff.

20. Petrarca, *I trionfi,* III, 56-57.

21. M. E. Wechsler, "Frauendienst und Vassalitat," in *Zeitschrift*
für romanische Sprache und Literatur, XXIV, pp. 159 ff.

22. T. Ribot, *La Psychologie des sentiments,* p. 244.

23. Salvianus, *De gubernatione dei,* VI, 72; VII, 16, 27; in Migne,
Patrologiae cursus, Vol. LIII, col. 120, 132, 135.

24. C. de Lollis, *Studi medievali,* I, p. 21.

25. P. Andraud, *La Vie et l'oeuvre du troubadour Raimon de*
Miraval, p. 146.

26. E. J. W. Gibb noted in this respect (*History of Ottoman*
Poetry, Vol. I, p. 24) : There are many poets who are primarily artistic
in words; these take such for what they are worth as decorative ad-
juncts, and work them into verses to produce some desired aesthetic

effect . . . While many poets were truly Sufis, others, and they are perhaps the majority, merely play with Sufi ideas and Sufi phrases . . . They found these ideas and phrases ready to hand, and these became, along with many things similarly acquired, so many "studio properties" for the poet, to be introduced into his words as occasion might suggest.

27. J. Anglade, *Les Troubadours*, p. 79.

28. Raymon Vidal, in *Histoire littéraire de la France*, Vol. XVIII, p. 634.

29. Ugo de Mataplana, in P. Andraud, *La Vie et l'oeuvre du troubadour Raimon de Miraval*, p. 138 f.

30. G. Paris, *Poèmes et légendes du moyen âge*, p. 173 f.

IV. CONCEPTION OF LOVE

1. Emil Lucka, *Die drei Stufen der Erotik*, Berlin, 1913, p. 137 f.

2. Louis Gillet, *Dante*, p. 22 f.

3. K. Weinhold, *Die deutschen Frauen in dem Mittelalter*, p. 181.

4. P. Andraud, *La Vie et l'oeuvre du troubadour Raimon de Miraval*, p. 162.

5. Guillaume de Malmesbury, *De gestis anglorum*, in *Recueil des historiens des Gaules et de la France*, Vol. XIII, p. 19.

6. Jaufré Gros, *Vita B. Bernardi abbati de Tirono*, *Rec. des historiens*, Vol. XIV, p. 169. The establishment of an "Abbey" of debauchery is attributed to Count Guilhem (Guillaume de Malmesbury, *loc. cit.;* cf. P. Rajna, "La badia di Niort," in *Romania*, VI, pp. 249 f.).

7. A. Jeanroy, *Les Chansons de Guillaume IX, duc d'Aquitaine*, p. 25.

8. *Ibid.*, p. xviii.

9. *Ibid.*, p. 15.

10. Boccaccio, *Decameron*, Third Day, I.

11. *Les Chansons de Guillaume IX*, p. 12 f.

12. *Les Poésies de Cercamon*, ed. A. Jeanroy, p. vii.

13. *Ibid.*, p. 2.

14. *Ibid.*, p. 7.

15. *Ibid.*, p. 13 f.

16. *Oeuvres de Marcabru*, ed. Dejeanne, p. 1. About two centuries

before Marcabru, Ibn Hazm said: "Who would trust a woman, but a fool?" (*Tauk-al-Hamama,* ed. Pétrof, p. 50).

17. *Ibid.,* p. 84.

18. *Ibid.,* p. 117.

19. *Bernart von Ventadorn,* ed. C. Appel, p. lxxiv.

20. *Ibid.,* p. 207 f.

21. *Ibid.,* p. 146.

22. *Ibid.,* p. 159; cf. pp. 114, 152, 183, 195.

23. *Les Chansons de Jaufré Rudel,* ed. A. Jeanroy, p. 15. Love inspired by a lady that the lover has never seen is a very widespread theme. We saw it above in the book of Ibn Hazm. Love of a distant princess occurs frequently in "A Thousand Nights and One." In fact, ordinarily a Muslim does not see his betrothed before the marriage. In the novel of *Flamenca* the hero falls passionately in love with a lady he has never seen. See: Lotte Zade, *Der Troubadour Jaufré Rudel und das Motiv der Fernliche in der Weltliteratur.*

24. *Ibid.,* pp. 8 and 2; Raynouard, *Choix des poésies,* Vol. III, p. 94.

25. Dante, *De vulgari eloquentia,* II, xi.

26. *Bertram de Born,* ed. Stimmung, VII, 431, p. 69. Dante, who abuses Bertram de Born so atrociously and unjustly in Hell (*Inferno,* XXVIII, 118 ff.) cites him elsewhere as a notable example of largess and liberality (*Convito,* IV, 11).

27. *Ibid.,* p. 130.

28. *Ibid.,* p. 123 f. The *gaillardises* of Guilhem de Poitiers are sometimes equaled by those of Bertram de Born. For example, the song *Ieu m'escondisc* (ed. Stimmung, 31, p. 120 f.).

29. *Les Chansons de Guilhem de Cabestanh,* ed. Arthur Längfors, p. 11.

30. *Ibid.,* p. 13.

31. *Les Poésies de Peire Vidal,* ed. J. Anglade, p. 6 f.

32. *Ibid.,* p. 46.

33. *Ibid.,* p. 58.

34. *Ibid.,* p. 63.

35. *Ibid.,* p. 63 f.

36. *Ibid.,* p. 145 f; cf. p. 136.

37. P. Meyer, *Recueil d'anciens textes bas-latins, provençaux et français,* I, 82.

38. J. Anglade, *Les Troubadours,* p. 130.

39. C. Raynouard, *Choix de poésies originales des troubadours,* Vol. III,

From p. 312: *Qu'aissi serai justiziatz*
e fis de gran damnatge,
s'il sieus gens cors blancs e prezatz
m'es estrans ni m'estai iratz.

From p. 305: *Mas quan veirai home de son linhatge*
lauzar l'ai tan tro que la boca m fen
tan d'amor port al sieu bel cors jauzen.

40. Dante, *Purgatorio*, canto, xxvi, 117.
41. U. A. Canello, *La Vita e le opere del trovatore Arnaldo Daniello*, p. 111.
42. *Ibid.*, p. 115 f.
43. Dante, *Purgatorio*, canto xxvi, 82.

Nostro peccato fu ermafrodito
ma perchè non servammo umana legge,
seguendo come bestie l'appetito
in obbrobrio di noi, per noi si legge.

44. U. A. Canello, *op. cit.*, p. 95.
45. Dante, *De vulgari eloquentia, II*, x.
46. U. Canello, *op. cit.*, p. 109. Petrarch imitated the famous phrase, *"chatz la lebre ab lo bou."*

Ed una cerva errante e fugitiva
Caccio con un bue zoppe e'nfermo e lento.

—*Sonetto*, CLVIII

47. *Ibid.*, p. 115.
48. *Ibid.*, p. 102.
49. *Ibid.*, p. 97 ff.
50. Raimon Jordan, in *Le Parnasse occitanien*, p. 200.
51. Gaucelm Faidit, in C. A. F. Mahn, *Gedichte der Troubadours*, Vol. I, p. 36.
52. Raimon de Durfort, in *Parnasse occitanien*, p. 75; Peire de Bussinhac, *ibid.*, p. 292; Trucs Molesc, "Ueber die in Italien befindlichen provenzalisiche Liederhandschriften," in *Archiv für das Studium der neueren Sprachen u. Literatur*, XXXIV, p. 200. "On the erotic poetry of the troubadours, one must cite some songs of Daude

de Prades, Canon of Maguelone, the coarse poems of Montan and his lady, and those of Mir Bernard and of Sifre" (Anglade, *Les Trouba-dours*, p. 316).

53. C. Raynouard, *Choix de poésies*, Vol. III, p. 218. *"Voluntatz qu'ai del vostre cors gen."* Cf. *ibid.*, p. 203 f.

54. *Ibid.*, Vol. III, p. 223.

55. We append the following examples:

Guilhem Adhemar, in C. Raynouard, *Choix des poésies*, Vol. III, p. 197.

> *E non envei el mon nulh home nat,*
> *si m vol mi dons tener vestit o nut,*
> *baizan lonc se, en luec de mollerat:*
> *anc no fon fag al nieu par tals honors*
> *cum er a mi s'en aissi s'esdeve;*
> *qu'el sieu cors blanc, gras e chauzit e le*
> *remir baizan, ni m tenc entre mos bratz.*

Peire Rogier, in Mahn, *Die Werke der Troubadours*, Vol. I, p. 120:

> *Molt mi fera gen secors*
> *s'una vetz ab nueg escura*
> *mi mezes lai o s'despuelha.*

Giraud de Salignac, in Raynouard, *Choix de poésies*, Vol. III, p. 395:

> *En vos podon complir tug mey voler.*

Bernard Arnaud de Montcuc: *Ibid.*, Vol. II, p. 217.

> *Dona, que m'esglai*
> *lo desir qu'ieu n'ay*
> *del vostre bel cors cortes,*
> *complit de totz bes.*

The same formulae were frequently used by the *trouvères* of the *langue d'oil*. Thus, for example, Seigneur de Couci, the most elegant among them, sings:

Que cele où j'ai mon coeur et mon penser
tiegne une foiz entre mes bras nuete.

—Châtelain de Coucy, *Chansons*, ed. Fr. Michel, p. 33;
cf. p. 31.

56. U. Canello, *Arnaldo Daniello*, pp. 99, 101.
57. Marcabru, *Poésies complètes*, ed. Dejeanne, p. 198.
58. *Ibid.*, p. 180.
59. J. Anglade, ed., *Peire Vidal*, p. 2.
60. Maria de Ventadorn, in *Parnasse occitanien*, p. 267.
61. "Razo" à un poème de Miraval, [cited by] P. A. Andraud, *Raimon de Miraval*, p. 102.
62. *Ibid.*, p. 124.
63. Andreas Capellanus, *De Amore*, ed. E. Trojel, p. 310 f.
64. Bernard de Ventadorn, cited in A. Langfors, *Les Chansons de Guilhem de Cabestanh*, p. 44. Cf. J. Anglade, ed., *Peire Vidal*, p. 2:

> *es fols qui.s vai vanan*
> *son joi.*

65. A. Langfors, *Guilhem de Cabestanh*, p. 14.
66. See Pätzold, *Die individuellen Eigenthumlichkeiten einiger hervorragender Troubadours*, para. 79.

We have seen that among the Arabs the corresponding term (*lauzengier*) had special connotations note (43). It has thus perplexed many commentators. Jeanroy said that the term "tells us hardly anything concerning its meaning" ("Etudes sur l'ancienne poésie provençale" in *Neuphilologischen Mitteilungen*, XXX, 1929, p. 225). Nevertheless, the *Breviari d'amor* are quite explicit: "*Lauzengier e mal parlador, car ilh fau les donas lunhar dels amadors am mal parlar*" (II, 641).

67. Marcabru, ed. Dejeanne, p. 116.
68. *Ibid.*, p. 179.
69. *Les Poésies de Peire Vidal*, ed. J. Anglade, p. 148 f.
70. C. Appel, "L'Enseignement de Garin le Brun", *Revue des langues romanes*, XXIII, p. 406 ff.
71. Marcabru, ed. Dejeanne, p. 26.
72. *Roman de Renard*, III, 303.
73. William Langland, *Piers the Plowman*, Passus I, 85; ed. W. W. Skeat, p. 27. "Hit is as derworthe a drur ie as decre god himseluen."

74. J. Bédier, *Le Roman de Tristan, par Thomas*, Vol. I, p. 259.

75. Dante, *Inferno*, canto xviii, line 133. In the *Convito* (III, 15), however, Dante speaks of *"drudi della filosofia,"* lovers of philosophy.

76. C. Appel, *Bernart von Ventadorn*, p. lxxiv.

77. F. Diez, *Die Gedichte der Troubadours*, p. 131.

78. P. Andraud, *Raimon de Miraval*, p. 34.

V. THE ALBIGENSES CRUSADE

1. *Monumenta Germaniae historica, Poetae latini*, Vol. I, p. 499.

2. "At this time . . . the Northern nobility, with much cruder mores, had scarcely any taste for poetical relaxation or for adventures which it could make the subject of poetry" (A. Jeanroy, *Origines de la poésie lyrique*, p. 76).

3. S. Munk, *Mélanges de philosophie juive et arabe*, p. 487 ff.

4. Georgius Cedrenus, *Historia universalis*, II, 153; Johannes Zonaras, *Epitome Historion*, II, xiv. "Dante only saw Muhammad as the author of a schismatic doctrine and Islamism as an Arian sect" (Renan, *Averroès et l'averroïsme*, p. 241).

5. Guizot, trans., *Chronique de Guillaume de Puy-Laurens*, Chapter VII.

6. St. Bernard, *Epistola*, CCXXI, in Migne, *Patrologia*, Vol. 182, col. 434.

7. *Aucassin et Nicolette*, Chapter VI.

8. C. Raynouard, *Lexique roman*, Vol. I, p. 382.

9. R. Altamira, *Historia de España*, Vol. I, p. 420 f.

10. Innocent III, *Epist.* LVII, LXXV, in Migne, *Patrologia*, Vol. CCXV, col. 355-57.

11. Dante, *Inferno*, XIX, 112; *Paradiso*, XXI, 135 f.

12. Petrarch, *Rime*, cxxxvii. Sonnets XIV and XVI are still more violent in their denunciation of the church: "Fiamma del ciel su le tue trecce piova" and "Fontana di diolore, albergo d'ira." (May fire from heaven rain down on your trickeries; fountain of affliction, hostel of wrath.) Similar comments are to be found elsewhere in Dante:

> The walls which were wont to be a house of prayer have become dens, and the hoods are sacks full of foul meal. But heavy usury is not exalted so counter to God's pleasure as the fruit which doth so madden the monk's heart.
>
> Par. XXII.

13. *Histoire littéraire de la France*, Vol. XX, p. 574.

> *Quar azir tort aissi cum suelh*
> *et am dreg, si cum fer ancse*
> *e qui qu'aia autre thesor*
> *Ieu ai leialtat en mon cor*
> *tant qu'enemic m'en son li plus leial;*
> *e si per so aziron, no m'en cal.*

14. The citations given are extracted from many different poems. K. Bartsch, *Chrestomathie provençale*, col. 173; *Histoire littéraire de la France*, Vol. XX, p. 577; Raynouard, *Lexique roman*, Vol. I, p. 451 f.; *Choix des poésies*, Vol. IV, p. 337.

15. V. Crescini, *Manualetto provenzale*, p. 328.

16. I. J. Döllinger, *Beiträge zur Sektengeschichte des Mittelalters*, Vol. I., pp. 120 f. Another dignitary, Julian of Palermo, came in 1201 to confirm the Cathars in Provence (C. Schmidt, *Histoire de la secte des Cathares ou Albigeois*, Vol. II, p. 145). The term "parfait" (perfect), which was applied to divinities (Pseudo-Denys l'Aréopagite, *Les Noms divins. Oeuvres*, trans. M. de Gandillac, p. 172), was current in the Orient as a hierarchical title among the Gnostic sects.

17. *Chanson de la croisade*, v. 497-500.

18. Guillaume le Breton, in the *Grandes Chroniques de France*, Vol. VI, p. 318. On the back of Lat. Ms. 5925, folio 291, the figure *vi* has been scratched out and first vii, then xvii substituted (Jules Viard, note in his edition of *Grandes Chroniques, loc. cit.*). The legate Milon, in his report to the Pope, wrote: "nostrique non parcentes ordini, sexui, vel aetati, fere viginti milli hominum in ore gladii peremerunt, factaque hostium strage permaxima spoliato est tota civitas et succensa, ultione divina in eam mirabiliter saeviente." (Our people put twenty thousand people, without regard to rank, sex or age, to the sword, and after enormous slaughter of the enemy, sacked the whole city and set it on fire, for the divine vengeance raged so wonderfully against it.) Indeed the impression which was produced by the massacre of Béziers was such that considerable effort was expended to attenuate the enormity of it. Pierre of Vaux-Cernai said: "a minimo ad maximum omnes fere necati" (*Historia Albigensium*, Chapter XVI). From the humblest to the greatest, almost all were killed. Aubri of Trois-Fontaines wrote: "sexaginta millibus hominum et amplius in ea trucidati" (*Alberici Monachi Trium Fontium Chronicon*, Hanoverae, 1698, p. 450). (Sixty thousand people and more.

were slaughtered.) Vincent de Beauvais put the number "above 70,-000" (*Speculum historiale,* Book XXX, col. ix), and Césaire de Heisterbach brought it to 100,000 (Book V, col. xxi).

19. Marchegay et Mabille, *Chroniques des églises d'Anjou,* p. 58: "Immanissimam stragem haereticorum et catholicorum quos non potuerunt discernere."

20. *Caesaris Heisterbacensis chronicon,* Book V, Chapter XXI.

21. V. Crescini, *Manualetto provenzale,* p. 333.

22. Pierre de Vaux-Cernai, *Historia Albigensium* c. xiv; *Chanson de la croisade,* verses 537-779.

23. Guillaume de Béziers, in *Histoire littéraire de la France,* Vol. XVIII, p. 552.

24. *Grandes Chroniques de France,* Vol. VI, p. 319.

25. A. Luchaire, *Innocent III: la croisade contre les Albigeois,* p. 182.

26. *Chanson de la croisade,* verse 1081 f.; Pierre de Vaux-Cernai, Chapter XXXVII.

27. Aiméric of Montréal is mentioned in the biography of Miraval, *Parnasse occitanien,* p. 221.

28. *Chanson de la croisade,* verse 1551 f.; Pierre de Vaux-Cernai, Chapter LII.

29. *Chanson de la croisade,* verse 1625 ff.

30. *Ibid.,* verses 9308-20.

31. Pierre de Vaux-Cernai, *Historia Albigensium,* p. 145; Sixteenth century translation, ed. Guibin et Lyon, p. 49.

32. Pierre de Vaux-Cernai, Chapter LII. The same expression is repeated in the following chapter in a reference to sixty people who were burned at Casses.

33. C. Raynouard, *Choix de poésies,* Vol. IV, p. 191.

34. Peire Cardenal, in *Histoire littéraire de la France,* Vol. XX, p. 572; *Parnasse occitanien,* p. 187.

35. C. Raynouard, *Lexique roman,* Vol. I, p. 481.

36. *Parnasse occitanien,* p. 320.

37. Pierre de Vaux-Cernai, c. lxxii. See the end of the prose version of the *Chanson de la croisade* for the fate with which the papal legate menaced Toulouse.

38. *Histoire littéraire de la France,* Vol. XX, p. 571.

39. Dante, *Paradiso,* VI, 133 ff., 128. Eleanor of Provence married Henry III of England, and her sister, Sanchea, married Richard, Duke of Cornwall, who was elected King of Rome. Dante, however, was

very poorly informed concerning Provençal affairs. He was unaware of the reconciliation of Bertam of Born with King Henry II (see *Inferno*, XXVIII, 118 f.). Like Petrarch, he paid homage to the sanctity of Folquet, Bishop of Toulouse (*Paradiso,* IX, 82 f.). The sources from which the great Ghibelline drew his information were evidently very Guelph.

40. Ford Madox Ford, *Provence*, p. 182.

41. J. Anglade, *Les Troubadours*, p. 177.

42. Guillaume de Saint-Pathus, *Vie de Saint Louis*, ed. H.-Fr. Delaborde, pp. 25, 26 f. Cf. Joinville, *Histoire de Saint Louis*, 53. After publishing an edict against blasphemy, Louis ordered it to be punished by "burning the lips of the blasphemer with a glowing hot iron." He organized a spy system to detect blasphemers. A certain knight who took a solemn oath on the "name of God" was condemned to have his lips burned with a red hot iron. A number of barons asked the king to grant him mercy, but the king would not listen to them and the knight was tortured. The victims were publicly exhibited in a pillory (ladder—*échelle*) with the entrails of beasts, filled with excrement, hung around their necks. The king had "échelles" erected for this purpose on the public squares in every town. Saint Louis did everything in his power "to chase the 'bougres' and other evil people from his kingdom, so that the land would be purged of them."

43. *Histoire générale de Languedoc*, Vol. VI, p. 790.

44. H. C. Lea, *A History of the Inquisition in the Middle Ages*, Vol. II, p. 109 f.

45. J. J. Salverda de Grave, *Le Troubadour Bertran d'Alamanon*, p. 39 ff.

46. Diez, *Die Poesie der Troubadours*, p. 55.

47. C. Raynouard, *Lexique roman*, Vol. I, p. 481.

48. H. C. Lea, *A History of the Inquisition in the Middle Ages*, Vol. II, p. 11.

49. *Ibid.*, p. 44 ff.

50. J. Anglade, *Le Troubadour Guiraut Riquier*, p. 336.

51. *Ibid.*

52. Jean de Nostredame, *Vies des plus célèbres et anciens poètes provençaux* (ed. Chabaneau-Anglade), p. 64. King Saint Louis demonstrated his piety by persecuting poets. "Il ne chantait pas les chançons du monde, ne ni soufrait pas que ceux qui estaient de sa mesniée les chantassent" (Guillaume de Saint Pathus, *Vie de Saint Louis*, p. 19). He did not sing worldly songs, nor did he suffer those

in his retinue to sing them. "Their songs, he felt, are hiccoughs which too much resemble ribaldry."

> Ne fut chançon nulle chantée
> du siécle, més de Notre Dame.
>
> . . . Un escuier il avait
> qui du siècle trop bien chantait.
> Il li deffent que plus n'en die,
> et il chante de dame Marie . . .
> A l'escuier mult grief estoit
> mès obéir li convenoit.
>
> —Achille Jubinal, *Nouveau recueil de contes, dits, fabliaux et autres pièces inédites du XIIIe, XIVe et XVe siècles.* Vol. II, p. 200 f., according to the Ms. sup. fr. 1132, B.N.

53. C. Raynouard, *Choix des poésies,* Vol. V, p. 230. Also H. C. Lea *op. cit.,* Vol. II, p. 11.

54. J. Anglade, *Les Troubadours,* p. 297.

55. J. Coulet, *Le Troubadour Guilhem Montanhagol,* p. 73.

56. *Ibid.,* p. 70.

57. *Ibid.,* pp. 148, 141 f.

58. "As a result of the error common among the ancients during the last days of paganism, who imagined that in each country the indigenes had appeared there like mushrooms, various authors were convinced that these savage men who still felt the baseness and imperfection of their origin were in no way distinguishable from beasts. Indeed these authors believed that these men had existed a long time before their soul developed to the extent that they were capable of that docility which is required by laws and polite society. Athenaeus, like others accepting this principle, wrote that in the earliest times men did not solemnize marriages, and that they were as indifferent as animals in this matter until the time of Cecrops, who in codifying laws required his subjects to take one spouse and to be content with one. This infection of the authors propagated itself, and the truths of the Christian religion did not always enlighten a scholar sufficiently to enable him to rid himself of the ideas that he had taken from the pagan authors . . . On the contrary, it seems evident to me that marriage has always been regarded by all people as a sacred and solemn

thing, which is respected by even the most barbarous nations. Indeed, although there are a large number of countries today which have maintained all of their savagery and which to us appear to live without laws, without religion, without civil order, we do not know one example of a people who do not observe some solemnities in the alliances which they contract and who are not jealous of conjugal fidelity. We have seen virginity respected from the most ancient times . . . This virtue was not widespread among all peoples at all times because of the necessity of the propagation of the human race, but within this necessity, conjugal chasity is respected and marriage, shameful in its practice, had laws of decency, of modesty, of pudency and of sentinence which nature inspires, which reason supports and which have been maintained in the midst of barbarism. I admit that among some people, at various times and places, depravity and coarse mores have introduced abuses in this matter and even shameful customs. But this has not been universal" (J. B. Lafiteau, *Moeurs des sauvages amériquains comparées aux moeurs des premiers temps,* Vol. I, pp. 535 f.).

The opinions of Père Lafiteau are not, however, shared by his confreres. The most intelligent among them, Père Paul Le Jeune, recounts: "I have been told that the savages were very chaste; I can not speak for all of them, not having seen them very often, but those with whom I have talked, men and women, are extremely lewd" (*Relation,* 1634, p. 117).

Jacques Cartier relates: "They have another wicked custom involving their daughters, who, from the time they are old enough to receive a man, are placed in a bordello abandoned to all who want them until they have found their mate. And we are speaking from experience, for we have seen the houses crowded with girls, like students in a French boy's school" (J. Cartier, *Bref Récit et succinct narration de la navigation faict en MDXXXV et MDXXXVI,* Paris, 1654, fol. 30 verso). For some time I have been examining the methods followed by professors of ethnographic sociology; their methods are identical to those of Père Lafiteau and of the troubadour Montanhagol (*The Mothers,* Vol. II, pp. 13 ff.).

59. J. Coulet, *Le Troubadour Guilhem Montanhagol,* 141.

60. *Ibid.,* p. 110 f.

61. *Ibid.,* p. 51 f.

62. Matfré Ermengaud, *Lo Breviari d'amor,* ed. G. Azais, Vol. II, pp. 2ff., 5 ff.

63. *Ibid.,* pp. 418 f.

64. C. A. F. Mahn, *Die Werke der Troubadours*, Vol. IV., p. 30; Cf. Anglade, *Le Troubadour Guiraut Riquier*, p. 243 f.

65. Gaucelm Faidit (1190-1240) in C. Raynouard, *Choix de poésies*, Vol. III, p. 293.

66. Gaucelm Faidit, in Mahn, *Gedichte der Troubadours*, Vol. I, p. 36; Pons de Capdoill, in Mahn, *Die Werke der Troubadours*, Vol. I, p. 353.

67. Guiraut Riquier, in Mahn, *Die Werke der Troubadours*, Vol. IV, p. 37.

68. Guillaume de Saint-Didier, in Raynouard, *Choix de poésies*, Vol. III, p. 300.

69. Guiraut Riquier, in Mahn, *Die Werke der Troubadours*, Vol. IV, p. 22.

70. Augier, in Raynouard, *op cit.*, Vol. III, p. 105. The same formula is found in a very licentious poem by one of the oldest of the troubadours Raimbaud d'Orange, *ibid.*, p. 251, where it is associated with an obscene play on words.

71. J. Anglade, *Les Troubadours*, p. 298.

72. C. de Lollis, *Vita e poesie di Sordello di Goito*, p. 200.

73. *Ibid.*, p. 182.

74. Granet, in Mahn, *Gedichte der Troubadours,* Vol. III, p. 203.

75. C. de Lollis, *op. cit.*, p. 172 ff.

76. J. J. Salveda de Grave, *Le Troubadour Bertran d'Alamanon,* p. 95: *"Mout m'es greu d'En Sordel, car l'es faillitz sos senz."*

77. A. Rossler, in *The Catholic Encyclopedia*, Vol. XV, p. 690.

78. The cult of the "virgin"—i.e. "unmarried"—goddess is discussed in detail in my work, *The Mothers*, Vol. II, pp. 450-455; Vol. III, pp. 168-171. The attributes of the universal goddess are identical with those of the Virgin Mary. See *ibid.*, Vol. III, pp. 183 ff.

79. Gautier de Coincy, *Miracles de la Sainte Vierge*, col. 349. Cf. *Sermones discipuli*, Exemplum XXXII.

80. *Les Miracles de Nostre Dame par personnages*, Paris, 1876-93, Vol. I, p. 96.

81. *Sermones Discipuli*, Exemplum XXIV; Cf. St. Alphonse de Liguori, *Les Gloires de Marie*, Vol. I, p. 222 f.

82. St. Alphonse de Liguori, *The Glories of Mary*, p. 547 f. (English translation by R. A. Coffin, 1868).

83. *Ibid.*, p. 179.

84. *Ibid.*, p. 231.

85. V. Lowinski, *Zum geistlichen Kunstlied*, pp. 10 f., 17; J. Anglade, *Le Troubadour Guiraut Riquier*, p. 285.

86. J. Anglade, *Les Troubadours,* p. 294.

87. V. Lowinski, *loc. cit.*

88. J. Anglade, *op. cit.,* p. 297. Cf. Mahn, *Die Werke der Troubadours,* Vol. IV, p. 75.

89. Mahn, *op. cit.,* Vol. IV, p. 75 f.

90. S. Stronski, *Le Troubadour Folquet de Marseille,* pp. 66 and 68. It is to be noted that of four hundred troubadours who have described the mortal anguish that the cruelty of their ladies caused them, not one, even in the romantic legends which we have concerning them, is said to have committed suicide because of love.

91. R. Zenker, *Die Gedichte des Folquet von Romans,* p. 13.

92. Bertran d'Alamanon, ed. J. J. Salveda de Grave, p. 119.

93. C. de Lollis, *Vita e poesie di Sordello,* p. 189.

94. *Ibid.,* p. 199.

VI. THE TROUBADOUR TRADITION
IN ITALY AND ENGLAND

1. Pietro Bembo, "Della volgare lingua," in *Prose scelte* (ed. Sonzogno, pp. 151 f.). From Dante up to the most recent critics, the Italians have exhibited the rare merit of recognizing the debt their literature owes to that of Provence, rather than abandoning themselves, as a result of a false conception of national pride, to the pursuit of speculations concerning an autochthonous origin of Italian literature.

2. Every reader of Dante must have wondered what was the book in which the lovers of Rimini were reading of the love of Lancelot:

> Noi leggevamo un giorno per diletto
> di Lancilotto, come amor lo strinse:
> soli eravamo e senza alcun sospetto.
>
> Per più fiate gli occhi ci sospinse
> quella lettura e scolorocci il viso;
> ma solo un punto fù quel che ci vinse.
> . . . . .
> Galeotto fu il libro e chi lo scrisse.
> We read one day for pastime, seated nigh,
>   Of Lancelot, how love enchain'd him too.
>   We were alone quite unsuspiciously.

But oft our eyes met, and our cheeks in hue
All o'er discolored by that reading were;
But one point only wholly us o'erthrew;

. . . .

Galahad was the book and he who wrote it.

—*Inferno* V, 127 ff.

Assuming that Francesca was sufficiently cultivated to read French, although it is hardly probable, one certainly can not attribute a similar linguistic knowledge to Paolo Malatesta, who had spent his life in the camps. Dante did not intend to inflict the ponderous prose of the French *Lancelot* on his lovers. In the twenty-sixth canto of Purgatory, speaking of Arnaud Daniel, he places the following words in the mouth of Guido Guinicelli:

Versi d' amore e prose di romanzi
soperchió tutti.

He surpassed all others in love verses and romantic prose.

Arnaud Daniel did, indeed, write some novels in prose. Unfortunately, we do not have any of these works, although they seem to have enjoyed considerable popularity in their time. Pulci mentions them many times in his *Morgante Maggiore*. Le Tasso, in one of his essays on epic poetry, mentions Arnaud Daniel, "who wrote *Lancelot*" (*Discorso secondo del poema eroico*, Vol. IV, p. 62; Cf. p. 210 ed. Florence, 1724). Cristoforo Landino, in his article on Dante, says that Arnaud Daniel composed a "*moralité*" (Chabaneau, *Hist. générale de Languedoc*, Vol. X, p. 222).

Canello offered a negative criticism of these items of evidence, but it is not clear that he succeeded in refuting Dante and Tasso. C. Fauriel (*Hist. litt. de la France,* Vol. XXII, pp. 212 ff.) thought that the German *Lanzelot* of Ulrich von Zatzihoven was a paraphrase of Arnaud Daniel's *Lancelot*, but this opinion was based on an error in reading (Cf. G. Paris, in *Romania,* X, 48 ff. and XII, p. 459 f., note). In the thirteenth century, narrative poems in blank verse were sometimes referred to as "prose"; in his *De vulgari eloquentia*, Dante, however, uses the term "prose" in a manner which conforms to our usage. In Spain any composition which was not intended to be sung was designated as "prose."

Dante, who never forewent an opportunity to express his admiration for Arnaud Daniel, has his lovers read his favorite author in the most poetically masterful episode of the *Divine Comedy*. Even the phrase, "seducers, like Galvain, were the book and its author," though in the form of a reproof, paid homage to the cleverness of the troubadour whom he regarded as his master.

3. Dante, *Convito*, I, ii. "A perpetuale infamia e depressione delli malvagi uomini d'Italia, che commendendano lo Volgare altrui, e il lore proprio dispregiano." The *Convito* is of earlier origin than *De vulgari eloquentia*. Dante appears to have altered his opinion later.

4. Dante, *Inferno*, xiii, 75.

5. A. Gaspary, *Die sicilianische Dichterschule des dreizehnsten Jahrhunderts*, pp. 17, 25, 30 and f.; Raynouard, *Choix de poésies originales*, Vol. III, p. 348.

6. Guittone d'Arezzo, *Rime*, canzone xxii.

7. *Histoire générale de Languedoc*, Vol. VI, p. 653.

8. *Le Antiche rime volgari*, ed. A. d'ancona c Comparetti, Vol. III, p. 89 f. C. de Lollis explained the relations between de Davanzati and the Provençals: "Sul canzionere di Chiaro Davanzati," *Giornale storico della letteratura italiana*, Supp. I, pp. 82 f., iii f. On his relations with Guinicelli and the poets of the *stil nuovo*, see: N. Zingarelli: "Dante"; *Storia letteraria d'Italia*, Vol. V., p. 57 f., and C. J. G. W. Koken, *Guittones von Arezzo Dichtung und sein Verhältniss zu Guinicelli von Bologna*.

9. Guittone d'Arezzo, *Rime*, Vol. I, p. 16 f.

10. Dante, *De vulgari eloquentia* I, xv.

11. Dante, *Purgatorio*, canto XXVI, line 97 f.

12. *Vita nuova*, XXV, 6.

13. "Las Razos de trobar," *Romania* VIII, 344 f.

14. *Poeti del primo secolo della lingua italiana*, Vol. I, p. 93.

15. *Ibid.*, Vol. I, p. 70.

16. *Ibid.*, p. 90.

17. *Ibid.*, p. 96.

18. *Codex vaticanus*, No. 3793.

19. G. Salvadori, *La Poesia giovanile e la canzon d'amore di Guido Cavalcanti*, p. 95.

20. *Rimatori del dolce stil nuovo*, p. 12 ff., pp. 29, 36, 39.

21. E. Monaci, *Crestomazia dei primi secali*, p. 59·

> Pero ch'amore no se po vedere
> e no si trata corporolamente
> manti no son de si fole sapere

che credono ch'amor sia niente.
(Pier delle Vigne)

22. Dante, *Inferno* X, 52 ff.

23. Roger Bacon, *Opus majus*, ed. S. Jebb (1735), p. 44.

24. C. B. Jourdain, *Recherches critiques sur l'âge et l'origine des traductions d'Aristote*, pp. 95 ff.

25. Dante, *Convito*, II, xiv. The treatise, *Diarwani ilm alnudjrum*, by Ibn Kathir al-Farghani, an astronomer who flourished in the ninth century, had been translated by Gérard de Crémone and by Jean de Séville (Johannes Hispalensis) under the title *Liber aggregationibus scientiae stellarum*. Dante's citation from it is found in Chapter VIII.

26. *Ibid.*, II, Chapter VI.

27. *Ibid.*, II, Chapter III. Averroès, *Summa*, III, ed. de Venise, 1562, Ch. II, p. 144.

28. *Ibid.*, II, Chapter IV. Al-Bitrodji (Alpetragius) was translated by Calo Calonymos under the title *Planetarum theoria*. The work was printed at Venice in 1531. See S. Munk, *Mélanges de philosophie juive et arabe*, pp. 518 ff.

It could be alleged that Dante drew his Arabic astronomy from Albertus Magnus, whom he had read and who cited the same authorities. But a second-hand knowledge would not account for the fundamental interest which Dante exhibited from the *Vita nuova* onwards in Arabic science and thought. Moreover, Albertus Magnus (who Dante called "Albert the German," *Alberto da Magna*) was a violent anti-Averroist; Dante, on the other hand, was an admirer of Ibn Roschd. The case of Siger de Brabant is conclusive. Condemned at Paris for Averroism, Siger came to die in Italy (on Siger, see: *Histoire littéraire de la France*, Vol. XXI, pp. 96 ff.; Mandonnet, *Siger de Brabant et l'averroïsme latin au XIIIᵉ siècle*, Louvain, 1911). Braving Church authority, Dante placed Siger in Paradise among the great masters of theology and lavished praise on him (*Paradiso*, X, pp. 135 ff.). Thus it was not through Albertus Magnus that Dante came to know the science of the Arabs.

29. *Ibid.*, II, xiv.

30. *Ibid.*, II, vii.

31. *Ibid.*, III, xiv.

32. *Ibid.*, III, ii.

33. *Ibid.*, II, xiv.

34. *Ibid.*, III, xiv.

35. *Ibid.,* I, i.
36. *Ibid.,* II, v.
37. *Ibid.,* III, xi.
38. *Ibid.,* III, xiv.
39. *Ibid.,* III, xii.

40. Ibn Masarra (833-931) was the first to introduce the neo-Platonic doctrines of the Alexandrian school into Spain; thus he exerted a considerable influence on his successors of the same gnostic and mystic tendencies, in particular on Ibn Arabi and on Ibn Gebirol. He travelled to Syria and brought back a so-called Empedoclean philosophy. The trait which particularly attracted the attention of his contemporaries and his successors was the similarity of his doctrines to those of pantheism, insofar as he postulated the existence of a universal substance, common to all created beings. But he avoided an absolute pantheism by supposing that this universal substance was an emanation of another substance, that of the Creator. "The partial souls," he said, "are parts of the universal soul." "The property of the universal soul," he said, moreover, "is love; for in the contemplation of the intellect, with its beauty and its brightness, the partial soul loves it as one, desperately in love, loves the object of his love" (S. Munk, *Mélanges de philosophie juive et arabe,* p. 244).

Thus he is responsible for the transmission into Europe of those doctrines which were so widespread in the Middle Ages. Giordano Bruno was to be burned alive at Rome three centuries later for having expressed the same doctrines. The unifying character of all philosophical thought causes it inevitably to lead to monism, that is pantheism. One of the factors which forced the thinkers of the Middle Ages to adopt neo-Platonic mysticism is that it provided them a means of eluding pantheism, which was contrary to the Islamic as well as the Christian religion. Ibn Masarra, himself, was persecuted; this was the reason for his flight from Spain to the East.

In order to understand Arabic philosophic and scientific thought it is necessary to keep in mind that its development under the Omeyades of the East and the West was made possible by the religious scepticism of those princes and of the first Abassids, who were themselves *muta'zil,* that is to say rationalists. The decay of Islamic civilization coincided with the advent to power of fanatics who were inflamed with the zeal of neophytes.

The Arabs only knew Plato through the Alexandrine school; thus they often confused neo-Platonic ideas with those of Plato. They even imposed a neo-Platonic cast on Aristotle and attributed to him a *Theology* which was actually a forgery that came from Syria, the great "home of forgeries." The same confusion was later transmitted to the Christian Middle Ages.

Jamal ad-Din al-Qufti has a note on Ibn Masarra in the article on Empedocles in his *Dictionnaire des philosophes*. See S. Munk, *op. cit.,* pp. 241 ff.; Amari, *Storia del Musulmani di Sicilia,* Vol. II, pp. 100 f.; M. Asín Palacios, *Abenmassarra y su escuela,* Madrid, 1914; A. González Palencia, *Historia de la literatura arábigo-española,* pp. 206 ff.

41. Asín Palacios, *Dante y el Islam,* p. 78. It is known that Palacios developed the theory that the *Divine Comedy* is, in conception and in detail, completely derived from this legend of the voyage of Mahomet into the other world, as it was told by Ibn Arabi in the *Futuhat* (Miguel Asín Palacios, *op. cit.,* and *La escatología musulmana en la Divina Comedia,* Madrid, 1919. French translation by Cabaton, 1928. Cf. André Bellessort, "Dante et Mahomet," *Revue des Deux-Mondes,* April 1, 1920; Blochet, "L'acension au ciel du prophète Mohammed," *Revue de l'histoire des religions de toutes les nations,* Vol. XLI, 1901; Carra de Vaux, "Fragments d'eschatologie musulmane," in *Compte rendu du troisième Congrès scientifique international des catholiques,* Brussels, 1905; Asín Palacios, "Historia y crítica de una polémica," *Boletín de la Academia Española,* 1924.

In my opinion, the thesis was presented with more certainty than was warranted. The theme of a voyage into the other world is universal; it is encountered in all phases of culture, even the most primitive. Versions of it abound in the Middle Ages. It has long been the custom to compare them with Dante's poem (see Ancona, *I precursori di Dante*). Palacios replies that these versions are of later origin than the Arabic tales, which is true, and that they are derived from the latter, which is extremely doubtful. There is no need to make recourse to Arabian tradition to explain their origin; the theme abounds in all of Celtic literature. Moreover the conception of the *Divine Comedy* can be accounted for without any need for invoking Arabian inspiration. However, it is also necessary in a different connection to keep in mind that Dante's entire intellectual culture, and that of the Middle Ages as well, issued from Arabic works or was actually transmitted by the Arabs. Hence it is quite natural that, being imbued with a culture and thought of Arabic origin, Dante manifested this filiation of his spirit in his great poem as well as in the rest of his works. Although the notion of a voyage to the world beyond the grave is too widespread for it to be necessary to assume that Dante borrowed the notion from the Arabic tradition, the same cannot be said for the manner in which he made use of it. The philosophical novel is a peculiarly Arabic type. Thus, for example, Ibn Tofail, when he presents his theory of the development of innate thought (a quite erroneous conception, by the way), did it in the form of a philosophical novel, a sort of a Robinson Crusoe tale, dealing with a child who miraculously grew up on a desert isle (see Munk, *Mélanges,* pp. 412 ff.). Thus, if we have understood the sources of Dante's inspiration, we should not have been surprised to have noted that throughout the tour the whole arrangement and architecture of the world beyond the grave, the circles of the inferno, those of the hill of Purgatory and of the spheres of Paradise, as well as their location, and innumerable details of the punishment received by the damned and the pleasures enjoyed by the saints, correspond exactly to those which Al-Arabi gave in his elaboration of the Islamic legend. This is not a proof of the Arabian source of Dante's education, but the confirmation of that which we should have noted much earlier.

It is scarcely important that we cannot trace exactly and with certainty the route by which knowledge of Al-Arabi's work came to Dante. Most of the books which pre-date the printing press are lost (no manuscript of the work of any Arabian philosopher is extant; all of their works have come down to us through Hebrew or Latin translations), and what we know about the literary history of the twelfth and thirteen centuries is indeed small compared with what we do not know. Signs which can buttress conjectures concerning the sources of the education of Brunetto Latini's student certainly are not lacking. And that is the most for which we have any right to hope.

42. Dante, *Convito,* I, ii. Cf. *De monarchia,* I, 9.

43. *Ibid.,* III, v.

44. Asín Palacios *op. cit.,* p. 156.

45. Dante, *Convito,* II, v.

46. *Ibid.,* II, vi.

"Theology has designated all of the celestial essences by their revelatory names which our divine initiator has divided into three orders. The first permanently encompasses God ... these are the thrones ... which in Hebrew are called *cherubin* and *seraphin* ... The second order is composed of powers, of lordships and of forces ... The third constitutes the last celestial hierarchy, the order of angels and of principalities" (Denys l'Aréopagite, *La Hiérarchie céleste*, trans. Maurice de Gandillac, pp. 205 f.).

"In order to explain the action of pure energy, or of God, on matter, the Arab peripatetics borrowed some neo-Platonic doctrines and put the *Intelligences of the spheres* between God and the world, by proposing a sort of emanation . . . In substance the Arabic doctrine is this. The celestial spheres, which are nine in number, each have a soul which is the source of their movement. In addition to the supreme Intelligence, there are nine other *Intelligences* which emanate from the latter . . . The last of these separate *Intelligences*, which presides over the sphere nearest to us (that of the moon), is the *active intellect,* through whose influence the *passive intellect,* which is in us, is developed . . .

According to Ibn Sina, as cited by Ibn Tofail, this philosophy is the cryptic meaning of Aristotle's words. We find again among the Arabs this distinction between exoteric Aristotle and esoteric Aristotle, which was later adopted by the Italian Platonic school along with the mystic doctrines of the Kabbale, just as the *Ischrakyyin* of the Arabs became absorbed in Sufi mysticism" (S. Munk, *Mélanges de philosophie juive et arabe,* pp. 331 f.).

47. S. Munk, *op. cit.,* p. 158.

48. *Rimatori del dolce stil nuovo,* pp. 3 f.

49. *Ibid.,* p. 11.

50. Dante, *Convito,* II, xi; IV, xxi.

51. *Ibid.,* III.

52. Purgatorio, xxvi, line 119.

53. On the life of Sordello, see C. De Lollis, *Vita e poesie di Sordello di Goito,* Halle, 1896.

54. Purg., xxiv, lines 55 ff.

55. *Rimatori del dolce stil nuovo,* pp. 60 f.

56. Giovanni Boccaccio, *Trattatello in laude di Dante,* x, XII: "Tra cotanta virtù, scienza, quanta dimostrata è di sopra essere stata in questo mirifico poeta, truovo amplissimo luogo la lussuria, e non solamente ne' giovani anni, ma ancora ne' maturi."

57. Purg., xxxi, line 40.

58. Parad., v, line 99.

59. Inf., xxii, lines 14-15.

60. Rime, lxxiii.

61. Purg., xxiii, line 115.

62. Lip., p. 174.

63. Purg., xxxi, line 54.

64. *Ibid.,* line 45.

65. Purg., xxx, lines 136 ff.

66. Rime, lvi, lvii, lviii.

67. Purg., xxxi, line 59; Rime, lxxxvii-lxxxix.

68. Vita nuova, 36-38.

69. Purg., xxiv, lines 37 ff.

70. Rime, c-ciii.

71. Rime, cxvi.

72. The case of Petrarch and Laura is a very curious example of a literary "canard." None of the rather numerous authors, many of whom were Petrarch's contemporaries, such as Domenico Aretino, Coluccio Salutati, Vergerio, Filippo Villani, Manetti, Leonardo Bruni, who wrote on Petrarch during the century after his death, made any mention of an actual Laura. The notion that the poetic effusions of the grave clerk were related to a flesh-and-blood lady did not occur to them. Undoubtedly it would have seemed to them far too ridiculous a contrast to the character and habits of the worthy canon. It was only around a century later, at the court of the Medicis that the question was debated for the first time. The role of Petrarch's "Laura" was assigned, indeed with little conviction, to various ladies. In the middle of the eighteenth century, the abbot de Sade proposed one of his female ancestors, Lady Laura de Sade, as a candidate for the role (*Mémoires de la vie de Pétrarque,* Amsterdam, 1764-1767). The abbot unearthed all of the identification papers of the Lady Laura, her baptismal certificate, her marriage contract, etc.; he even insisted on showing her ashes to prove that she was really dead. Obviously none of this had anything to do with Petrarch. The only item that appears to have even the slightest relation to the affair is a note on the margin of a manuscript of Virgil, relating to the death of "Laura," which is said to be in Petrarch's handwriting. Tassoni and Vellutello claimed that it was not. Even assuming that it were, it does not prove anything with respect to the Lady de Sade. Nevertheless, while Petrarch was reputed to have been distraught with love for "Laura," he was in the process of fathering two children of an unknown lady at Vaucluse—probably a lady of low birth, likely his housekeeper or cook. It may be that the note on the Virgil manuscript refers to the death of this person; or indeed it could with equal likelihood simply be a literary

memorandum noting that it was time to kill "Laura." This would appear reasonable enough after the production of some 207 sonnets and a number of canzoni, sestinas, and madrigals.

In summary, there is not a shadow of proof. Moreover, most of the more reliable authorities, Settembrini, C. Cantu, Camerini, Costero, Leopardi, reject the Abbé de Sade's story.

The name "Laura" very likely is drawn from Arnaud Daniel, Petrarch's favorite troubadour, who enjoyed making puns on the word *"l'aura."* One asks himself why Petrarch, during the greater part of his life, delivered this tide of poetic elegance with respect to an imaginary "Laura." To emphasize the question implies a failure to take into account the strength of literary tradition. In the thirteenth and fourteenth centuries one could conceive of no other lyric theme than Love, such as it was imagined that the troubadours had conceived it, just as in the nineteenth century one could only conceive of a novel as a love story. This type of tradition is singularly tenacious. The Arabs rigorously prescribed not only the form of their *qasīdas,* but the subject of the first lines, that of the second group of lines, and so on. Likewise, the epic tradition prescribed, from the time of Homer, themes of severity, the invocation of the muse, the counsel in heaven, combat details, the divine messenger in human form, etc., and until Camoens and Milton the epic poem had been constrained to follow these rules.

73. Dante, *La Vita nuova,* 42.

74. Bettinelli, *Saisone,* p. 194.

75. S. T. Coleridge, *Notes and Lectures upon Shakespeare . . . with other literary remains,* ed. H. Coleridge (London, 1849), Vol. II, p. 23.

76. A. Tassoni, *Considerazioni sopra le rime del Petrarca . . . col confronto di luoghi de' poeti antichi di vari tempi,* Modona, 1609; P. Bembo, *Della volgare lingua,* Lib. I.

While pretending to defend Petrarch against the imputations of plagiarism made by Jehan de Nostradamus, Tassoni very effectively reinforced these accusations and provided them detailed support. Bembo did it with even more delicacy. The case of the Catalan poet, Auzias March, is rather piquant. He was a contemporary of Petrarch (1379-1459). He retained the troubadour tradition into the fifteenth century, and wrote "in limousin." The similarity of his work to that of Petrarch extends even to his having met his lady in the church on Good Friday and to the extolling of her in a long series of sonnets after her death. Many modern authors cite him as an imitator of Petrarch. But their contemporaries, Odovillo Gomez and Giacopo Antonio de Ferrare, allege contrarily that it was Petrarch who robbed him (A. Tassoni, *op. cit.,* p. 4; cf. Venanzio Todesco, "Auzias March," in *Archivum romanicum,* Vol. XI, 1927, pp. 213 ff.). Let it suffice to pose the question of precedence; it is useless to pursue it. Ch-Ant. Gidel (*Les Troubadours et Pétrarque*) cites a number of similarities between Petrarch and the troubadours, most of which are drawn from Tassoni and which are rather poorly chosen.

77. Petrarch, *Triumph I* (The Triumph of Love), Part IV, lines 38-57.

> . . . e poi v'era un drapello
> Di portamenti e di volgari strani:
> Fra tutti il primo Arnaldo Daniello,
> Gran maestro d'amor, ch'alla sua terra
> Ancor fa onor col suo dir strano e bello.
> Eranvi quei ch'Amor si leve afferra:
> L'un Piero e l'altro, e'l men famoso Arnaldo;
> E quei che fur conquisi con più guerra:
> I'dico l'uno, e l'altro Raimbaldo
> Che cantò pur Beatrice e Monferrato,
> E'l vecchio Pier d'Alvernia, con Giraldo,
> Folco, que' ch'a Marsiglia il nome ha dato
> Ed a Genova tolto, ed all'estremo
> Cangiò per miglior patria abito e stato;
> Giaufrè Rudel, ch'usò la vela e'l remo
> A cercar la sua morte, e quel Guiglielmo
> Che per cantare h'al fior de' suoi di scemo,
> Amerigo, Bernardo, Ugo e Gauselmo
> E molti altri ne vidi a cui la lingua
> Lancia e spada fu sempre, e targia ed elmo.

78. Arthur Quiller Couch, *The Art of Writing,* Lecture IX.

79. *The Poems of Sir Thomas Wiat,* ed., A. K. Foxwell, Vol. I, pp. 272, 279, 301.

The *murabba'* form occurs, in but rare instances, throughout English poetry posterior to the fifteenth century. It is almost exclusively confined to lyrics intended or supposed to be sung. It has also been employed in humorous ditties. See Sir Philip Sydneis Song, in Percy's *The Faery Pastorall or Forrest of Elves.*

80. Othello, Act III, Scene 3, line 330.

81. Henry VI, Part II, Act IV, Scene 1.

82. Purg., canto xi, line 115.

83. Hamlet, Act IV, Scene 3.

84. *Inferno,* canto xxvi, line 118: "Take thought of the seed from which you spring. You were not born to live as brutes, but to follow virtue and knowledge."

85. Macbeth, Act V, Scene 3.

86. Sestina, I.

87. Tertullian, *De cultu faeminarum,* in Migne, *Patrologia, series prima,* Vol. I, col. 1305.

88. Ambroise, *Commentaria in Epistola ad Corinthis prima,* in Migne, *Patrologia,* Vol. XVII, col. 221 f.; cf. Athanasius, *In passionem et crucen domini,* XXX, in Migne, *Series graeca,* Vol. XXVII, col. 236; *De virginitate,* in Migne, *ibid.,* Vol. XVII, col. 279; Ambroise, *De Virginibus,* Migne, *Series prima,* Vol. XIV, col. 192 f.

89. Tertullian, *Apologeticus,* in Migne, *Series prima,* Vol. I, col. 535.

90. Tertullian, *De monogamia,* III, in Migne, *ibid.,* Vol. III, col. 535.

91. *L'Histoire ecclésiastique d'Eusèbe,* trans. C. de Seyssel (Paris, 1532).

92. Ambroise, *Exhortatio virginitatis,* in Migne, *ibid.,* Vol. XVI, col. 343 f.; cf. Tertullian, *Ad uxorem,* IX, 3, 5, in Migne, *ibid.,* Vol. I, col. 1278.

93. Ambroise, *Exhortatio virginitatis,* in Migne, *ibid.,* Vol. XVI, col. 346.

94. Clement of Alexander, *Paedagogus,* II, 2, in Migne, *Series graeca,* Vol. VIII, col. 429.

Index